D0433621

Collins Guide to the Countryside

Collins Guide to
THE COUNTRYSIDE

Illustrations by John Wilkinson
Text by Richard Fitter and Alastair Fitter

COLLINS
8 Grafton Street, London W1

ARTIST'S ACKNOWLEDGEMENT
The artist would like to thank his wife Anne,
and Audrey and Peter Chantree for their help and
enthusiasm in organising the field trips to many
of the various landscapes depicted in the book.
He would also like to express his gratitude to
Norman Arlott for his invaluable help with the
illustrations of birds.

William Collins Sons & Co Ltd
London, Glasgow, Sydney, Auckland, Toronto, Johannesburg

First published 1984
© in the illustrations, John Wilkinson 1984
© in the text Richard Fitter, Alastair Fitter, 1984

Additional bird illustration by Norman Arlott
Cartography by David Perrott
Calendar artwork by Stuart Perry

Filmset by Ace Filmsetting, Frome, Somerset
Origination by Adroit Photolitho, Birmingham
Map origination by Bridge Graphics Ltd, Hull
Printed and bound by Printer Industria Gráfica S.A.
Sant Vicenç dels Horts   Barcelona   D.L.B. 4969-1984

Contents

About this Book

This book presents a complete picture of the natural history and ecology of the British Isles. It explains which animals and plants are to be found in different parts of the countryside, and why; it tells you what can be seen at any time of the year; and it shows you where all the outstanding areas of natural history and landscape interest are to be found. It is a book both to be read and to be referred to.

Most guides are intended to allow the reader to identify different groups of animals or plants – whether in the field or in the home. While the numerous paintings in this book will undoubtedly help in the identification of most of the common, and some of the rarer, plants and animals in Britain and Ireland, identification is not the primary aim of the book. *Collins Guide to the Countryside* is much more an aid to the recognition of, and the enjoyment of, wild animals and plants. If you know what you are likely to find in, for example, an oakwood in spring, or on a heather moorland in autumn, you are not only more likely to see it and recognize it, but you will have a far better idea of why it is there, how it relates to the rest of the wildlife community, and what it is doing. This knowledge is not only an important part of identification; it is an essential basis for the understanding of the countryside, and the key to the enormous pleasure that can be derived from the British countryside.

The book is divided into three main sections.

The Habitats (pages 22–149). This section deals in turn with the six major habitats of the British Isles – Farmland (pages 22–43), Towns and Gardens (pages 44–57), Woodland (pages 58–91), Heath, Moor and Mountain (pages 92–111), Fresh Water (pages 112–127), and The Coast (pages 128–149). Within each of these broad divisions are descriptions and illustration of the more specialized habitats of which they are composed, and of the plants that live there and give them their character. There are also accounts of the wild mammals, reptiles and amphibians, birds and insects that make up the wild animal community of each habitat.

The result is an ecological portrait of the British Isles. Anyone who wants an overview of the whys and wherefores of the countryside would do well to read this section through from beginning to end. However, it serves an equally valuable reference function, particularly if used in advance of a trip to one of the habitats described. In either case, knowing what to expect can be half the fun of a coflntry walk.

The Calendar (pages 150–175). The tables in the calendar allow you to see at a glance what is happening in the countryside at any time of the year. For ease of reference, the tables are divided into the same major habitat divisions as the previous section, and the calendar itself should be used in conjunction with the habitat text and illustrations. The colour shading, and the symbols, represent the full range of activities of the plant or animal concerned – whether plants are in flower or in fruit, whether birds are singing, nesting or migrating, when tadpoles are to be found and when butterflies are emerging. A full explanation of shading and symbols, and of how to interpret the calendar in terms of the annual life-cycle of a plant or animal can be found on pages 150–151.

The Gazetteer (pages 176–229) contains a series of maps covering the whole of Britain and Ireland showing the location of places of natural history and landscape interest. The accompanying text gives a brief description of each of them, and picks out major points of interest. A key to the Gazetteer maps will be found on pages 176–177.

In addition to these main sections, there is an *Introduction*, giving the essential background to the climate and geology of the British Isles, and explaining the basic ecological concepts used in the book, the *Index*, gives references for all the species in the book to text, illustrations and calendar; and since Latin names have been omitted from the text to make it more readable, the Latin name of each species in the book has also been given in the index.

INTRODUCTION

'God made the country and man made the town'. William Cowper's saying was already dated when he coined it in the middle of the eighteenth century. The countryside we see today is almost entirely man-made and ironically its beauty, which we are now steadily and systematically destroying, was being created by the activities of land-owners at around the very time when Cowper uttered his *mot*.

While man has in a sense created the countryside, Nature still largely determines how he does so, what parts he ploughs, what crops he grows and what animals he raises where, and even where he can safely build. Climate and the soil are the underlying factors which so greatly influence the human environment, and which are reflected in the kinds of plants and animals that occur in the country-side. A trinity of influences thus affect every acre of Britain and determine its wildlife: the turbulent atmosphere of the Earth, inter-acting with the Atlantic Ocean; the underlying rocks, which deter-mine the character of the soil; and the activities of man over the past several thousand years.

The reasons why wild snakeshead fritillaries grow abundantly in Magdalen Meadow at Oxford are that Oxford enjoys a relatively mild climate through being so close to the Atlantic, that the rich alluvial soil has a high water table since it is so close to the River Cherwell, and that for many years the owners have not allowed cattle to graze it in Spring, but have instead harvested the haycrop in mid-summer – the very word meadow means a grass field that is not grazed until after the hay is brought in.

Climate

Climate is in many ways the most important factor of all, for it sets the overall range within which each animal and plant can survive. Moscow and Winnipeg, with their long, cold, snowbound winters, both lie in the same latitudes as Britain, but we escape such winters through a combination of our predominantly westerly winds and the mild waters of the North Atlantic Drift, popularly known as the Gulf Stream. The westerly winds are warm because they travel for hundreds of miles over those warm waters before reaching us; by contrast, when they give way to an easterly airflow in winter, we feel air that has been cooled by travelling equally far over the cold, frozen lands of Asia. But it is the westerlies that prevail, producing a mild year-round climate further north than anywhere else in the northern hemisphere, which might lead one to suppose that it is Britain, not the United States, which is God's own country.

Britain is nevertheless uncomfortably near to the Arctic. Unst in the extreme north of Shetland is only 6° south of the Arctic circle and more than 10° north of the 50th parallel, which just cuts the tip of the Lizard Peninsula in Cornwall. As a result Britain is a constant battleground between polar air descending from the north and east—and occasionally giving us Arctic

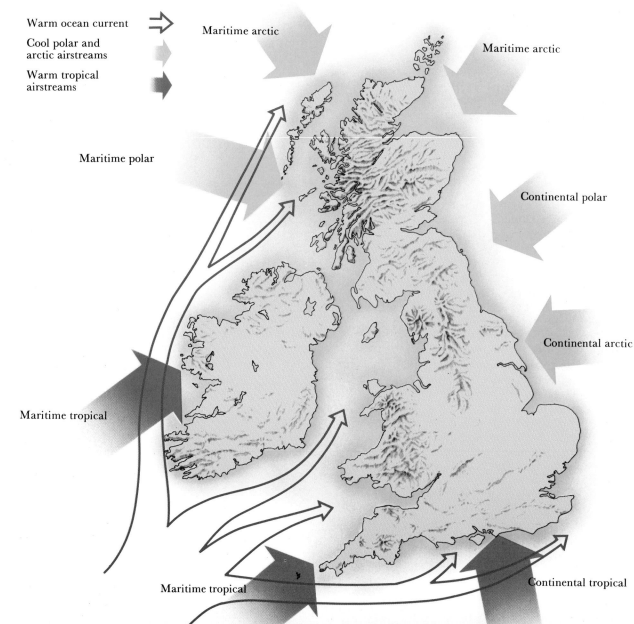

Warm ocean current

Cool polar and arctic airstreams

Warm tropical airstreams

Maritime arctic

Maritime arctic

Maritime polar

Continental polar

Continental arctic

Maritime tropical

Maritime tropical

Continental tropical

winters such as 1962/3, 1978/9 and 1981/2—and warm air from the south and west—which produces snowfree winters in lowland Britain, as in 1975/6. Our summers too can vary from wet horrors (1980) to extreme drought (1921 and 1976).

The British climate, while on average one of the most equable in the world, is thus capable of every extreme, of cold and heat, and of rainfall and drought, and of rapid transitions from one to another, as when the 1976 drought, the worst for about 200 years, was immediately succeeded by the wettest autumn for 50 years. All this keeps both people and wildlife on their toes. To live in Britain requires the ability to adapt and to cope with extremes. No British animal or plant appears to have been exterminated by the 1962/3 winter or the 1976 summer, and some plants, for example mountain avens, have adapted to life both at sea-level and on near-Arctic mountain tops in Scotland.

Some creatures, on the other hand, are not quite adaptable enough – our climate is outside their range of tolerance. The European pond tortoise was found in prehistoric Britain, as fossil remains show, when summers were warmer. Now only the occasional summer is warm enough to allow its eggs to hatch, and it has become extinct.

Above: the beech is a widespread European plant which reaches its north-western limit in southern England.
Below: European pond tortoise, a warmth-demanding creature now extinct in Britain, but common during warmer prehistoric times.

Above: mountain avens, an Arctic-Alpine plant found at sea level in northern Scotland.

Temperature

The two elements of climate that have the greatest impact on plants and animals are temperature and rainfall. It is warmer in the south and wetter in the west, so that, roughly speaking, you can divide the British Isles into four quadrants.

the **south-east** is warm and dry, especially in summer and in parts of East Anglia, where elements of the steppe flora of Eastern Europe, such as the field wormwood and the Spanish campion, grow on the Breckland heaths of the Norfolk–Suffolk border.

the **north-east** is the cool, dry quadrant, being closest to the Arctic air and furthest from the Atlantic westerlies. Plants characteristic of Scandinavia have their outposts here, notably the delicate twinflower.

Twinflower

Spanish campion

Pale butterwort

Spanish campion

Twinflower

Cornish heath

Cornish heath

Pale butterwort

the **south-west** is warm and wet and is the home of the so-called Lusitanian flora, whose headquarters is in the Iberian peninsula (Lusitania was Roman Portugal) and which includes three notable heaths – Dorset heath around Poole Harbour in Dorset, Cornish heath on the Lizard peninsula, and Irish heath in the far west of Ireland.

the **north-west** is cooler and wetter, perhaps explaining Manchester's bad reputation, but cooler is a relative term and it is much warmer than Labrador at the same latitude on the opposite side of the Atlantic, but outside the balmy influence of the Gulf Stream. Because of that provider of warmth, in winter the west of Britain is generally warmer than the east, and there is an Atlantic flora, less warmth-demanding than the Lusitanian plants, but equally frost-sensitive, which can be found up to the far north-west of Scotland. Pale butterwort is an example.

January and July isotherms

16°C	} July
12°C	
5°C	} January
3°C	

The key moment in the British spring is the time, which may vary from late or even mid February (in years such as 1957, for instance) to early April (1963), when the mean temperature rises for several days above 6°C (42°F), for this, coupled with the lengthening of the days, stimulates both the growth of many plants and the breeding cycle of many resident birds. This first flush of spring almost invariably occurs earlier in the south-west than elsewhere, and earlier on the coast than inland: whereas primroses may bloom almost throughout the winter in Cornwall, in northern Scotland they do not start until April and may go on well into June. The temperature differences are greater in summer than in winter: the northern isles have an average July temperature some 4°C lower than that of the Thames Valley, but in January the average temperature of the two is similar, though parts of central Scotland are much colder. In winter the temperature differences are between east and west, not north and south, and the west is noticeably warmer, thanks to the beneficial influence of that universal provider – perhaps our most reliable energy source – the Gulf Stream. The amount of sunshine is less important, for Shetland has the unbelievably exiguous daily average of half an hour in December, but it has the same average winter temperature as Middlesex.

There is another temperature gradient which you experience as you go up into the mountains, for the temperature falls by about 1°C for every 200 m altitude (1°F per 300 feet). At a sufficient height the climate becomes so severe, with low temperatures and high winds, that trees fail to grow, and the tree-line is reached. In Britain the tree-line is hard to see because grazing by sheep stops tree regeneration, but in the Peak District, for instance, oak and ash ascend to only 300 m (1000 ft), while birch struggles on for another 100 m or so; the natural tree-line would probably be above 600 m. At such heights (and on exposed coasts) wind is very important, as is witnessed by the semi-horizontal wind-cut trees sometimes seen there.

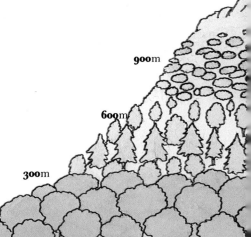

900m

600m

300m

Rainfall

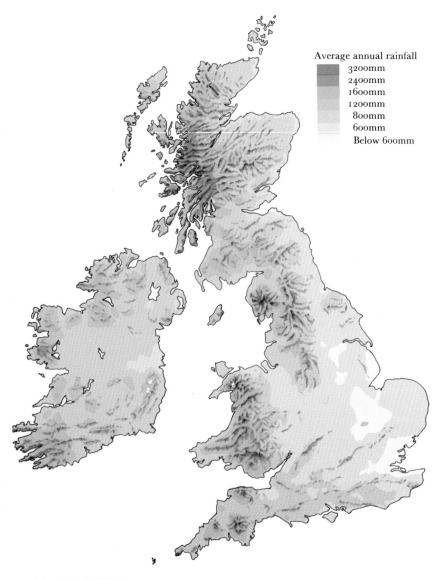

Average annual rainfall
- 3200mm
- 2400mm
- 1600mm
- 1200mm
- 800mm
- 600mm
- Below 600mm

Rainfall is the other great climatic factor. It especially affects plant growth, for plants use enormous quantities of water in transpiration, largely to keep themselves cool, but it is also important for some smaller animals that have little control over their evaporation. Other animals are influenced indirectly through their dependence on plants. The total amount of rain which falls in a year on different parts of Britain varies over a very wide range. It may be as little as around 500 mm (20 in) on the Essex shore of the Thames estuary – hence the reputation of Southend as a resort – but over 2000 mm over large parts of upland Britain, rising to as much as 5000 mm in a few very wet places, such as the top of Snowdon.

The wetness of the climate experienced by a plant, however, depends not simply on rainfall, but on the balance between rainfall and evaporation. Long periods of sunny weather in summer can produce severe water deficits, and the annual average lowland rainfall of 600–1000 mm is diminished by around 400 mm by evaporation. Fortunately nowhere in the British Isles suffers from potential evaporation losses greater than the annual rainfall, or our countryside would look very different; nevertheless south Essex is clearly a dry area by any standards. In fact wherever the annual rainfall falls below 750 mm the land is likely to dry out in summer.

This propensity to drought has pronounced effects on plant distribution. Ferns for example, which are rather primitive plants and need moisture to reproduce, are relatively scarce in eastern Britain, whereas a lot of small annuals which grow on sandy soils that dry out in summer, such as several clovers, are much commoner in the east. However, the survival of a plant depends not on the general climate of the area but on the microclimate of the exact spot where it is growing. This is why several 'western' ferns such as Tunbridge filmyfern and hay-scented buckler fern are found in the deep, damp wooded ghylls of the Sussex Weald, far from their main distribution. The steep valleys and deep shade provide a microclimate similar to the climate of western Britain.

Equally, even in the driest parts of the country, the lie of the land can cause the ground to become waterlogged and peat may form, for in waterlogged soils there is no air for the microbes that normally break down dead vegetation. Then, far from suffering from water shortage, plants may have to cope with an excess, and with the problems of growing in airless soil. To see such effects one has only to go to the fenlands of Cambridgeshire, now largely drained and with only a few surviving remnants such as Wicken Fen. Once, all the land between Cambridge and Boston was a vast fen, thousands of acres of waterlogged peatlands. Nowadays the land is drained and in summer farmers have to irrigate their crops!

Left: common polypody is the only vascular plant in the British flora that commonly grows as an epiphyte on trees. It is not a parasite; in the damp climate of the west of Britain, it can get all the water it needs from moisture trickling down the trunks of the trees. Right: conversely, haresfoot clover is the commonest of a group of small clovers which are indicators of dry soils, and are commonest in eastern areas.

Haresfoot clover

Soils

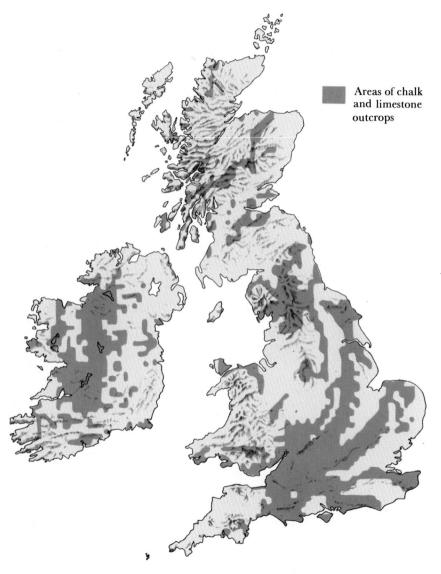

Areas of chalk and limestone outcrops

Climate, then, determines the overall distribution of our wildlife and the general shape of the countryside, with microclimate acting as a sort of 'fine tuning'. But in any one area you can find many different communities of plants and animals, and much of the reason for this can be sought in differences in the underlying soil. If a severe climate can render even the most fertile soil barren, so a soil can counteract even the most favourable climate, if it contains insufficient nutrients or some toxin. For soil provides the mineral nutrients of plants, and so of the animals which feed on them. Plant root systems absorb both the essential minerals, such as nitrogen, phosphorus and potassium in solution, and also the water required to transport these and to cool the leaves.

Soil itself is a complex of mineral particles, derived from the erosion and disintegration of rocks, and organic matter, the remains of animals and plants, the whole broken down and worked upon by climate, heating and freezing, wetting and drying. The nature of the soil, both its texture and its chemical composition, is determined by the underlying rocks and by the site where it develops – a poorly drained hollow will develop a very different soil from a ridge. Texture depends upon the size of the mineral particles and the amount of organic matter, and controls drain-

age: large sand particles allow rapid drainage, but small clay particles retain water better, so that clay soils become wet and sticky in winter but remain moist for longer in summer. A loamy soil, so beloved of gardeners, has a good mixture of particles of different sizes.

Though texture is important, for many plants cannot survive waterlogging, chemical composition is as strong a factor. Climate provides two great divides – wet and dry, and hot and cold; similarly soil has two – wet and dry again, and acid and calcareous. Calcareous soils are formed from basic rocks such as limestone and chalk, which are more or less pure forms of calcium carbonate, and also from some volcanic rocks which are rich in calcium; acid soils are either formed on very base-poor rocks, such as sandstones, shales, or granite, or have been heavily leached by rain over a long period, so that all the bases have been lost.

This brings us to another important dichotomy in Britain – the geographical one between Highland Britain and Lowland Britain that comes from drawing a line from Teesside to Exeter. This line divides the higher and wilder hills of the north and west from the low hills and downs of the south and east. In the north and west the farmland is mainly pasture on acid soils under

Heather moorland

heathlands of the New Forest, Dorset, the Surrey Greensand and the East Anglian heaths. Similarly the wet north and west have limestone hills, formed of the older and harder carboniferous limestone, more resistant to erosion, and there are outcrops of limestone as far north as Durness in Sutherland, where such a typical lime-lover as the dark red helleborine grows. Indeed most of the rare alpine plants of the Highlands, many of them exquisitely beautiful, grow only where veins of base-rich rocks occur, on such mountains as Ben Lawers in Perthshire or the hills that surround Glen Clova in Angus. The extra fertility this imparts to the soil can often be seen from far off in the greener vegetation, particularly in blanket peat areas and you will rarely find a botanist climbing a hill entirely composed of acid rocks.

Chalk downland and dark red helleborine, a plant of the limestone hills of the north and west

heavy rainfall, whereas in the south and east the soils are drier and more often calcareous or neutral and the farms are more often arable. In Britain the calcareous rocks are on the whole the younger ones, and these are found in the south-east; as you travel north-west from the Thames Valley to the Scottish Highlands you move over progressively older rocks. The result is that the differences in vegetation are so great that a naturalist landing from a helicopter in a fog would know which half of Britain he was in — when the fog cleared!

The greatest contrast is between the chalk vegetation of the southern downs, with its array of special shrubs – wayfaring tree, dogwood, spindle and privet – and colourful flowers such as cowslip, bee orchid, rockrose and salad burnet, and the moors of the north and west, where heather is king, accompanied by tormentil, bilberry, heath milkwort and a handful of others, with rowan as the principal tree. Animals are less eclectic, for the skylark and wheatear are found on both, but ring ouzel, red grouse and merlin live only on the moors, and stone curlew, corn bunting and quail only on the downs. In between are a wide range of less fussy animals and plants, often common weeds which will grow on any but the wettest or most acid soil.

But the details of the picture are more complex than this. Although the south and east is rich in basic soils, with the chalk of the downs and Chilterns and the oolitic limestone stretching from the Dorset coast through the Cotswolds to Yorkshire, it also has acid soils that form the

History of the Landscape

Left to themselves the forces of nature once produced – and might again if everybody emigrated – an almost completely forested Britain. When men first arrived, the lowlands were mainly mixed oakwood, with birch and pine on the northern hills. The lowland rivers were not constrained within artificial banks, but spread themselves across broad floodplains dense with alder carr, and the flatter upland areas, in the wetter period that followed the 'climatic optimum' 7–8000 years ago, began to disappear under a carpet of wet peat – blanket bog. The first farmers, who arrived around 3000 BC, made little impact on the landscape. Their primitive tools meant that they could not plough the heavy valley soils, and they were largely confined to the dry downlands. The once wooded southern downs became first arable and then grassland, prevented from reverting to woodland by grazing cattle and sheep. On these downs thrived a neolithic civilisation capable of such architectural and engineering feats as Stonehenge and Avebury.

As technology improved and iron implements became available, so settlement spread to the valleys; the rivers were driven back behind raised banks and by the Roman period, simple drainage systems were created. With the freedom from flooding and waterlogging that

I

these advances conferred, the rich alluvial soils were brought under the plough, until by the end of the Middle Ages, the countryside of Britain would have become unrecognisable to one of those early neolithic farmers. Yet the forests still remained: some were protected for the royal hunting, but every village, too, had its woodland, an essential part of the rural economy, providing wood for building and timber for fuel. The next great change came with the enclosures, when the vast open common fields were fenced and hedged in by landowners and so many of the 'deserted villages' that dot East Yorkshire and parts of the Midlands, for example, were first abandoned, their economy undermined.

1. Prehistoric settlements in a clearing in the ancient woodland in lowland Britain. The river banks are as yet unmanaged.

2. Mediaeval village, *ca* 1200 A.D. The settlement has grown and much of the forest has been cleared for agriculture. Notice the strip fields and the absence of hedgerows.

2

History of the Landscape

Man is changing the countryside all the time. From the Middle Ages until 100 years ago many woodlands were hazel coppice with oak standards, the latter used for building and for ships' timbers, the coppiced hazel for hurdles and other agricultural uses, as well as for fuel. Now coppice woodland is a rarity, but plantations of conifers, virtually unknown a few hundred years ago, march across vast areas of the country. At the end of the Middle Ages there were few hedges in the Midlands; two periods of enclosures made the Midlands into a predominantly hedged countryside.

Since the second World War the destruction of hedges to make prairie-like arable fields has restored the countryside in many areas to what it must have looked like when most parishes consisted mainly of three large open fields – except that there are no earth baulks between the strips of arable, and no longer is one-third of all farmland left fallow each year. In one large area of Huntingdonshire, cited in the *New Naturalist* book *Hedges*, the length of hedge was halved in the 5 years to 1970 alone, and in that decade Britain as a whole was losing 2000 miles of hedge a year. It is thought that more than 140,000 miles of hedges have been destroyed since 1945, out of a total of 620,000 miles, but mainly in the east. Indeed

3

80% of trees and half the hedges have been lost in some eastern counties during the past 25 or so years.

If you stand on any eminence in the south of England, such as Bredon Hill in Gloucestershire or Leith Hill in Surrey, you get the impression of a predominantly wooded landscape. This is largely due to the hedgerow trees. Now that perhaps as many as 11.5 million elms have died in the great Dutch elm disease epidemic, and now that most mechanical hedge trimmers chop off the saplings that once grew into hedgerow trees, the prospect from these hills may soon be greatly changed. We today would think it less beautiful, just as we find the bare northern hills more beautiful than those clad with conifers. But those who enjoy the countryside 50 years hence may not agree: they may like their hills wooded and their lowlands bare.

3. Eighteenth century: the town has grown, but the mediaeval bridge still suffices. There is much less woodland. The open fields of the mediaeval landscape have been enclosed by hedges.

4. The modern landscape. The hedges have disappeared and the mediaeval bridge has been replaced by a modern one. There is even less woodland, and some of what remains is composed of imported conifers. The river bank now boasts a power station in its favourite site.

4

The Ecological Framework

In one sense this whole book is about **ecology**. This is a term that once used to mean something specific to the few people who knew of it, but now can mean almost anything from wholemeal bread to non-returnable bottles, and tends to arouse strong emotions. Strictly speaking, ecology is the science of the interactions of animals and plants and their relationship with their environment. The whole of this introductory chapter has been concerned with the ecological framework of Britain, for the climate, the soil and human influence are three of the most important components of the environment of animals and plants.

A useful concept in ecology is that of the **niche**, the position that a species occupies in the community. Since small mammals, such as mice and voles, are largely nocturnal in their above-ground activity, wherever they are found there is a niche for a nocturnal predator. Which is why owls are found almost throughout the world. Similarly when man creates a new habitat – such as railway tracks, with their accompanying cinder beds – he creates new niches; railway tracks suited well the Oxford ragwort which originally grew on lava beds on Mt Etna!

Each species has its own way of life – its niche – and together the different species make up a **community** in which all are dependent on each other, directly or indirectly. But such communities, be they oakwoods, saltmarshes or even railway sidings, are not static systems. Some are stable over long periods of time (oakwoods, for example), but even there individual trees die and are replaced by others. Other communities are more transitory: when ground is disturbed or laid bare, either by human activity or some natural catastrophe, the initial pioneer plants, the first colonists, will grow for a while before being succeeded by others, which in turn will be replaced. These orderly, sometimes predictable changes are known as **succession**, and the changes continue until some community is reached which changes little or not at all, when the climax is attained.

Consider a sand-dune: when it is young few plants can grow on it, only those, such as marram-grass, which are adapted to life on the shifting, blowing sand. The marram stabilizes the sand and gradually a fixed-dune community develops, with plants such as thyme and perhaps bee orchids. This community can be maintained by grazing, for sheep will eat the saplings that would otherwise invade and turn the dune into, perhaps, pine woodland, as in the sequence of illustrations below.

Over most of inland Britain succession will lead eventually to oak woodland, for this is the commonest climax community here. You can see succession in miniature in every wood, for wherever a tree has fallen, light floods into the woodland floor and herbs and small shrubs such as bramble thrive. Fast-growing trees such as sycamore or ash quickly appear and race towards 'the little patch of blue' overhead; beneath them, growing more slowly but more tolerant of shade, come the oak or beech saplings, one of which will eventually fill that hole. But perhaps the simplest way to watch succession is to stop cultivating your vegetable garden.

One of the key concepts in ecology is the **food chain**, which is a scientific expression of the idea that 'big fleas have little fleas upon their backs to bite 'em'. It demonstrates the dependence of all organisms on others in a community. An earthworm eats fallen leaves, a blackbird eats the earthworm and a sparrowhawk the blackbird; or a waterflea consumes microscopic algae in a lake, a minnow the waterflea, a pike the minnow, and finally a heron eats the pike. All such chains must start with a plant, since these are the producers in the community, fixing energy from the sun. Each animal in the chain uses some energy for growth, and burns up much more in respiration, leaving less for whatever eats it. As a result food-chains rarely contain more than four or five links in a line, but they always have side-branches, for example other birds which eat earthworms or other fish which eat minnows. Some animals, such as the field vole, can start many chains, being preyed on by such different predators as foxes, kestrels, short-eared owls and hen harriers. Food chains are therefore better called foodwebs; their complexity emphasises the inter-connectedness of natural communities.

At the top of the food-webs sit the large predators, not preyed upon by other organisms to any significant extent. Man is such a 'top predator'. But the webs do not stop there. When top predators die, their bodies are decomposed by animals, fungi, and bacteria in the soil, and so they are the basis of a whole new set of foodwebs based on decomposers.

The animals at the top of food chains are particularly vulnerable to man's activities, either because he destroys them directly as competitors for his food supply, or because he destroys their habitat. Large birds of prey and the larger carnivores, the wolf, bear, golden eagle (in England and Wales) and osprey, for instance, were all killed off in an attempt to protect farm stock or game. Many others such as the pine marten, polecat, kite and sparrowhawk, have been greatly reduced in numbers for the same reason. For-tunately some, particularly the sparrowhawk and osprey, have responded to protection and are returning. In contrast such prime pests as the brown rat, rabbit, grey squirrel and muskrat were all brought in by man for one reason or another, and it is arguable that by destroying their natural predators in the supposed interests of game preservation, we have made the situation far worse and given these pests free rein. Many game mammals and birds have been deliberately released in the country-side, which would be a less interest-ing place without the fallow deer and the pheasant, red-legged part-ridge, little owl and Canada goose. Even the native roe deer and red squirrel have been re-introduced into some areas, having become ex-tinct because their habitat had been earlier destroyed. Similarly many mallard, common partridges, brown trout and red deer, natives all, may be of introduced origin, such is the need of sportsmen to augment the stocks they consistently overshoot and overfish.

The flora, too, has been changed by man. Probably we have gained more plants than we have lost in this way. Railway tracks, particu-larly, are homes to many immi-grants, such as buddleia, Michael-mas daisies, Canadian goldenrod and Oxford ragwort.

FARMLAND

Over much of Britain the 'countryside' is a landscape of green fields, brown fields, and scattered small woodlands, linked together with a network of hedges – or increasingly wire fences. This heavily farmed landscape is in no way wild, but it is so much the dominant type that we will begin with it. The green fields may be of grass or of any one of a dozen or so common crops; the brown fields are the crop fields, early in the year after ploughing, and are called arable. This is the most man-made part of our countryside, and for its beauty we must thank the tree-planting mania of our eighteenth century ancestors. Many of those trees are now being felled or killed by disease, and sadly we shall hand down to our descendants a more monotonous scene. Despite its artificiality, it is still one of the most important habitats in Britain for wildlife, both animal and plant. The grasslands and hedges, in particular, harbour a wide variety of wildlife.

Farming practices have changed considerably, even in the last twenty years. It is worrying that many agricultural landscapes, which were havens for wildlife very recently, have now been almost sterilised by modern farming methods. New economic pressures on farmers have produced a head-on conflict of interest between agriculture and conservation. Often good nature conservation practice involves maintaining agricultural methods that were commonplace a generation ago, a point not fully grasped by those who believe that conservationists wish to lock away the land and leave it wholly unutilised. As a society, we have failed to solve this conflict; our countryside is paying the price.

Arable Land

Land is cultivated in order to grow crops. Inevitably, therefore, the wild flowers of arable land are nearly always treated as weeds. Ironically, most of these plants are deeply dependent on man's activities for their survival. Five thousand years ago, when most of Britain was wooded and agriculture was non-existent, they must have been rare plants. It is probable that many have migrated across Europe with the spread of agriculture, seizing the new opportunities presented, and presumably evolving as they travelled, to cope with the changes in climate. Their persistence in crops is a reflection of their ecological similarity to those crops, for our crop plants probably often originated from the weeds which sprang up around settlements and which early man found he could put to profitable use.

The plants of ploughed fields are quite different from those of meadows, pastures or even leys (see pp. 26–29). The great majority are annuals, which can grow from seed right through their life-cycle to the production of flowers and new seed in the interval between ploughings, though a few, such as couch grass or twitch, are perennial. First, there is a group of opportunist weeds which flower almost throughout the year, except during periods of hard frost. These include groundsel, common chickweed, red dead-nettle, shep-

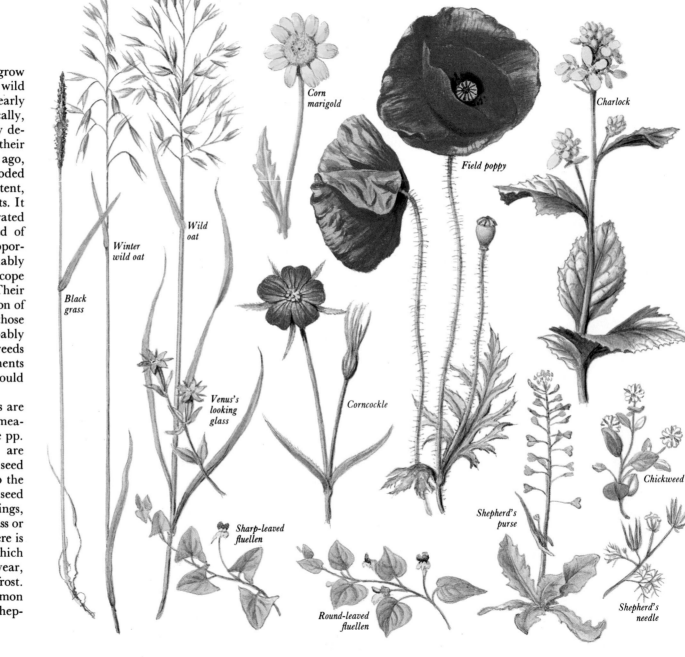

Corn marigold

Field poppy

Charlock

Wild oat

Winter wild oat

Black grass

Venus's looking glass

Corncockle

Chickweed

Shepherd's purse

Sharp-leaved fluellen

Round-leaved fluellen

Shepherd's needle

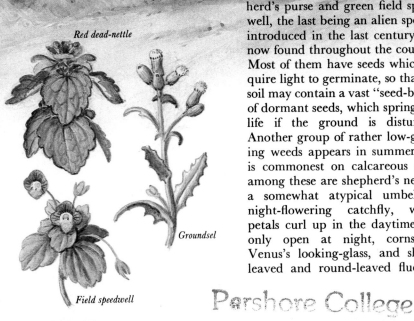

Red dead-nettle

Groundsel

Field speedwell

herd's purse and green field speed-well, the last being an alien species, introduced in the last century and now found throughout the country. Most of them have seeds which require light to germinate, so that the soil may contain a vast "seed-bank" of dormant seeds, which spring into life if the ground is disturbed. Another group of rather low-growing weeds appears in summer and is commonest on calcareous soils; among these are shepherd's needle, a somewhat atypical umbellifer, night-flowering catchfly, whose petals curl up in the daytime and only open at night, cornsalad, Venus's looking-glass, and sharp-leaved and round-leaved fluellen.

Unlike the first group which simply germinate and grow to fruit whenever the ground is bare, these plants fit in their annual life-cycle with the farmer's crops. Some of these summer-flowering weeds are more widespread, and heartsease and scarlet pimpernel can be found in most cornfields.

The most famous plants of arable fields are those which used to turn whole cornfields red, yellow or blue, but which modern herbicides and improved standards of seed purity have almost eliminated. The two which most often survive are the yellow charlock, a relative of mustard and oil-seed rape, corn marigold, and the brilliant scarlet field

poppy. Two others which are virtually extinct in Britain are the blue cornflower and corncockle; the latter has exceedingly poisonous seeds, so its loss should not be mourned too deeply.

One result of the use of selective herbicides has been to encourage other weeds, just as unwelcome. Herbicides used on a crop must not kill the crop, and those used kill dicotyledonous weeds but not monocotyledons, such as grasses, for cereals are grasses too. This opens the door, therefore, to monocotyledonous weeds, especially grasses, and such weed grasses as the wild oat, winter wild oat and black grass or black twitch can thrive.

Dyer's greenweed

Common sorrel

Sneezewort

Meadow fescue

Greater burnet

Pepper saxifrage

Meadow thistle

Meadow buttercup

Meadows and Pastures

Grassy fields, which look simply green and uniform to the superficial glance, are actually of several kinds, with very different floras. First there are grass leys, mostly of ryegrass and other palatable grasses, often mown eventually for silage or hay. This is grass as a crop, and such fields are ploughed regularly in a rotation that may include cereals, sugar-beet, potatoes or several other crops. Few other plants have time to establish themselves in leys. Secondly there are pastures, where cattle or sheep graze through much of the year; again few of the more attractive plants survive this intensive process, except where rather special conditions prevail.

It is the hayfields or meadows that produce the finest floral displays, especially those old-established meadows that have not been ploughed for many years. Regrettably such meadows are fast falling to the plough and the ley, and really old unploughed lowland grassland is one of the most endangered habitats in Britain. At its peak in late May and early June such hayfields are ablaze with the yellow of meadow buttercup and a little later tinged red with the spikes of common sorrel. In really old grassland, as on Ot-moor in Oxfordshire, plants such as greater burnet, sneezewort, dyer's greenweed, meadow thistle and pepper saxifrage jostle for position

with a host of others. Pastures at this time of year have little more than a few buttercups and thistles, which are both distasteful to cattle.

In the upland valleys of Wales and the Pennines, hay meadows reach their peak of magnificence. There, the soils are too thin to plough and fertilisers and herbicides are still used sparingly. In early July the meadows of Swaledale turn a rich violet-blue with clumps of wood cranesbill, and the tall spikes of melancholy thistle, a bigger version of meadow thistle, stand out.

Back in the lowlands, particularly on the heavy clay soils of the Midlands, you will see parallel ridges sloping up the hills in grassy fields. This "ridge and furrow" is a relic of the days when the heavy clay-lands had to be ploughed by teams of horses and did not drain properly without these ridges and furrows. Modern drainage techniques have bypassed them, but they still provide a fascinating ecological miniature. In such a field in winter, water often stands in the furrows; this wetter habitat favours the creeping buttercup. On the sides of the ridges meadow buttercup thrives, while sometimes on the very tops of the ridges bulbous buttercup, which cannot grow in waterlogged soil, may be found. So the yellow sheet of buttercups in May may hide a complex pattern.

Chalk Downs

The chalk downs that sweep across southern England were once covered almost entirely by grassland, maintained for centuries by the teeth of the tens of thousands of sheep that used to roam the great sheep-walks. Later their place was taken by rabbits, but since the devastating myxomatosis epidemic of 1953 much of the grassland has turned to scrub and young woodland and a unique habitat for wild plants is gradually disappearing.

Grassland, of course, is made up of grasses, and most of the commoner downland grasses are also found on other types of soil. Meadow oat-grass, the delightful quaking grass with its dangling lantern-like flowers, and red and sheep's fescues, are all widespread; only crested hair-grass is restricted in any way to chalk and limestone soils. Also common is glaucous sedge, sometimes misleadingly called carnation grass, but this can easily be distinguished from the true grasses by its triangular stems.

Some of the more colourful wild flowers too – for example birdsfoot trefoil and wild thyme – as well as the ubiquitous ribwort plantain, are widespread grassland plants, but many others, if not exclusively found on chalk and limestone, are distinctly uncommon elsewhere. The stemless thistle, bane of picnickers, carline thistle with its silvery bracts, rough hawkbit, burnet saxifrage (actually a white-flowered umbellifer), the edible salad burnet, hoary plantain, cowslip and small scabious, are all good indicators of a soil rich in lime.

The great glory of chalk grassland, however, is the extraordinary constellation of rare and showy plants, which are found only here. Most striking of all is the gorgeous Easter-flowering pasque flower, with its boss of golden stamens adorning an open bell of deep violet-purple petals. Almost equally showy are the deep violet flowers of the clustered bell-flower and the pale purple Chiltern gentian.

Even these, spectacular though they may be, cannot compare in interest with the great variety of orchids that grow more profusely on the downs than anywhere else in Britain. Of the chalk grassland orchids, both the dainty pyramidal and elegant fragrant orchids are pollinated by moths which they attract at night by scent. There are also insect mimics – the bee and the early and late spider orchids – as well as the manikin group, represented here by the man and monkey orchids, which get their names from the fact that the lower lips of the flowers resemble a human (or at least a primate) body, with tiny arms and legs. Another great rarity, the lizard orchid, has a 'tail' 5 cm long and is notable for its erratic appearances, usually after hot, dry summers.

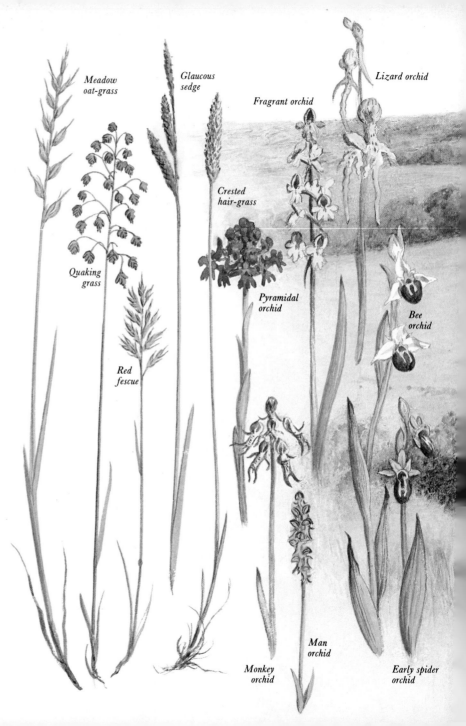

Meadow oat-grass

Glaucous sedge

Lizard orchid

Fragrant orchid

Crested hair-grass

Quaking grass

Pyramidal orchid

Bee orchid

Red fescue

Monkey orchid

Man orchid

Early spider orchid

Cowslip

Small scabious

Rough hawkbit

Clustered bellflower

Pasque flower

Chiltern gentian

Hoary plantain

Birds-foot trefoil

Hedges

Hedges form a link between cultivated land and woodland—literally as well as figuratively. They are a quintessential, although disappearing, part of the English countryside, and their presence immeasurably enriches the wildlife of the cultivated areas they divide.

Hedge is a word with several meanings; basically it is a boundary, often stock-proof, and in many parts of western Britain such boundaries are massive banks of earth or stone, which may or may not carry what the rest of England calls a hedge on top. To make a hedge of shrubs, hawthorn is the ideal plant, for it is very thorny and fast-growing, but it does not sucker, in contrast to the even thornier blackthorn, which would turn the whole field into a blackthorn thicket if left to itself. Hawthorn, also known as quickthorn or just quick, was the main species used when the hedged landscape of England was being planted up during the enclosure of the common fields, which lasted from the late Middle Ages to the mid-nineteenth century.

Not all hedges date from the enclosures. Many, especially those on parish boundaries, are hundreds of years old, though few can trace their lineage back for a thousand years, as can the Black Hedge near Princes Risborough, Buckinghamshire, which was mentioned in an Anglo-Saxon Charter in A.D. 900. Such ancient hedges are a part of our heritage that should be preserved no less carefully than ancient buildings. They have not survived by chance; they have been carefully managed by layering at intervals. Without layering, which involves half-cutting through the stronger stems, laying them almost flat, and twining other stems around them, they would quickly become leggy and no longer stock-proof. The sight of a newly-layered hedge is nowadays regrettably rare and bodes ill for the future survival of the hedge in the farming landscape.

A remarkably simple way of estimating the age of a hedge has been worked out by Max Hooper in one of the most fascinating volumes in the *New Naturalist* series (published by Collins). Just pace out 30 metres of hedge and the number of different species of shrubs in that stretch is the approximate age of the hedge in centuries. Obviously you need to do this on several stretches and take an average, and it assumes that the hedge was planted with a single species, as most were. The method was worked out in the east Midlands, and the equation may be different in areas where more or fewer species of shrubs naturally occur. This relationship is particularly interesting because it gives us an insight into the rate at which new

Hawthorn

English oak

English elm

Privet

Spindle

Blackthorn

Dog rose

Wych elm

Hazel

Dogwood

Field maple

Ash

species of plants invade existing communities. In practice of course, this is unlikely to be as regular as one per century, since in the early stages of such colonisation, the chances of a new species appearing are much higher than later on, when most of them are in the hedge already.

Hedges and small copses are almost the only places where woody plants can grow in farmland. Over the years other shrubs, notably blackthorn, elder and dog rose invade the planted hawthorn hedges, and in calcareous soils several of the special chalk shrubs—dogwood, privet, spindle and wayfaring tree—

can usually be found. Where tree saplings have been allowed to grow up in the shelter of the hedge, oak, ash, and elm appear at intervals and provide the shade that was once welcomed by cattle but is now disliked by farmers for its effects on crop yields. Many of the elms, now almost annihilated by the Dutch elm disease epidemic, may once have been planted by farmers who fed the foliage to their stock. The trees we see now may be the direct descendants, propagated by suckers, of trees first planted in the Iron Age, for modern British summers are rarely hot enough for the common elm —as distinct from the native wych

elm—to produce viable fruit.

Some hedges are not planted, but were originally the borders of woods. Now the wood may have been felled, leaving only the hedge, whose origin is usually betrayed by the great variety of shrubs in it. They can also be distinguished by the woodland plants that grow along them, such as wood anemone, bluebell and red campion. Such hedges also often give themselves away by their shape, winding their way across the countryside, instead of cutting across at right angles, as enclosure hedges typically do. It is sometimes possible to trace the outline of a now lost wood, by looking for such hedges.

Flowers of the Hedgerow

Few hedges do not have a bank or strip of grassland on which wild flowers can grow, and most hedges alongside roads have quite broad verges, which constitute one of the principal refuges for wild flowers in a heavily farmed countryside (see pp. 36–37). Sometimes these verges are disproportionately wide, and this usually indicates that the road was used for stock driving, or at least was so heavily used that, in winter, several tracks were available, and as each became impassable with mud a new one would be used.

In the West Country road and also railway banks are often covered with primroses early in the year, but the wild daffodils on motorway banks in the daffodil districts of Gloucestershire and Herefordshire have of course been planted. In May hedgebanks all over lowland England turn white with Queen Anne's lace, a general term for white-flowered umbellifers, which are distinguished by having their small flowers arranged radially, as if on the spokes of an umbrella. First to appear, with a few spikes even at the end of March in the south, is cow parsley which reaches its glorious peak in May. A few weeks later it is succeeded by the much less showy rough chervil, easily told by the purple spots on its stem—cow parsley's stem is either green or purple but never spotted—and in July the

succession is wound up by the still smaller and wirier upright hedge parsley. The much larger hogweed, reaches a peak in May and June and lingers on into the autumn. Our native hogweed, up to a metre or so tall, must not be confused with the alien giant hogweed which reaches two metres and has umbels up to 50 cm across, compared with 20–30 cm in the native plant. Giant hogweed often grows on waste ground, and contact with it can make human skin blister.

Many shade-loving plants such as red campion, greater stitchwort, herb robert, lords and ladies, garlic mustard, herb bennet and bush vetch frequently grow on hedge banks, either within the latticework of fields and hedges of true farmland, or along the network of roads and lanes. Ferns, too, which can only reproduce in moist spots, are often found in the ditches beneath hedges.

Hedges are also the main home of a very distinctive type of plant—climbers. The two bryonies, black and white, which are quite unrelated, are common in hedges. Both are the sole British representatives of large tropical families, the white bryony being related to cucumbers and melons and the black to the yams. Other climbers include old man's beard or traveller's joy (the wild *Clematis*) on chalk and limestone, and several vetches.

Traveller's joy

Upright hedge parsley

White bryony

Black bryony

Cow parsley

Rough chervil

Lords and
ladies

Red
campion

Garlic
mustard

Greater
Stitchwort

Herb
bennet

Herb robert

Bush
vetch

Greater plantain

White clover

Rye grass

Smooth meadow-grass

Annual meadow-grass

Meadow foxtail

Creeping bent

Sweet vernal grass

Couch grass

Footpaths

Footpaths today are used largely for recreation, and provide one of the pleasanter ways of seeing the countryside. Few study the footpath they are walking on, but footpaths do in fact have a distinctive and interesting vegetation of their own.

Just as the wild plants, such as daisies, dandelions and plantains, that survive on mown lawns, do so because their leaves form ground-hugging rosettes which are missed by the mower blades, so plants of footpaths are adapted to resist the trampling effect of human and animal feet. Trampling combines vertical pressure with a twisting action as the ball of the foot leaves the ground. Mild trampling has little effect, but as it becomes more intense it causes damage to the leaves and eventually may uproot or kill plants. The centre of a well-used footpath is therefore bare, but beside it there is a zonation of plants progressively less able to withstand trampling. The most resistant, nearest the middle, are greater plantain and annual meadow grass, followed by smooth meadow grass, ryegrass and white clover. Other common grasses such as creeping bent and even the pestilential weed couch grass or twitch, are quickly killed off by the patter of feet.

In the age of the automobile, all important roads (and even some footpaths) have metalled surfaces.

But it is not long since the great highways of Britain were mud or gravel tracks. Some still survive as 'green lanes': a few are very ancient, such as the Icknield Way and the Ridgeway, the pre-Roman track that connects Dorset to Norfolk and runs along the foot of the Chilterns and the crest of the Berkshire Downs. The great mediaeval drove roads, along which drovers brought their cattle and sheep from Wales, northern England and Scotland to market, survive too in places – the Drift in Lincolnshire is an example. These old tracks are often as wide as a modern trunk road, since the churning of hooves quickly reduced them to mud, forcing the drovers into parallel tracks alongside.

The modern equivalent of these great tracks are the long-distance footpaths that have been created by the linking together of traditional rights of way. The best known is the Pennine Way, from Edale in Derby-shire to Yetholm in the Cheviots. The Offa's Dyke Path, the Pem-brokeshire, Devon and Cornwall Coast Paths, and the Downs Way are others. Even the old Icknield Way and Ridgeway route has been opened to modern feet in this way. The most recent is the Ebor Way, from Helmsley *via* York to Ilkley, the final link in a 450-mile chain stretching from Oakham in Rutland to Windermere in the Lake District.

Roadsides

Meadow cranesbill

White campion

Upright hedge parsley

Silverweed

In an intensively cultivated arable countryside, such as in parts of Lincolnshire or the Fenlands, the road verges and their accompanying hedges (where they survive) form the last refuge for many forms of wildlife. Road verges reflect the fauna and flora of the often now lost natural vegetation of the surrounding countryside: in the limestone Cotswolds, for example, the handsome, lime-loving, blue meadow cranesbill appears on many minor roads (the major ones are too often sprayed with selective herbicides that favour grasses), and on the chalk downs of southern England the marbled white butterfly, whose caterpillars feed on horseshoe vetch, may still be seen, or six-spot burnet moths, perhaps, feeding on field scabious. On neutral or acid soils, however, most roadsides have a different, often richer flora than the adjacent fields, partly because of the fertilizing effect of dust and other materials from the road; this is very clearly seen where roads cross heather moorland.

The flora of road verges is astonishingly diverse and reflects not only the local geology, climate and so on, but also the range of management that the verges receive. Some are regularly mown or grazed, and these tend to have the most interesting flora; others receive herbicide sprays and can be ineffably dull. The most colourful are usually those that have been recently disturbed, by road-works for example. In the first year, the habitat resembles an arable field, with field poppy, scentless mayweed, charlock, and other annual weeds very abundant. In the second year there is often a profusion of biennial species such as hogweed, and mullein, which forms a rosette of leaves in its first year, a massive flowering spike in its second, and then dies. Finally, the roadside reverts to the longer-lived perennials, with white and red campion, silverweed, greater knapweed, common mallow, yarrow, mugwort and others enlivening many a country drive.

Motorways might seem a particularly unpromising habitat for wildlife, but even here, distinctive local communities of plants and animals have developed. The broad, unmown and relatively inaccessible stretches of grassland that border many motorways form a refuge for small mammals, the prey for kestrels which can often be seen hovering above them. Drifts of salt, which is sprayed each winter to combat ice on the road, have turned the central reservations of some motorways into the ideal habitat for a number of salt-marsh and maritime plants, such as the sea meadow grass, although it is a brave or foolhardy motorist who stops to admire them.

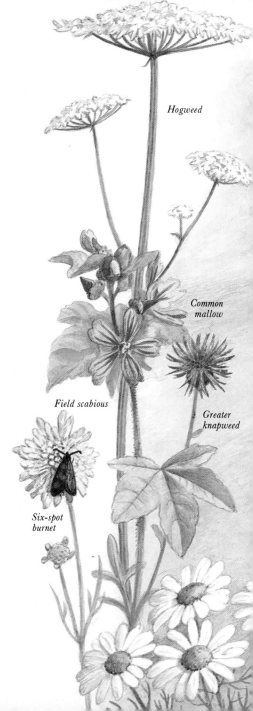

Hogweed

Common mallow

Greater knapweed

Field scabious

Six-spot burnet

Field poppy

Yarrow

Scentless mayweed

Mugwort

Great mullein

Common mallow

Farmland Animals

Rabbit

Hare

Because it is so cultivated, not many larger animals have been able to adapt themselves to life in an agricultural countryside, but among the few are the rabbit, the brown hare, and their predator (at any rate occasionally) the fox. Rabbits were introduced to Britain for their valuable fur and meat in the Middle Ages, but the hare and fox are native. Perhaps because game preservers have killed off so many of their natural predators, mainly the larger birds of prey, but also polecats and martens, rabbits and also brown rats (another introduced species) tend to get out of hand in the countryside, and become great pests to the farmer. When there is a severe infestation rabbits often graze the edges of cornfields right down, but do not often go far into the middle. There are certain wild plants which rabbits do not like, such as elder, ragwort and houndstongue and these often grow conspicuously near rabbit warrens when all other vegetation has been grazed to the ground and much bare earth revealed. Desperate farmers spread the myxomatosis virus in Britain in the middle 1950s (an act which has since been made illegal, though doubtless it still goes on) with the result that during the later 1950s and early 60s there were rather few rabbits in the countryside. However, the population is now steadily recovering, though minor local epidemics are constantly breaking out, so it may be that rabbits will never again reach the plague proportions they once did.

The fox is the only remaining major mammalian predator of farmland, if the badger is regarded as a mainly woodland species, but contrary to legend it does not feed primarily on rabbits. The fox owes its success to being an omnivore; it will eat almost anything, animal or vegetable, live or dead, and probably at most times its staple diet is mice and voles, which are always numerous in farmland. However, it is not above competing with blackbirds and thrushes for earth-

Fox

Weasel

Field vole

Bank vole

Brown rat

Stoat

Harvest mouse

Mole

worms, and eats blackberries and other wild fruits in season. Foxes do not, of course, graze, like rodents or ungulates, but get their nourishment at secondhand by feeding on animals that graze.

Apart from the common or brown rat, mainly found near farm buildings, the commonest farmland rodents are the field vole and the house mouse. The term 'field mouse' used to be applied to both the short-tailed field mouse, now called field vole, and the long-tailed field mouse, now called wood mouse, because it is in fact much commoner in woods than fields. Voles can be easily told from mice by their blunt, not pointed muzzles. The field vole is

the commonest small mammal in the open countryside, farmland, rough grazings and moors, and is preyed on by many birds of prey as well as by foxes, stoats and weasels. When it produces population explosions, the so-called vole plagues, large numbers of predators, such as short-eared owls and kestrels, move· in and are wrongly praised for bringing the plague to an end. We now know that these vole plagues collapse for a variety of reasons within the vole population itself.

The house mouse, familiar and unwelcome denizen of our houses, is also widespread in the open countryside, and not just in corn

ricks, which anyway are now largely a thing of the past. In hedgerows, however, they are usually less common than the wood mice which have colonised these linear woodlands. Brown rats also come into the hedgerows about harvest time, but may live all the year round in fields of root crops, which provide them with a permanent food supply.

The tiny harvest mouse inhabits all kinds of thick vegetation, in farmland especially along field headlands and in rough grassy banks. It is the only British mouse that nests well above ground level; in early winter these cricket-ball-sized nests of dried vegetation can be quite easily found attached to dead stalks.

Farmland Birds

Many of the birds most often seen on farmland are really woodland birds that have stayed on as a result of the survival of trees and shrubs in the latticework of hedges. This is why blackbirds, song thrushes, green woodpeckers, wrens and chaffinches all feature in the list of farmland birds. Some woodland birds, notably the rook and woodpigeon, do rely very heavily on farmland for their sustenance. So much so in fact that they have become most unpopular with farmers, rooks for digging up the sprouting corn, and woodpigeons for grazing down brassica crops in hard weather. Rooks make up for this by also feeding on many farm pests, such as wireworms, but nobody has a good word to say for the woodpigeon.

Rooks are members of the Crow Family, and are best told from their close relative the carrion crow by the bare patch at the base of the bill. Otherwise both have an all black plumage, though at close range the rook has a purplish sheen, and the crow a greenish one. Rooks too usually go in flocks, while carrion crows more often than not are in ones or twos. However crows do flock and rooks do go singly, so this is not an infallible distinction. The woodpigeon is much more easily told from the smaller stockdove, which sometimes joins it in the fields, by the conspicuous white patches on each wing in flight and on each side of its neck. Juveniles lack the white neck patches. Occasionally feral pigeons from the towns feed in the fields, and those which still approximate to the basic rockdove pattern can then be told by their white rumps, which the stockdove lacks, while the stockdove has two dark bars on the wing, which the other pigeons lack.

The birds which live all the time on the open farmland are rather few, but include corn bunting, skylark and the two partridges, common and red-legged. The corn bunting, unlike most other song birds, does not require an elevated song-post, but is quite content to utter its jangly little song from a clod of earth, though if there is a post or a dead thistle available, it will use these too. The skylark has tackled the songpost problem in a different way, it mounts up into the sky and hangs or hovers there uttering the second most popular song in the poetry stakes (assuming the nightingale to be the first). Both therefore can survive in a totally hedgeless farming countryside, such as the Fens or other parts of eastern England. The two partridges, the native grey and the introduced red-legged, do not sing, or require any elevation to complete their annual behaviour cycle, though the red-legged partridge will sometimes fly up on to a stack to utter its challenging steam-hammer-like call. They are therefore ideally suited to life in farmland, and it is only a change in farming practice, which has reduced the amount of insect food available for their chicks, that has led to their recent widespread decline. When farmers first introduced herbicides to reduce the weed flora of their cornfields, none of them had any idea that they were spelling the doom of partridge shooting by also removing the insects that feed on the weeds. The red-legged partridge, a native of south-west Europe, has been able to adapt itself better and is now the commoner of the two species in many parts of England. It was originally brought here in the 18th and 19th centuries by landowners who had overshot their stocks of native grey partridges.

The kestrel also thrives in farming countryside, so long as a hollow tree or ruined building survives nearby where it can lay its eggs – it makes no nest. For the kestrel, like the fox, feeds on the mice and voles that are the real beneficiaries of any move to extend arable cultivation. Like the skylark, the kestrel has developed a hovering technique, which makes it the easiest British bird of prey to identify, and has also made it a familiar sight above motorway banks, where voles thrive undisturbed.

Corn bunting

Skylark

Woodpigeon

Barn owl

Lapwing

Rook

Grey partridge

Red-legged partridge

Farmland Insects

Insect life is on the whole discouraged on farmland, but still survives and even thrives, to the great benefit of insect-eating birds and animals. The extensive monocultures essential to modern mechanised agriculture provide the ideal breeding ground for such pests as the wheat bulb-fly and frit fly, and so stimulate the fashionable modern remedies of spraying pesticides and pretreating seeds. These drastic remedies were not so necessary in the days of mixed farming, for a pest which attacked a ten acre field, could only do ten acres worth of damage before meeting some different crop; when a pest attacks a hundred acre field, it does that much more damage, and today a hundred acre field is easier to find than a ten acre one.

Among the more familiar insects, two of the commonest farmland butterflies are unwelcome: the large white and the small white have caterpillars which feed on cabbages and other brassicas in farm and garden. The damage they do is familiar, and the more striking because so few other insects feed on these plants. This is because they contain poisonous mustard oils which kill most insects, but which the white butterfly caterpillars are resistant to; indeed they go one better and use the scent of these toxins as an attractant, a way of identifying their food plant. Two other attractive butterflies, the small tortoiseshell and the peacock, have hairy black caterpillars that feed on stinging nettles, a primarily woodland plant that is common round farms, because it thrives on the fertile soils found there. Two of their relatives, the red admiral and painted lady, are ubiquitous migrants that arrive each summer from the Mediterranean; the brood they raise here returns southward in the autumn and few if any succeed in hibernating here, as the tortoiseshell and peacock do. These can be found in dark corners of most country houses in the winter months, and emerge, along with the brimstone butterfly, in early spring.

The chalk downs, insofar as they are still uncultivated, provide the richest and most attractive insect fauna to be found in the farmed landscape, with many beautiful butterflies found hardly anywhere else. Examples are the marbled white, whose caterpillars feed on grasses, the chalkhill and Adonis blues, with their food plant horseshoe vetch, which only grows on chalk and limestone, as well as a variety of butterflies found on grassland generally, such as small copper, small heath and common blue.

Two day-flying moths are also abundant: both have red hindwings and dark fore-wings with

Chalkhill blue

Adonis blue

Marbled white

Common blue

Small copper

Brimstone

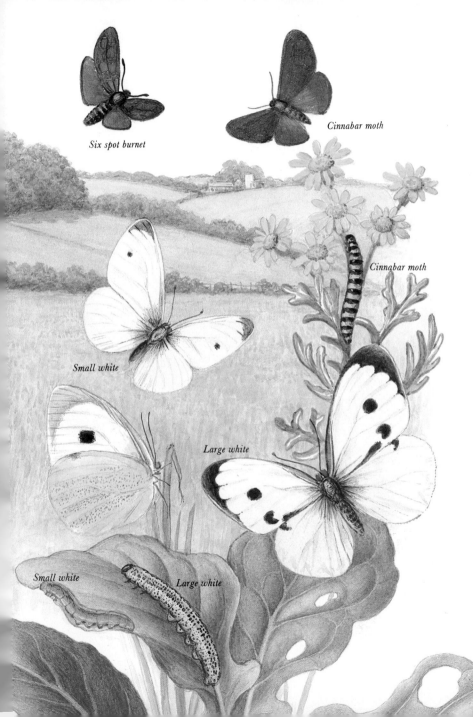

Six spot burnet

Cinnabar moth

Cinnabar moth

Small white

Small white

Large white

Large white

scarlet markings. The caterpillars of the cinnabar feed on ragwort, often stripping it bare in late summer. Ragwort is another very poisonous plant, but the cinnabar not only survives the poison but turns it to advantage by storing the poisons in its own body, becoming toxic itself, and then advertising the fact by the black and yellow stripes on the caterpillar, a universal danger signal in Nature. The burnet moths are superficially similar – the commonest is the 6-spot burnet – and are notable for their conspicuous chrysalises on grass stems.

Butterflies and moths are only the most conspicuous of the many insects and other invertebrates that live on farmland. The cockchafer is harmless enough, but its large white grub is disliked by farmers and gardeners, for the damage it does to their crops. The violet ground beetle, on the other hand, has nothing against it, being carnivorous. Ladybirds are positively beneficial, both they and their larvae feeding on aphids and scale insects.

Crane-flies or daddy-long-legs are two-winged flies that are accounted among the worst farmland pests. Their larvae are the hated leatherjackets which feed on the roots of grass and cereal crops. These too are relished by rooks, by way of recompense for any sprouting corn they may also dig up.

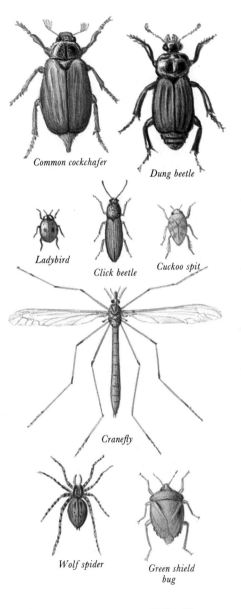

Common cockchafer

Dung beetle

Ladybird

Click beetle

Cuckoo spit

Cranefly

Wolf spider

Green shield bug

TOWNS AND GARDENS

Towns, villages and their associated industries and gardens form one of the most important habitats available for wildlife in a developed country like Britain. They are richer in terms of actual numbers of animals and plants than many natural habitats, such as moorland, upland lakes and sand dunes. There are many reasons for this: partly it may be because some human activities enrich the soil – pollute it if you like – with nitrogen and phosphorus and other essential minerals; partly it is because some animals can adapt very well to living in close proximity to man – it is curious for instance that finches can do this much better than the closely allied buntings; and certainly an important factor is that man actually introduces, usually inadvertently, quite alien and sometimes rather exotic species. Some of these, such as the gaudy and invasive Himalayan balsam, which lines urban rivers and canals, are highly successful in their new home; others survive a year or two, but eventually succumb to frost, perhaps, or competition from native species.

One of the questions which ecologists would most like to know the answer to, is what makes some species into successful invaders, for most of the major pests of crops are introduced from another country. One of the most important things seems to be the existence of natural enemies. Most plants and animals are probably not limited in numbers or abundance by the availability of food (for animals) or nutrients (for plants), but by the activity of predators or grazing animals. If a species invades a new area, it may be able to leapfrog ahead of its enemies and then flourish for a while. Sometimes the native grazing animals or predators learn to use this new food source; on other occasions its enemies themselves find their way to the new site; and sometimes man speeds the process up by introducing them deliberately as a means of biological control. This last method can have dangerous consequences, of course, since the newly introduced predator or parasite may find native species to its liking as well.

Urban Habitats

The habitats available to plants in built-up areas are remarkably varied. Most plentiful are those corresponding to rocks, cinder wastes such as occur around volcanoes, and bare gravelly ground as might be found by swift-flowing rivers. These are more familiar to us as walls, railway tracks and gravel paths, and are favoured by pioneer plants, those that first colonise bare or disturbed ground, where they thrive in the absence of competition. Gardeners spend much of their time preparing an ideal habitat for such plants, in the form of bare flower and vegetable beds. The plants that gratefully take advantage of their efforts are the ones they call weeds. Most garden weeds are annuals, often similar to cornfield weeds (pp. 24–25), but a few, such as couch grass, bindweed and ground elder are perennials and hard to eradicate.

Grassland is the other major habitat for plants in our towns and villages, and is usually mown. Mown grassland, which we normally call a lawn, has few natural equivalents, perhaps the closest being the closely cropped swards produced by intensive grazing by rabbits for example. Plants which thrive on lawns have one or more of several adaptations: a rosette of leaves, never touched by the mower, such as in plantains, dandelions and hawkbits; constant and rapid flowering, like the common daisy, which rears its bright head almost as soon as the mower has passed over; or the ability to regrow leaves from the base, which is why lawns are largely composed of grasses, for this is their distinctive feature. The plants of unmown or infrequently mown grassland in towns and villages are much like those of rough grassland anywhere,

and especially on the roadsides and at the edges of cultivated fields.

Plant-eating insects and other invertebrates usually follow their plant hosts, but some invertebrates find quite distinct habitats in towns, unconnected with vascular plants. Buildings provide a rich foodstore for insects and other invertebrates that feed on timber (woodworm), fabrics (clothes moths, house moth), foodstuffs (various beetles) and even for those whose habitat is human (bed bug, flea, head louse). Some butterflies are especially associated with towns, such as the cabbage whites, which feed on cabbages and Brussels sprouts in the numerous vegetable gardens, and such migratory species as the red admiral and painted lady, which find their way on to the flower beds and shrubberies of both parks and gardens, the buddleia being an

especially favoured bush, so much so that it is sometimes called the butterfly bush. If there are stinging nettles not far away, both peacocks and small tortoiseshells, whose caterpillars feed on nettles, will join the fray on the buddleias and also on Michaelmas daisies.

To birds a built-up area provides a mixture between open woodland —for most towns have a great many trees in both streets and gardens— and inland cliffs. It is the cliff-like quality of buildings and bridges that appeals particularly to the feral pigeons, which are established in almost all major areas, whereas the woodpigeon has adapted itself to town life largely because there are so many tall trees in which it can nest safely, while it exploits the rich food supply provided by gardeners and park keepers. The locally distributed black redstart, a robin-like bird that

Dandelion

Cabbage white

Black bindweed

Field bindweed

Greater plantain

is a relative of the redstart of the woods, also takes advantage of the cliff-like or cave-like qualities of the urban habitat, for it likes to build its nest on a concealed ledge, as does also the swallow, which was long ago driven out of most town centres by the lack of aerial insect life due to atmospheric pollution. For the same reason that highly adapted urban bird the house martin, which builds its mud nest under the eaves of often surprisingly new houses, is now rarely seen in city centres. The swift, perhaps the commonest of the three in towns nowadays, comes surprisingly far into the centre of some towns, perhaps as a tribute to the success of recent laws to enforce purer air. For nesting sites it depends on the survival of old houses with open eaves, under which it makes its scanty nest.

One of the most surprising urban animals is the fox, a scavenger which has made itself fully at home in the inner and outer suburbs of many towns, where it competes with (and probably also eats) both domestic and feral cats for much of its prey, which consists of small birds, rats, mice and human refuse of various kinds.

The familiar but unwanted house mouse is the commonest urban mammal but can also be found in open country. It is truly commensal with man, and arrived in the baggage of some of our ancestors more than two thousand years ago. The brown rat is a more recent immigrant, reaching our shores only in the eighteenth century. However, it soon made up for lost time and is an even more unwelcome denizen of warehouses, rubbish dumps, sewers and other places where it can find an easy living.

House martin

Swallow

Red admiral *Buddleia*

Daisy

Garden Birds

Song thrush

Mistle thrush

winter

Starling

summer

Hedge sparrow

♀

House sparrow

Blackbird

♂

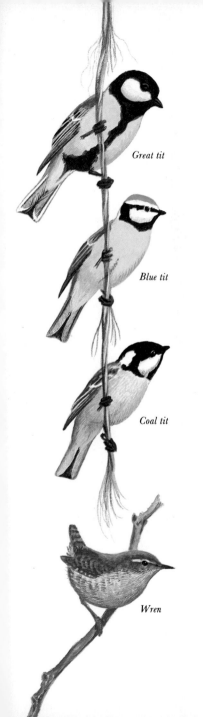

Great tit

Blue tit

Coal tit

Wren

Goldcrest

Robin

Greenfinch

Chaffinch

Spotted
flycatcher

To a bird a garden is equivalent to open woodland or scrub, with the added advantage of lawns mown not by deer but by mowing machines. In consequence the birds of gardens are for the most part those of woodland, and the birds that have succeeded in adapting themselves to life in and around human settlements are largely woodland birds that do not mind the presence of man. The archetype of the tame garden bird is the robin, which over much of Europe is still a shy bird of deep woodland. In Britain, however, it characteristically waits upon the gardener when it sees him digging, and darts down to secure small earthworms and other tasty morsels as he turns the soil over. It is of some interest that a robin has been seen doing exactly the same thing with a mole, whose excavations were being upheaved into a molehill. The robin has another interesting adaptation, in that instead of building its nest on a crevice in a tree or on a ledge in a river bank, it very often uses such artificial crannies as discarded pots or kettles, or ledges inside garden

sheds or garages. A nest is even on record in the pocket of an old gardening jacket hanging in a hedge.

The blackbird and the two thrushes, mistle and song, are all three woodland birds that find gardens much to their liking, although their nesting sites are more orthodox, most often in the fork of a tree or shrub. Sometimes too they nest in creeper on the wall of a house or barn, a site also much favoured by both the house sparrow and the spotted flycatcher. Thrushes are especially dependent on the food they get from lawns and flowerbeds, and for this reason they are often found at a higher density in gardens than in their original woodland habitat.

But where blackbirds live at a high density in urban habitats, they may be driven to use nest sites almost as strange as the robin's, such as drain-pipes, window ledges and lamp standards. A nest has even been found on a traffic light at a busy London junction.

The three common species of garden tit are the great, blue and coal, all woodland species. Where the householder puts up nestboxes for them, they will usually use these in preference to natural holes; certainly unless they are put up too close together, tit-boxes are almost invariably occupied. Coal tits usually require the presence of at least one conifer nearby, but these are not

Garden Birds

Carrion crow

Jackdaw

Jay

Magpie

uncommon in suburban gardens, and also often yield a goldcrest or two, perhaps more often outside the breeding season than in it. It is worth remembering in this connection that the yew is a conifer.

Two other primarily insect-eating garden birds that in the wild live mainly in woods and scrub are the hedgesparrow or dunnock and the wren, the latter having nearly as eccentric a choice of nest sites as the robin. Among seed-eaters the chaffinch and greenfinch are the principal frequenters of gardens, if we except the house sparrow, which is omnivorous and has lived with man for so long that one can only guess at what its original habitat may have been. It nests not only in holes in trees and buildings, but also in open sites against walls or even in low trees and shrubs like a greenfinch.

D. Summers-Smith, in the *New Naturalist* book on the house sparrow, suggests that the ancestral sparrow was probably a bird living in tropical Africa, that built large untidy domed nests in the branches of trees and shrubs, much like many of the weaver birds today. Thus tree nesting, now rather exceptional, may have been the original habit and the widespread hole nesting an adaptation to living with man, who had an unfortunate habit of cutting down the trees near his settlements for firewood.

Because of the need to adapt to the frequent presence of human beings, most garden birds are fairly small, but some members of the crow and pigeon family have to some extent become garden birds, at any rate in larger gardens. Carrion crows, jays and magpies may all

nest in large gardens and parks; jackdaws are well known for their association with old buildings, but are not in the ordinary sense garden birds, though in some built-up areas they are common enough. Woodpigeons, likewise, are birds of parks and squares rather than gardens, but a large, well tree-fringed garden is likely to attract a nesting pair. However, the recently arrived collared dove shows more signs of joining the garden bird association. Its colonisation of western Europe, including the British Isles, is one of the most dramatic ornithological events ever recorded. It has all happened since 1930, and mainly in the last few years. The first collared doves arrived in Britain in the early 1950s, and within 15 or 20 years the bird had colonised almost the whole archipelago.

Woodpigeon

Collared dove

Waste Ground

Considering the price of land, areas of waste ground are surprisingly common in towns. The cycle of urban demolition and renewal often involves long periods during which ground is left bare, and these areas can provide welcome oases of wildlife in the glass and concrete desert.

When a piece of waste ground is abandoned, it will first be colonized by those plant opportunists whose seeds are brought in by birds or are light enough to be borne on the wind, including such shrubs as goat willow (or great sallow) and hawthorn, as well as the common annual weeds of cultivation, for example groundsel, shepherd's purse, red dead-nettle and common field speedwell. These weeds are soon supplanted by coarse grasses, such as couch and false oat-grass and then by various biennials and perennials, including thistles, nettles and rosebay. Because waste ground is seldom disturbed, annual weeds are relatively uncommon. It is also rarely grazed, which favours plants other than grasses. As a result, the most characteristic plants of waste ground are the perennial weeds, particularly such conspicuous ones as rosebay willowherb, Oxford ragwort, creeping and spear thistles, and, where the soil is more fertile, stinging nettle.

Rosebay was once an uncommon woodland plant; it was known as fireweed because it so often colonized ground after fires. Some time early this century, either a mutation arose or a new variety was introduced, perhaps from North America, and rosebay took off, rather as the collared dove has in the last 30 years. It was one of the two most conspicuous weeds of the London bombed sites during and after the last war. The other was the Oxford ragwort.

Introduced from the lava wastes of Mt Etna in Sicily, and elsewhere in the Mediterranean, Oxford ragwort escaped from the Oxford Botanic Garden onto the city walls some time in the early 19th century. From there, when the railways came, its feathery fruits were blown by the draught of the trains all along the Great Western Railway. A plant adapted to life on the lava wastes had no difficulty in colonizing the cinders of railway tracks, and when it eventually arrived in London, the wartime bombing provided it with acres of suitable habitat. Today Oxford ragwort is one of the commonest waste ground plants throughout England and Wales and is starting to move into Scotland.

Few vertebrates make their homes on waste ground, although goldfinches will often visit thistle heads in autumn to feast on the seeds, and flocks of house sparrows can be seen on fruiting patches of fat-hen in August. The brown rat is probably the most characteristic mammal, although early risers might catch sight of a fox, an animal that is increasingly taking up life in towns. The insect life, however, is a good deal more interesting. Elephant hawk-moth caterpillars may often be found on rosebay, small tortoiseshell and peacock butterfly larvae on nettles, and also the warningly black-and-yellow striped caterpillars of cinnabar moth on Oxford ragwort, though less frequently than on what appears to be their favourite food plant, common ragwort. These caterpillars ingest poisonous chemicals from the ragwort which do no harm to them but which deter predators, hence the warning colours. The adults of many of these caterpillars, particularly red admiral, small tortoiseshell and peacock butterflies, find the flowers of buddleia, a garden plant now common on waste ground, quite irresistible – it is sometimes known as butterfly bush.

Small tortoiseshell

Red Admiral

Peacock

Goat willow

Shepherd's purse

Red dead-nettle

Hawthorn

Groundsel

Common field speedwell

Rosebay willow-herb

Nettle

Peacock

Spear thistle

Goldfinch

Oxford ragwort

Elephant hawk-moth

Small tortoise-shell

Fat-hen

Hoary cress

House sparrow

Cinnabar moth

Creeping thistle

Robin

Maidenhair
spleenwort

Hairy
rock cress

Wren

Wall pepper

Aubrietia

Snapdragon

Wild pink

Canterbury
bell

Wallflower

Ivy-leaved
toadflax

Walls

Great tit

Spotted flycatcher
Red admiral
Peacock
Xanthoria
Small tortoiseshell

In any built up area there are inevitably numerous walls, some of which provide an important habitat for plants and their associated insects. Except in districts where drystone walling is practised, the mortar which joins the bricks or stones together provides, as soon as it starts to disintegrate, a splendid seed-bed. Since mortar contains a high proportion of lime, it may provide the only suitable habitat for calcicolous plants in a district where the soils are predominantly acid. Most householders and managers of buildings take some action when the mortar of their walls begins to disintegrate and plants start to grow in it. Hence walls are only suitable for plants when they are neglected, and in most districts the neglected walls are those round gardens, or belonging to ruined buildings. Mosses, sometimes followed by lichens, are among the first colonists of a neglected wall or roof, and many other plants of bare ground, such as thyme-leaved sandwort, wall-pepper, hairy rock-cress and thale cress are found on walls. There is, however, one plant, which in Britain grows on walls and almost nowhere else. This is ivy-leaved toadflax, sometimes known as mother of thousands (a name also applied to several other plants), which was introduced in the early 17th century, and escaped from a garden in South Essex to colonise virtually the whole of England and Wales and the greater part also of Scotland and Ireland.

Certain ancient abbey and castle ruins, such as Beaulieu Abbey in Hampshire, Fountains Abbey in Yorkshire and Ludlow Castle in Shropshire, have a special flora that presumably originally escaped from medieval gardens and has remained on these medieval walls ever since. This includes the wallflower, the snapdragon, the common pink and even the Canterbury bell together with the more modern aubrietia. Beaulieu Abbey also has winter savory, a culinary herb.

Walls heat up very much on a hot summer's day and then provide a splendid basking place for such butterflies as the peacock, the small tortoiseshell and the red admiral. Those moths which hide during the day by relying on their camouflage effect against tree trunks may also rest similarly on stone walls, for example the red underwing.

If a wall is so neglected that bricks or stones start to fall out of it, the resultant cavities provide splendid nesting places for such birds as robin, wren and spotted flycatcher, and if they are deep enough, also for great, blue and coal tits. The wryneck, now a very rare bird in Britain, has also been known to nest in a wall. Where the wall is better maintained, however, there may be few footholds for plants with roots, and the main inhabitants then will be more primitive, rootless types – mosses, lichens and algae. A very characteristic group of mosses grows on the tops of walls, including *Tortula muralis* and several *Grimmia* and *Bryum* species. All form neat cushions and have long hair-tipped leaves, and they are capable of drying out to a remarkable extent without harm, and of recovering rapidly when permitted.

The champion for resisting desiccation, however, are lichens, curious symbiotic associations of fungi and algae, which can withstand astonishing extremes. In experiments, they have been stored in liquid nitrogen, and have still come back to full activity afterwards. They form colonies in places where other plants are unable to survive, and walls are an excellent habitat for them. Lichens grow very slowly, sometimes less than a centimetre in a year, but alas are very sensitive to atmospheric pollution. Some species have long since disappeared from industrial areas, but a few persist and, as the air becomes cleaner again, others are moving back. In city centres, very few are found, *Lecanora muralis* being the commonest, but the orange *Xanthoria parietina* is often found too. The varying sensitivity of lichens has been used to monitor pollution.

Wildlife in a Park

Town parks present a very different habitat from even large gardens. They are more frequented by people for more of the day, so that fewer shy creatures frequent them. Parks also have larger expanses of mown grassland, more trees, proportionately fewer shrubs, and a great deal more water, often a large pond or even a lake. Few town gardens have more than a goldfish pond.

So although parks and gardens have many birds in common, both have species that are not so often seen in the other. Members of the crow tribe, for instance the carrion crow, jackdaw, magpie and jay, are much more likely to be seen in large parks, the crows and magpies nesting in trees, the jackdaws in holes in trees and the jays in shelter-belts or shrubberies. Woodpigeons are also much commoner in parks than gardens, and in larger parks, especially if there are old trees, stockdoves as well as jackdaws will compete for any nest holes they may contain. If the park is right in the middle of the built-up area, there are also likely to be feral pigeons feeding on the lawns and pathways, and often perching in the trees, a slightly unusual habit for a bird which is basically a rock-lover. Most parks do not contain suitable buildings for feral pigeons to nest in, so they are likely to fly outside to find their nest sites.

It is the presence of quite large expanses of open water that provides the main difference between the avifaunas of parks and gardens. Most park lakes hold mallard, moorhen, coot and mute swan throughout the year and tufted duck, pochard and sometimes great crested grebe in the winter. Many urban parks have concrete banks, and so do not provide suitable nesting sites for water birds, but if rushes, reeds or other vegetation are allowed to grow around the edges, the moorhens and coots, and perhaps even the grebes, will nest. An alternative is to provide floating platforms, on which the coots at least will readily build. Mallards do not in any case necessarily nest very close to water, and in most town parks they will resort to cavities in trees, whence the ducklings have to jump hazardously long before they can fly in order to reach the safety of the water. In winter also there are many gulls on urban park lakes, especially black-headed gulls in their white-headed winter plumage, but also common gulls, and in some areas also herring and lesser black-headed gulls. In Regent's Park, London, and on old houses by the nearby Regent's Canal, a few pairs of herring gulls actually breed: it is strange to hear their wild ringing spring cry, recalling the sea cliffs of the north and west, amid the roar of the traffic. The same park holds a small heronry, a feature not usually found in parks in the middle of large urban areas, though not infrequent further out, for instance formerly at Wanstead Park in Essex. Herons, of course, are rare visitors to gardens, but when they do alight, usually early in the morning, they are often unwelcome, for they have probably come to remove the goldfish from some proud owner's pool. For the same reason the handsome kingfisher is liable to be unpopular on its rare visits.

Deer, usually fallow deer, are sometimes found in town parks, but rarely nowadays right in the middle. Richmond Park in Surrey, for instance, has both red and fallow deer, but this is an extensive park, large enough to give the illusion of being in the country, if visited early in the morning before too many other people are about. Park deer, of course, have to be fed in winter, and can scarcely be regarded as wild animals. Foxes, however, live in, or at least visit, many town parks, and are genuinely wild. It is some years, however, since badgers could be found either in Richmond Park or on Hampstead Heath. Much the most likely wild mammal to be seen in any town park is the introduced grey squirrel, a native of North America.

Carrion crow

Herring gull

Common gull

Black-headed gull

Coot

Moorhen

Tufted duck

Mute swan cygnets

Pochard

Mallard duck

Mallard drake

Mute swan

WOODLAND

Between the retreat of the glaciers after the last Ice Age, about 12,000 years ago, and the beginning of the Iron Age, when heavy axes and ploughs were first available, nearly all of Britain was covered with forest. Oakwoods were found in the south, with alder and willow in the valleys, and these gave way to pine and birch woods further north. As the climate fluctuated in the first 6,000 or 7,000 years, various trees advanced and receded, birch and pine spreading over the whole country in the coldest periods, and lime, elm, and beech moving into the oakwoods as the climate warmed. All parts of Britain, except for peat bogs, riverbeds, sea shores, mountain tops and unstable cliffs and banks were wooded, because left to itself the land of Britain can support trees, and in the process of ecological succession trees are a natural endpoint, the climax vegetation which nothing can supplant.

Over the next 4,000 years people began to clear this immense forest, at first slowly and on the lighter, drier upland soils, but eventually as tools improved moving down on to the more fertile, but heavier and wetter valley soils. Already by 2,000 B.C. large parts of the chalk plateaux of southern England were cleared and by Roman and Saxon times the process was in full swing.

Few if any of the woods scattered over the countryside today have been forest right back to prehistoric times. Most were felled and either regenerated naturally or have been replanted. A few, such as Wychwood in Oxfordshire, are probably virgin in that sense, though heavily managed, like all our woodlands. What we think of as a natural woodland is the result of an ancient and sophisticated cropping system, the coppice with standards, described on p. 63, now rarely practised. Most broad-leaved woodlands are now either fox coverts or pheasant reserves. The few truly ancient woods have a much richer flora, since many woodland plants reproduce vegetatively (by rhizomes, suckers, bulbs, corms, and the like) and are poor recolonizers of planted woods.

Deciduous Woods

Beech

Small-leaved lime

Sessile oak

Silver birch

Whitebeam

Wych elm

Hornbeam

Sweet chestnut

The major forest tree of lowland Britain today is the pedunculate oak which is dominant on all the wetter, heavier soils of lowland England and is widespread in the west and north as well. Sometimes it forms pure woods, but more often it is associated with trees such as ash, sycamore, and English elm, all of which are capable of forming a wood on their own. Scattered trees of rowan, wild cherry, crab apple, and aspen are all typical of such oak-woods.

On drier soils, and particularly in upland areas the pedunculate oak gives way to the sessile oak or sometimes to silver birch. On dry chalk and limestone soils in the south, however, either beech or small-leaved lime can be the main canopy tree. Hornbeam, whitebeam, wych elm, and sweet chestnut are all trees that grow on these drier soils. Hornbeam is a tree primarily of the sandy soils of south-eastern England and is not native in the north and west, while whitebeam, so-called from the silvery underside of its leaves, is commonest on the chalk. There are in fact many different species of whitebeam, some confined to a few inaccessible limestone cliffs, and in some cases found only in Britain in the world, but they are all hard to distinguish from the common species. Sweet chestnut is, of course, not native in Britain at all, having been introduced for its fruits and possibly its timber. It is sometimes said to have been introduced by the Romans, as chestnut wood has been found by archaeologists at Roman sites, but they may well have imported the timber.

Where the soil is wet or water-logged the tree that thrives best is alder, but on less fertile soils downy birch can also form large woods. Willows and poplars, particularly white willow, crack willow, grey poplar, and black poplar, all grow on very wet soils.

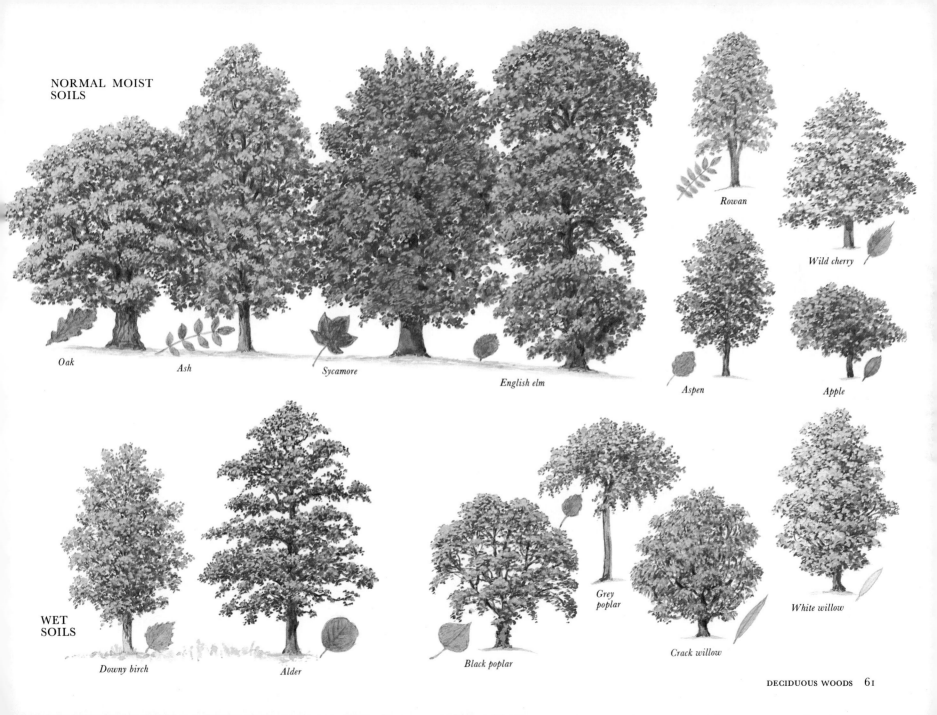

NORMAL MOIST
SOILS

Oak

Ash

Sycamore

English elm

Rowan

Wild cherry

Aspen

Apple

WET
SOILS

Downy birch

Alder

Black poplar

Grey
poplar

Crack willow

White willow

Early
purple
orchid

Bluebell

Bugle

Wood anemone

Oakwood

Oakwoods take many forms, depending upon how they are managed. The quintessential English lowland oakwood is the coppice with standards, with a canopy of spaced oaks rising out of a dense shrub layer of hazel, but often with a wide variety of other shrubs, including wild cherry, crab apple, and field maple. At a lower level may be found smaller shrubs, such as blackthorn, flowering on bare black twigs before its leaves appear, and the attractive red-stemmed dogwood. Scrambling up the trunks will be ivy and honeysuckle, the last thickly scenting the air on warm June evenings. Such a wood was cleared on a regular cycle, leaving just enough young oaks to be the standards of the next generation, and providing timber for building and fuel, and oak bark for tanning, a regular supply of hazel canes from the coppiced hazel, and a rich autumn diet of acorns for the village pigs. Once one of the lynchpins of the rural economy, the coppicing system has long ceased to be profitable and is now rarely practised. The development of the shrub layers depends upon how complete the canopy of oak branches is overhead, for the shrubs grow and produce leaves at the same time as the oaks. The plants that grow on the floor of the wood, however, will always be shaded in summer; whether by the trees or the shrubs, and they have escaped this problem by making use of the brief period in spring, lasting from March to May, when the sun is high enough to light the woodland floor but the trees and shrubs have yet to spread their leaves. In May the herb layer of an oakwood reaches a magnificent zenith. Sheets of primroses or in a few Cambridgeshire and Essex woods, the rarer and polyanthus-like oxlip may cover the ground, or the air may reek with the culinary aroma of the wild garlic or ramsons, another carpeter. The real champion for ground cover, though, is the bluebell, perhaps the best-known springtime woodland plant. Other typical plants of this season are wood anemone, nodding daintily in the wind, and early purple orchid. All these plants share one feature: they have some underground storage organ (bulb, rhizome, corm, or whatever) which enables them to produce leaves very early in spring when it may be too cold for normal growth, so that they are ready to make use of the brief window in the canopy.

The flora of oakwoods is rich. Other notable plants are bugle, creeping along the ground, red campion, with its separate male and female flowers, and yellow archangel, whose variegated-leaved form is familiar to gardeners.

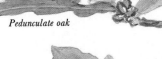

Pedunculate oak

Field maple

Blackthorn

Primrose

Red campion

Ramsons

Yellow archangel

Ivy

Honeysuckle

Hazel

*Sessile
oak*

Downy birch

*Midland
hawthorn*

*Bird
cherry*

Hornbeam

Wych elm

Ash

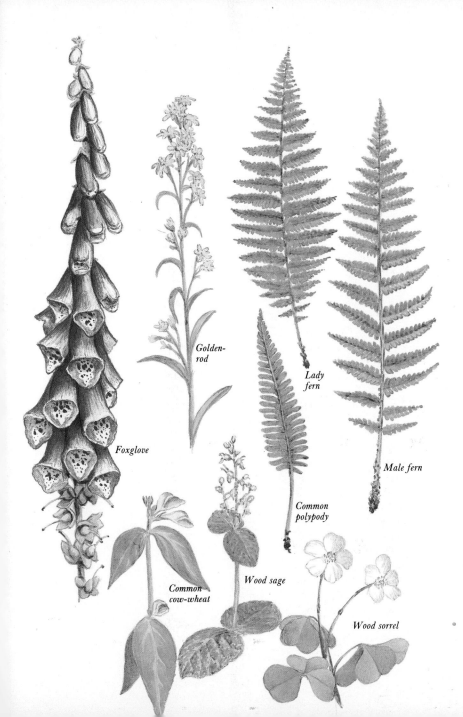

Foxglove

Golden-rod

Lady fern

Male fern

Common polypody

Common cow-wheat

Wood sage

Wood sorrel

Sessile Oakwood

Whereas the pedunculate oak dominates the lowlands, the sessile, or durmast oak is much the commoner of the two in Britain's upland areas. Sessile means stalkless, and the two types of oak can easily be distinguished by the long-stalked acorns and lobed leaf-bases of the pedunculate oak, and the almost unstalked acorns and unlobed leaf bases of the sessile oak. However, where the two grow together, as in parts of lowland Britain, there are many trees of intermediate appearance, due to hybridization.

Lowland sessile oakwood occurs mainly in the south-east, for example in the Blean woods of northeast Kent, now a national nature reserve. The wild flowers are the same as those of pedunculate oakwood, but sessile oakwoods differ in often having hornbeam as well as Midland hawthorn growing in them. Hornbeam is an attractive tree, best known for the pollarded specimens in Epping Forest, Essex, but it does not grow naturally further north or west than the Chilterns. The Midland (or woodland) hawthorn is characteristic of ancient woodlands and differs from the common hawthorn in having much less deeply lobed leaves and two stones instead of one within the fruit or haw.

Upland sessile oakwoods, however, have a very different tree, shrub and ground flora from their lowland counterparts. Birch, often the damp-ground species downy birch, rowan, wych elm and ash are common, and so is the bird cherry, which never comes into the lowlands at all. It is a much smaller tree than the common lowland wild cherry and is easily recognized by its long drooping flower-spikes, similar to those of the cherry-laurel. The wild flowers include many plants characteristic of lowland heaths, such as golden-rod, foxglove, common cow-wheat, wood sorrel and wood-sage; others, such as the great wood-rush, are mainly confined to the uplands.

Upland oakwood is very different in appearance from lowland wood. The soil is often poor and the trees are stunted, and twisted by the wind. In the west country, where the rainfall is high and the atmosphere within the wood permanently moist, sessile oakwood takes on its most distinctive form. Here, the conditions are ideal for mosses and ferns, and buckler ferns, male fern and the elegant lady fern are all common. One fern, the polypody, typically grows as an epiphyte, actually on the branches of the trees. Where the rainfall is high enough, the branches of the wood may be festooned with polypody, creating the impression of the interior of some tropical jungle, mysteriously transported thousands of miles to the alien British landscape.

Beechwoods

Most beech in Britain is planted; native beechwoods are almost confined to the chalk of south-eastern England. North-west of the Chiltern escarpment there are only a few on the Cotswold escarpment and the South Wales limestone. Our summers are too cool to enable beech to regenerate in upland Britain. Ash grows vigorously at the edge of many beechwoods and in clearings, but is soon shaded out, as are the silvery whitebeam and the wild cherry, at its best in spring when the cherry blossom adorns the edges of the Chiltern beechwoods just as the first pale green leaves appear on the beeches. Beech is a most demanding tree, and shades out not only most other trees, but almost all shrubs and all but a few herbs that can grow in deep shade. Holly, yew, and in open patches elder are among the few shrubs likely to be seen in beechwoods. Technically both spurge-laurel and its relative mezereon with its handsome fragrant pink-purple flowers are shrubs, but they are small ones, not often growing more than a metre high. Both are typical of beechwoods, and now that fewer people dig mezereon up, it is once more spreading, at least in the Chilterns. The two most characteristic plants of beechwoods, both of which form extensive carpeting communities, are dog's mercury and wood sanicle. In among them may grow herb paris, a relative of the trilliums of our gardens, sweet woodruff, bluebells, and the wood dog violet, flowering ten days before the common dog violet, from which it is best told by its narrower flower with a purple spur. Both our native hellebores, local rather than rare, are more often found in beechwoods than elsewhere, if only because beech more often grows on their preferred limy soils than does oak. Beechwood also has its own array of special orchids, notably the three *Cephalanthera* helleborines, the large white, which is not uncommon, the sword-leaved, which is widespread but very local, and the red, which is now exceedingly rare. In one recent year only a single plant flowered in the whole of Britain. The less attractive *Epipactis* helleborines are also very characteristic of beechwoods, and one, *E. leptochila*, is almost confined to them. Fly orchids are not infrequent, but strangest of all are the two saprophytic orchids, the frequent birdsnest orchid and the very rare ghost orchid, now only in two woods in the Chilterns. Together with yellow birdsnest, which is not an orchid, these plants have no chlorophyll or green leaves and so do not need light. They feed on rotting vegetation with the aid of a fungus partner, and so are able to thrive in the deep shade of beechwoods.

Narrow-leaved helleborine

Red helleborine

White helleborine

Mezereon

Herb paris

Stinking hellebore

Dog's mercury

Sanicle

Sweet violet

Ashwoods

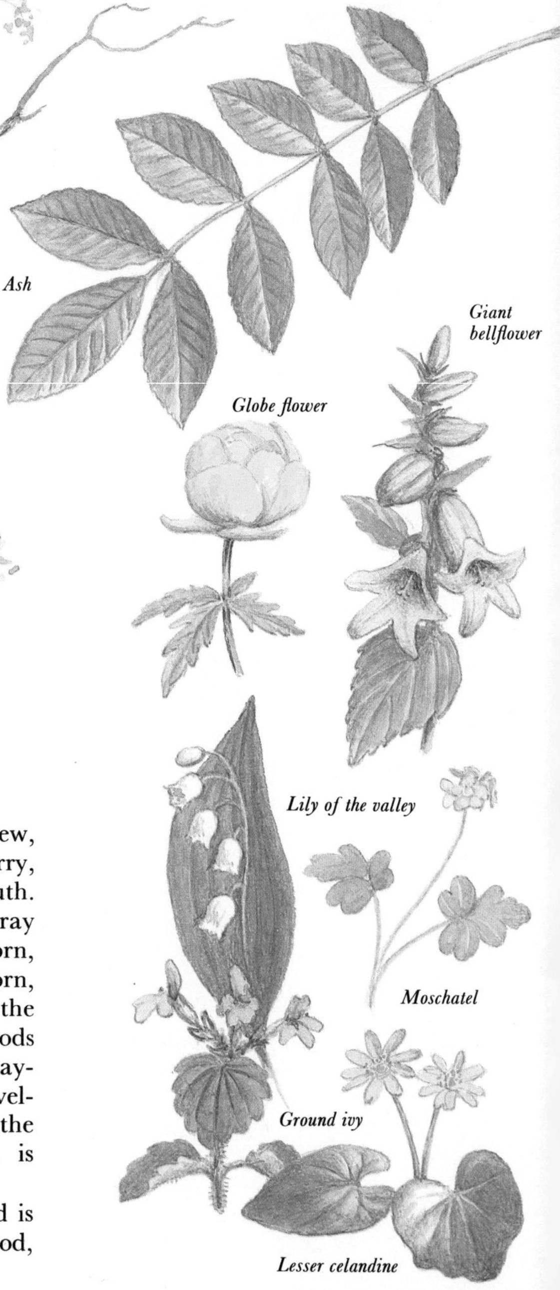

Ash

Giant
bellflower

Globe flower

Lily of the valley

Moschatel

Ground ivy

Lesser celandine

The British tree flora is so impoverished that few other trees besides oak and beech form pure woods, and these are not at all common. Ash, birch and alder occur with sufficient frequency to merit a mention. Elmwoods are rare, and usually result from the suckering of a group of planted common elms.

Pure ashwoods are found mainly on the limestone in the north and west of England, especially in the Mendips and the Peak District. They share many features with the also calcareous beechwoods, but whereas ash is often found growing on the outskirts of beechwoods, especially in the Chilterns, beech does not grow in or near pure ashwoods. If it did, it would soon replace the ash, as it does in the Chilterns. In fact ash only makes pure woods in Britain in places beyond the capacity of beech to reproduce itself. Where they grow together, beech seems always to dominate in the end.

The trees that do grow along with the ash in ash-woods are wych elm, maple and aspen, accompanied in the Mendips by whitebeam and yew, and in Derbyshire by bird cherry, which does not grow in the south. Ashwoods also have a normal array of lime-loving shrubs, hawthorn, hazel, dogwood, spindle, buckthorn, sallow, privet and elder. Again the Somerset and Derbyshire woods differ, the Mendips having wayfaring tree, honeysuckle and traveller's joy, which are lacking in the Peak. Ivy, a woody climber, is common in both.

The field layer in an ashwood is much richer than in a beechwood,

for the tree itself casts a much lighter shade than beech. On damper soils ramsons and lesser celandine, and on drier soils dog's mercury, moschatel, ground ivy and in places lily of the valley form carpeting communities. Wood anemone, columbine, giant bellflower, Jacob's ladder and globe flower are among the more attractive and colourful plants of ashwoods, some of which grow also in oak and beechwoods.

In the Pennines, ashwood extends higher than almost any other type, but voracious sheep usually prevent its regeneration. On limestone pavement, however, the saplings can grow in the deep grykes away from the sheep and a wood can become established. Such a wood, like that at Colt Park on the slopes of Ingleborough 1100 feet (330 m) above sea level, tends to have a very open canopy and a very rich shrub and herb layer, both again profiting from the freedom from grazing. Ferns are abundant, including wall-rue and maidenhair spleenwort, along with the unmistakable hart's tongue. Flowering plants include dog's mercury, ramsons, red campion, and wood sorrel, as well as some much scarcer plants, such as angular Solomon's seal and baneberry, with its fluffy white flowers and striking black berries, which, in Britain, is almost confined to Yorkshire.

Columbine

Jacob's ladder

Angular Solomon's seal

Baneberry

Birchwoods

There are two birches capable of forming a tree in Britain, the downy birch *Betula pubescens* and the silver birch *B. pendula*, though where they grow together they hybridise freely and confusingly. Generally downy birch prefers wetter soils than silver birches. Small groves of birches are a familiar sight on the edges of lowland heaths in England, and these are most often silver birch, but if left to themselves they rapidly turn into oakwood. Oak is a slower growing but very competitive tree, whereas birch is almost a tree-weed, one of the first woody plants to spring up when an area is cleared. This difference is reflected in their seeds: those of oak, the acorns, are large and of little value for dispersal, whereas birch seeds are light and winged and can travel great distances on the wind. If a birch seed falls in a wood, however, it contains no reserves to succour the shaded seedling, which quickly dies, whereas the young oak can live off its seed reserves for a long time. So if the heath is not burned, birches quickly spring up among the heather, but in time the oaks will move in, their acorns perhaps transported by some hoarding squirrel or jay.

Downy birch is often found on the surface of peat bogs and fens when drainage of the surrounding farmland makes them dry enough to allow trees to grow. The biggest such birchwood is at Holme Fen in the drained fenland near Huntingdon, and the remnants of the old peat bog flora survive there. Sometimes these sites are much richer, though, with a wide range of fenland plants, such as meadowsweet, yellow loosestrife, and skullcap, along with shrubs such as guelder rose (which is not a rose, but a *Viburnum*) and dog rose (which is), under the rather open canopy.

In the Scottish Highlands, however, downy birch is the main deciduous forest tree, replacing oak on acid soils, much as ash replaces beech on the limestone. In the far north of Scotland the downy birch is even represented by a distinct, Arctic subspecies, *carpatica*, which in the rest of Europe is only found in the mountains. These northern birchwoods often contain much rowan and a scattering of sallows, aspen, bird cherry, and hazel, with alder in damp places, but the tallest are rarely above 10 m (30 feet) high. The ground flora is rather similar to that of the surrounding grasslands, with much sweet vernal grass, wavy hair-grass, and soft grass, mixed with both common and white bents. In among these grow tormentil, heath bedstraw, and common dog violet, with few woodland plants, except perhaps wood sorrel and wood sage, but with some typical northern plants, such as goldenrod and chickweed wintergreen.

Silver
birch

Downy
birch

Yellow
loosestrife

Skullcap

Guelder
rose

Meadow-
sweet

Dog rose

Golden-rod

Alder Carr and Other Woods

Marsh marigold

Tussock sedge

Alder

Buckthorn

Alder buckthorn

Apart from oak, ash, beech and birch, the only other deciduous tree that frequently forms pure woods in Britain, widespread but rather local in distribution, is the alder. They also have a name of their own, carr. Alder carr is one of the later stages of a fen that is drying out and is often accompanied by ash, downy birch, aspen and various willows or sallows. The ground in an alderwood is always damp and often wet, since the alder grows best in wet places, so that only the most devoted naturalists normally penetrate into its interior. The fact that the dominant plant of the field layer, as in so many wet woods, is often the stinging nettle makes it an even less inviting place for an afternoon stroll. The rest of the ground flora is much less related to those of dry woodlands than it is to that of marshes and fens, with such typical species as meadowsweet, marsh marigold, goosegrass, great willow-herb and hemp agrimony. Quite often there are massive tufts of the tussock sedge, which if they grow close together can make walking in alder carr even more difficult. These tussocks are often the remnants of an earlier fen flora and are in fact the cause of the establishment of the alder carr. Being raised above the water level they provide drier sites on which the alder seedlings can establish.

Alder is interesting in being unable to regenerate under its own canopy, so that the trees in alder carr tend to be all of an age. As the carr matures, the ground may have been raised by silting around the alders sufficiently to allow trees of drier soils to invade, for example birch or oak, but it is not certain that this happens often. More frequently perhaps *Sphagnum* mosses invade the carr and start the process of bog formation. Alternatively a new generation of alders may grow up as the old ones die back. Alder is a short-lived tree, rarely much exceeding a century, and like the birch relies on being able to colonise new areas by good dispersal and rapid establishment. Underneath the dense alder canopy few shrubs grow well, but the buckthorn and its relative alder buckthorn are often abundant. Two ferns are also often abundant in alder woods, the elegant, creeping marsh fern and the imposing royal fern. The latter forms huge mounds, up to half a metre high, from which emerge the great 2-metre fronds, brown at the tips where the spores form.

Other Woods

Other trees form woods in Britain occasionally. Elmwoods were once an occasional sight in southern Britain, before the advent of Dutch elm disease. They tended to be formed by the invasion of an existing wood by the suckers of elms planted along its edges, and often were rather disturbed in other ways. Frequently the ground under elms is carpeted in nettles, a sign of human activity, for nettles require a very fertile soil.

An increasing woodland type is sycamore wood. Sycamore is not native, but was introduced, probably in the sixteenth century. It is the most vigorous broad-leaved tree in upland areas and often forms small woods. The leaf litter deposited by sycamore is very heavy and tends to suppress the ground flora.

In Wales and south-west Scotland woods tend to be very mixed, with oaks (sometimes both species), ash, wych elm, birch, alder, hazel, holly and others all intermingling. Such woods often have a correspondingly rich ground flora.

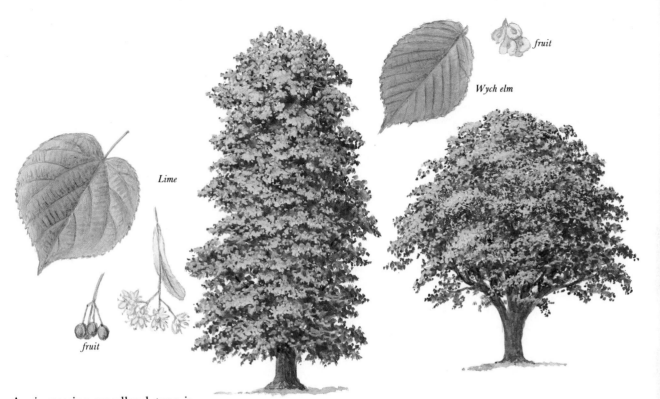

fruit

Wych elm

Lime

fruit

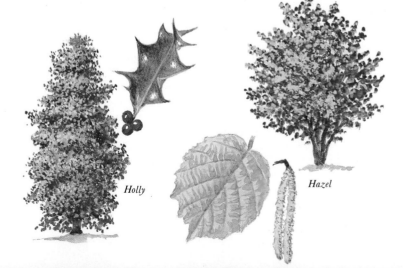

Holly

Hazel

Woodland Mammals

The flora and fauna of woodlands are both very rich. The complexity of the habitat provides for many different ways of earning a living, and their productivity offers a rich harvest for the residents. Which woodland tree (see p. 60) forms the canopy depends upon soil, climate and management, and in turn determines the associated shrubs and herbs. Most plant-eating insects are very specific as to their food plant. This is because most plants contain various chemical deterrents, some obvious like the formic acid in a stinging nettle, but most much more subtle, and so the insects can only feed on that plant whose poison they have learnt to deal with. Carnivores, however, further up the food chain, are less choosy and so are more generally distributed than the plants and insects.

Not all mammals are carnivores, of course. The wood mouse will eat almost any part of a plant, although specialises in seeds and shoots. More voracious and so more damaging is the grey squirrel, introduced from North America, which strips bark from trees, especially sycamore and beech, and so kills them. Foresters fear too the depredations of two deer, the native roe deer, and the larger, introduced fallow deer, with its characteristic flattened antlers. Roe are much commoner than many realise, and over much of Britain almost every wood of any size will harbour a pair, often only detected when snow gives away their tracks. Two other introduced deer are both now quite common. The Japanese sika looks like a small, dark fallow deer, but with antlers like the red deer; the dog-sized Chinese muntjac originated from Woburn Park in Bedfordshire.

Some carnivorous mammals, such as the shrews and the mainly nocturnal hedgehog are primarily insect, worm, and slug eaters. Two shrews occur in our woods—the common shrew, most often seen dead, and the minute pygmy shrew, less than 2 inches (5 cm) long. Shrews are so small for a warm-blooded animal, that they lose heat rapidly and have to spend most of their time hunting for food, simply to stay alive. The badger is an omnivore, eating almost anything from acorns and bluebell bulbs to worms, young rabbits, and carrion. Badgers build complex underground tunnels with large entrance holes, and if left undisturbed will occupy the same site for many years, gradually digging new chambers and holes, until a wide area becomes pock-marked with entrances, all linked by regularly used trackways. The fox, the largest true carnivore in Britain, will also eat fruit or bulbs. Only the stoat and weasel eat nothing but meat.

Fox

Stoat

Weasel

Hedgehog

Grey
squirrel

Badger

Fallow deer

Roe deer

Muntjac

Sika deer

Bank vole

Wood mouse

Common shrew

Pygmy shrew

WOODLAND MAMMALS 75

Woodland Birds I

Mature natural broad-leaved woods are wonderful places for birds. The different layers of plants—tree canopy, shrubs, and herbs—and the variety of plant and insect species provides a wealth of habitats and food sources. The number of insects that can be shaken from a branch of an oak tree in June is prodigious, so the birds of the woodlands are mainly insect-eaters.

Tree trunks are much used by birds as nest-sites, being relatively safe from predators. Woodpeckers, of course, drill out their nest-holes there and get most of their food by extracting wood-boring insects from the trunks, although the green woodpecker is more often seen on the ground, carefully picking off ants from their nest with its long tongue. Many other species, particularly starlings, use old woodpecker holes, but nuthatches reduce the size of the hole with dried mud, making it difficult for predators to enter. Nuthatches run up and down tree-trunks and feed on nuts when they are available, while treecreepers prefer to run up the trunk and then fly down to the base of a nearby tree. Treecreepers pry insect food out of the cracks in the bark with their long, curved beaks.

Tits too often feed on tree-trunks, but also on the ground and in trees, wherever insects, seeds, or other small food is to be had. Great tit,

Nuthatch

Spotted
flycatcher

Pied
flycatcher

Lesser spotted
woodpecker

Tree-
creeper

Great spotted
woodpecker

Green woodpecker

Blackcap

Garden warbler

Wood warbler

Chiffchaff

Long-tailed tit

Marsh tit

Blue tit

Great tit

blue tit, and marsh tit are common, and long-tailed tits, though usually nesting in more open places, can be seen in winter flying from tree to tree in small parties.

None of these are exclusively insect-eaters; those that are—the flycatchers and the warblers—are all summer visitors, for in winter their food is dormant. The spotted flycatcher is much the commoner and is usually first noticed by its habit of selecting a perch, darting out to catch a fly, and returning. The pied flycatcher has less regular flycatching behaviour and often feeds on the ground; it is commonest in Wales and western England.

Five warblers are characteristic of these woods and all are more often heard than seen. The chiffchaff and willow warbler are so similar that they can hardly be distinguished in the field, except by song, from which the chiffchaff gets its name. Less frequent is the again very similar

wood warbler, with a trilling song, while the larger garden warbler and blackcap are widespread.

The birds on these pages feed mainly in the trees, for that is where most of the insects are. But there are plenty of other food sources in a wood, such as seeds and leaves, earthworms, snails and other ground animals, and small mammals and even other birds.

Of seed eaters the woodpigeon is the largest and so has a considerable appetite, making it a considerable pest on farmland. Pigeons cannot eat very hard or large seeds, however, for their beaks are rather flimsy and they rely on grinding their food up in their gizzards. Finches, in contrast, are real seed specialists, with beaks designed to crush seeds. The hawfinch is the champion of all, with its massive parrot-like beak, quite out of proportion with its body, but it is a shy and rather scarce bird, and so sel-

Buzzard

Tawny owl

Sparrowhawk

Woodland Birds

dom seen. The two common finches are the brilliantly-coloured bullfinch, with its characteristic white rump, and its love of fruit-tree buds, and the equally colourful chaffinch. In winter bramblings, a Scandinavian visitor and another white-rumped finch, often join flocks of chaffinches, especially under beeches, and sometimes gain their summer plumage before leaving in spring. Another woodland finch is the redpoll, mainly found in birch and alder woods, feeding on the catkins, where it is joined in winter by flocks of siskins, which breed in conifers.

Most birds are much more catholic in their food requirements. Thrushes will eat snails, worms, and fruit, but still have preferences. Song thrushes eat mainly snails, bringing several to one place to crush on a special stone, the 'anvil'. Blackbirds eat worms and fruit, while the larger mistle thrushes have a similar but more vegetarian diet. Wrens are primarily insect eaters. Another worm-eater is the woodcock, most often seen either when flushes from the ground where it is almost perfectly camouflaged, or 'roding' on spring evenings, flying along a repeated circuit and calling 'twis-ick' at regular intervals, interspersed with a curious little growl.

Among the more carnivorous birds are two great opportunists,

magpie and jay, both with harsh, chattering calls, and both opportunistic feeders and hoarders. Jays burying acorns are one of the characteristic sights of autumn, while the thieving magpie is an artistic cliché.

Three big carnivores breed in woods, though they often hunt over fields and moors. The tawny owl is nocturnal and so not often seen, though frequently heard, for it is the commonest British owl. Sometimes its daytime roosting place is discovered, perhaps by a startled foraging blackbird or great tit, whose alarm call quickly attracts other birds, which mob the owl in an attempt to force it to leave their territory. Sparrowhawk and buzzard are both round-winged birds of prey, and so easily distinguished from the more pointed-winged falcons such as kestrel and peregrine. The buzzard is a typical sight, soaring above oakwoods and moors in the north and west, while the much smaller sparrowhawk is more likely to be seen flashing along a hedgerow close to the ground. In a few remote valleys in Wales there survive, too, a small number of another tree-nesting bird of prey, the red kite. Though their nesting sites are closely guarded, they may be seen soaring over nearby moors and fields, as like as not searching for carrion which is their main diet at certain times of year.

Jay

Chaffinch

Redpoll

Magpie

Brambling

Woodpigeon

Bullfinch

Hawfinch

Wren

Blackbird

Mistle thrush

Woodcock

Song thrush

Woodland Butterflies and Moths

Woods have a rich fauna of butterflies and even more moths. Some, such as the caterpillars of the beautiful fritillary butterflies, feed on various species of wild violet near the ground, and many butterflies such as the fritillaries and the rare white admiral, fly up and down the rides on sunny days and bask or sip nectar on thistles and other tall plants. Others fly higher up, among the leaves of the trees, in particular the purple hairstreak, whose caterpillars feed on oak leaves, and the rare and beautiful purple emperor. The most characteristic of all woodland butterflies is the speckled wood, whose males occupy sun-flecks as territories, while the females fly high in the canopy, choosing from among the dancing males illuminated beneath them. Woodlands are immensely rich, too, in moths, but most fly at night and are rarely seen. Often an agile yellow underwing can be disturbed in the leaf litter where it is hiding, and lost again in a flash of yellow as it scuttles off. Many other moths have strikingly marked or brilliantly coloured hindwings; those of the red underwing are bright crimson, while the eyed hawkmoth has realistic 'eyes' which can be flashed at predators which disturb it. Their forewings, however, are at first sight dull, and cover the hindwings when the moth is at rest; in fact they are exquisitely

camouflaged, particularly in some of the large geometrid moths, such as the mottled beauty or the peppered moth. Of course such disguise is only of use on a clean tree-trunk: once it becomes blackened with soot it makes the moth more conspicuous, and several such moths have evolved dark races in industrial areas, which are again well camouflaged on the dirty trunks.

This phenomenon, known as industrial melanism, is one of the best studied cases of evolution in action. The first black peppered moths were recorded in Manchester in 1848, and rapidly spread in polluted urban areas, so that now almost all the peppered moths in these areas are black, while the speckled form persists in the unpolluted countryside in the far north and west. By placing the two forms on lichen- or soot-covered tree trunks, experimenters have shown that the 'wrong' form is much more likely to be eaten by birds, and it is this selection which has caused this piece of evolution. In these times of cleaner air the normal speckled moth is starting to make a comeback. Black or melanic races of several species of moth are known, but are usually much rarer than the normal type, probably because they are more conspicuous and so more likely to be eaten.

The leaves of the trees and shrubs

in the woodland provide sustenance for many more larvae, especially of moths and sawflies. The oak carries the heaviest burden of such unwanted guests; many fewer species feed on elm, ash or beech, though quite a number, including the striking larvae of the puss and poplar hawk moths, consume the leaves of poplars or willows, while the handsome purple emperor and white admiral butterflies have larvae that feed on sallow and honeysuckle respectively. Several species of moth rank as forest pests because of the destructiveness of their larvae to the foliage of trees: the tiny green oak leaf-roller *Tortrix viridana* sometimes destroys so many leaves that the unfortunate oaks have to put forth a second crop, called Lammas leaves because they appear around the time of the ancient festival on August 2. Other well known defoliators are the winter and mottled umber moths, which attack oaks and many other broad-leaved trees, and the buff-tip, whose large, rather furry caterpillars can strip a tree branch in a remarkably short time. Birds are searching trees and bushes for food all the time, and caterpillars have evolved a variety of defences. Some like the vapourer are distasteful and advertise the fact, while others such as the ivy-feeding willow beauty have a remarkable similarity to bare twigs.

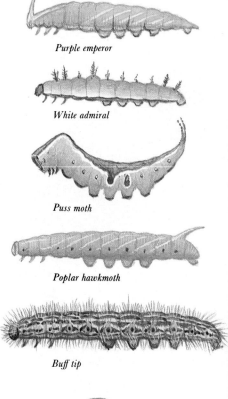

Purple emperor

White admiral

Puss moth

Poplar hawkmoth

Buff tip

Winter moth

Mottled umber

Willow beauty

Silver-washed
fritillary

Speckled wood

Yellow underwing

Red underwing

Purple emperor

White admiral

Eyed hawkmoth

Peppered moth

Woodland Insects

Woods are immensely rich places for the smaller animals that are often overlooked. The soil contains great numbers of worms, both the tiny and often parasitic eelworms and the larger and more innocuous earthworms. In addition it harbours countless springtails, very small and very primitive insects, which live in decaying leaf litter and have a curious forked spring, enabling them in some cases to jump up to several inches. Another group of insects that burrows in the soil is paradoxically one many of whose members fly—the Hymenoptera: ants, bees, and wasps. The two common wasps *Vespa vulgaris* and *V. germanica* and most bumblebees build nests underground, as do many ants. On the ground, too, are found slugs and snails, including the large black slug *Limax cinereogaster*, and the largest British land snail, the Roman snail, found in many calcareous woods. It owes its name to a belief that it was introduced by the Romans to satisfy their gourmet tastes —it is the famous *escargot* of French cuisine—but though often found near former Roman settlements, it also occurs well away from them, and has even been found in pre-Roman deposits. The other very noticeable group of woodland ground dwellers is the beetles, and among the enormous number which might be seen, the commonest per-haps is the violet ground beetle, a large and fierce hunter, which roams the woodland floor on long, slender legs.

Many woodland insects are hard to find and have to be sought out, but some will come and seek you out, in particular the blood-sucking tabanid flies popularly known as clegs or stouts, or in the Forest of Dean, for some inscrutable reason, as old maids. It is the females that batten on human beings and their domestic animals; the males spend a drone-like existence sipping nectar alongside the butterflies. The neighbourhood of ponies in the New Forest is particularly hazardous for humans, for there lurk two of the largest British clegs *Tabanus sudeticus* and *T. verralli*, and if their females find you before they find a pony, so much the worse for you.

A very curious byway in the insect world has resulted in the production of galls, made by tiny hymenopterous insects, on the leaves and twigs of trees. The best known galls are the oak apples and marble and spangle galls of oak, and the robin's pincushion often seen on wild roses. The gall-fly *Biorrhiza terminalis* which makes the oak apple is a good illustration of the remarkable Jekyll and Hyde existence of many of these gall-flies. The winged insect that emerges from an oak apple about midsummer flies off to lay its eggs on the root of an oak tree. These eggs produce a different kind of gall, from which in due course hatches a wingless insect that climbs up the tree to lay its eggs in a bud that in turn produces an oak apple. Not surprisingly the early entomologists thought this second form of the insect was a different species.

Although the most common kinds of black-and-yellow-striped wasp make their nests underground, two more of these plagues of the woodland picnicker, *Vespa sylvestris* and *V. norvegica*, hang similar ball-like papery nests from a branch. Their large relative the hornet, however, takes us into yet another microhabitat, rotten wood, since it usually makes its nest inside a hollow tree, often in a rotten branch. The hornet's fierce reaction when attacked or disturbed has made its nest into a proverb, but actually, left to itself, it is quite pacific. An insect which is often mistaken for a hornet, and looks even more fearsome with its outsize ovipositor, is the greater horntail or wood-wasp *Sirex gigas*. However, it has no sting, its huge weapon being used to bore into rotten trees, within which its larva spends the early part of its life. Another of the many insects whose larval stage takes place in rotten wood is the beetle *Scolytus scolytus* which carries the fungus which causes Dutch elm disease.

Springtail

Common wasp

German wasp

Bumble bee

Wood ant

Roman snail

Black slug

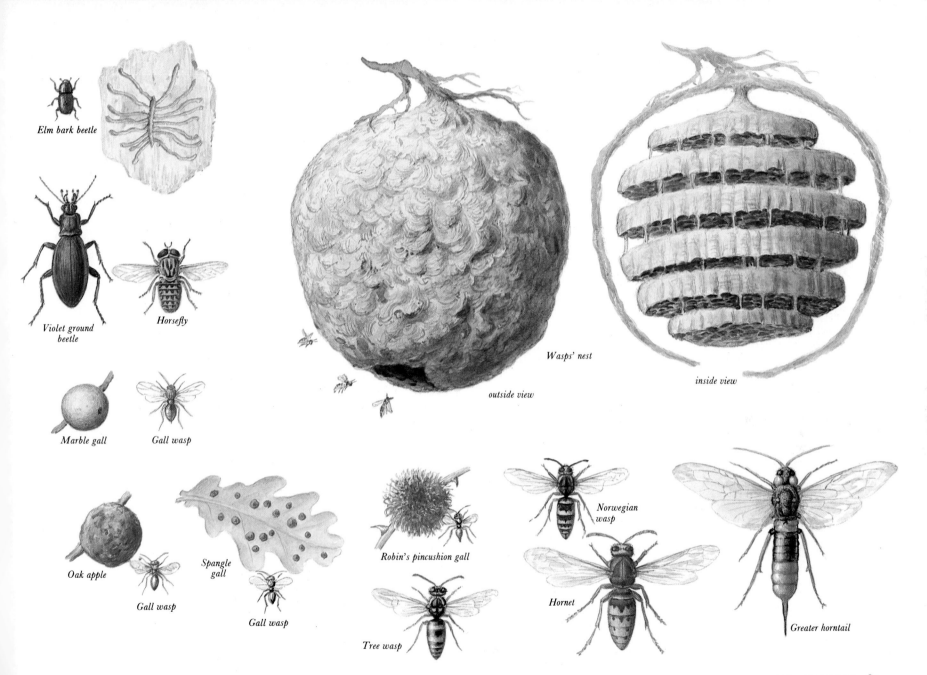

Elm bark beetle

Violet ground beetle

Horsefly

Marble gall

Gall wasp

Wasps' nest

outside view

inside view

Oak apple

Gall wasp

Spangle gall

Gall wasp

Robin's pincushion gall

Tree wasp

Norwegian wasp

Hornet

Greater horntail

Pinewoods

Conifers are more primitive than the flowering plants (angiosperms)—they belong to the gymnosperms. The only native conifer is Scots pine, but two other native gymnosperms—juniper (in Dumfriesshire) and yew (on the southern chalk)—exceptionally form woods. Unlike conifers their seeds have a fleshy coat. Scots pine is one of the commonest conifers in Britain, being often planted for amenity, but in fact genuine native pinewoods are found only in the Highlands of Scotland, where they form but a tiny remnant of the magnificent spread of highland forests that grew before Lowland Scottish and English timber merchants laid the Highlands waste in the 17th and 18th centuries. In the south the numerous patches of pine woodland on and near heathland result from 17th century plantings. Native pine is believed to have become extinct in southern England in the prehistoric period. Elsewhere in England, Wales and southern Scotland all the numerous coniferous plantations, often of Scots pine, but more often of Corsican pine, Norway or Sitka spruce, larch or Douglas fir, have appeared mainly since World War I, as a result of the activities of the Forestry Commission and the landowners whom it has grant-aided. As a general rule, the flora and fauna of these coniferous plantations is dull in the extreme, and the small patches of pinewood on the southern heaths have a flora naturally derived from the neighbouring heathlands.

In the Highlands, however, the native pinewoods, such as the Black Wood of Rannoch in Perthshire and Rothiemurchus on Speyside have a good fauna and flora of their own, including some species not found anywhere else. They are mainly pure pinewoods, but with occasional birches, sallows and rowans, and invariably have a good deal of heather *Calluna* and blaeberry, as the bilberry is called in Scotland. Cowberry is also a fairly constant con-

Cowberry

Bilberry

Juniper

Yew

Scots pine

Douglas fir

Norway spruce   Corsican pine   Larch   Yew   Juniper

stituent of pure pinewood, and sometimes juniper is also important. One does not go to a pure pine forest to see a fine display of wild flower bloom, for mosses and grasses are the commonest plants that actually cover the ground, especially brown bent, wavy hair-grass and soft grass. Even such common woodland and heathland species as wood sorrel, tormentil and common dog violet are rather infrequent in pinewoods. Among the rarer and more delectable species however, are several orchids and wintergreens, such as creeping lady's tresses, which grows almost exclusively under pines, lesser twayblade which hides its demure

charms in heather-shaded beds of sphagnum moss, and four species of true wintergreen as well as the chickweed wintergreen, a member of the Primrose family. The handsomest of the true wintergreens, the one-flowered and serrated wintergreens are also more happily named St. Olaf's candlestick and Yavering bells. The two others are the common and intermediate wintergreens. Most of the natural Scottish pinewoods consist of trees of very similar age. This appears to be because the regeneration of pine normally occurs after the burning of heather, providing the conditions suitable for seedling growth.

Pinewood Mammals

Red deer

The true pinewoods of Scotland are so small that inevitably they can have few mammals that do not also frequent the much more extensive surrounding moorlands. The red deer, for instance, was originally a woodland animal, but has been driven, by the destruction of the forests, out on to the moors. Even so it still takes shelter in the pinewoods when it needs to, and is indeed one of the main factors preventing these woodlands spreading out again on to the moors. Together with the omnipresent blackface sheep of the Highlands, the deer, both red and roe, are largely responsible for grazing down any pine seedlings that do manage to struggle through the heather. This is why most young pines in the Highlands are fairly near human habitations, for here the deer are less likely to penetrate.

The wild cat and the pine marten, the special predators of the Highlands, inhabit pinewoods as well as moors, but the red squirrel, which at least the marten preys on, is naturally confined to woods and plantations. Although at one time it was common in English broad-leaved woods, the red squirrel is primarily adapted to coniferous woodlands. This is why it has been largely displaced in England by the introduced grey squirrel, which is adapted to broad-leaved woodland, but survives in some numbers in its proper habitat of the Highland pine forests and plantations. The preferred food of the red squirrel is pine seeds, which it is well adapted to extract from their woody cones, but that of the grey squirrel is acorns. Both squirrels also eat a great deal of other vegetable matter, besides the hazel nuts which popular folklore imagines to be their staples, and make themselves unpopular by eating tree shoots in spring and stripping off the bark in winter.

The wild cat and pine marten are among the most elusive and little known British mammals. Both were once widespread. At the peak of their persecution, both retreated into their Highland fastnesses, where the inhospitable terrain and huge areas of unpopulated moor gave them the chance of survival, but in these more enlightened times, both are showing signs of spreading again.

Roe deer

Pine
marten

Red
squirrel

Wild cat

Scots pine

Pinewood Birds and Insects

Coal tit

Crested tit

Crossbill

Goldcrest

Siskin

The bird community of coniferous woods is much more distinct than the mammal population. Several species much prefer conifers to broad-leaved trees, and others are virtually confined to them. The coal tit and the goldcrest almost invariably breed in or near conifers, including isolated yew trees, and so are widespread wherever even ornamental conifers are found throughout Britain. In the autumn and winter, however, they join with other tits in foraging through broad-leaved woods as well. The marsh tit on the other hand almost never enters pinewoods, and the great tit is distinctly uncommon there. The crossbill is the classic example of a bird adapted to a specialised food source, since its crossed mandibles enable it to twist open cones in order to get at the seeds, instead of, as the squirrels do, tearing off the scales with their sharp teeth. Two groups of crossbills inhabit Britain, the long established Scottish crossbills of the Highland pine forests, and the more recently established population of the East Anglian brecklands and elsewhere in the south, the result of an invasion from northern Europe.

Other specialities of the Highland pinewoods are the siskin, which like the redpoll of the alderwoods has recently shown signs of spreading southwards, and the crested tit, which remains confined to its north-ern fastnesses. Many southern bird-watchers will see half a dozen new species on their first visit to the Speyside woodlands near Aviemore: besides crossbill, siskin and crested tit, osprey, capercaillie and black grouse can also be seen quite easily, not to mention three or four others as you ascend the Cairngorms. The capercaillie is a startling bird to encounter unexpectedly, as a family party of half a dozen turkey-sized birds suddenly explodes from the heather. The original Highland stock became extinct during the devastation of the Highlands in the 18th century, and the present population derives entirely from a few pairs introduced from Sweden in the first half of the last century. The native black grouse, which is really a bird of the forest edge, is much scarcer than it used to be, and occurs also in other parts of Highland Britain. Both blackgame and capers are protected from the wrath of the foresters only by their status as game birds, for both feed largely on the young shoots of trees. Black grouse are noted for their communal court-ship habits, involving many mock battles between competing cocks at a spring assembly called a lek.

Capercaillie

Whereas many of the insects and other invertebrates of deciduous woods tend to be associated with several different tree species, those of pinewoods are a very distinct group. Partly this is likely to be because pine needles are a very different diet from any other sort of leaf, and partly because the pine forests are found mainly in Scotland, in a very different climate.

One of the most obvious pinewood insects is the wood ant, which though not confined to pinewoods, certainly prefers them. The huge mounds made by wood ant colonies may be 2 or 3 feet (60 to 90 cms) high, and have a circumference of anything up to 30 feet (10 m). Such a mound is inhabited and fiercely guarded by 100,000 or so ants. Although the outside appears to be just a pile of twigs and other fragments, inside there is a complex system of tunnels and galleries which continue underground, while leading away from the nest are clearly marked tracks, the result of generations of ants marching back and forth to collect food.

The most striking pinewood moth is not found at all in Scotland, where pines are commonest. The pine hawkmoth is a southern insect, found only in the south of England, in East Anglia, where it has profited from the great increase in plantations over the last century. At rest, it is beautifully camouflaged. Another southern species is the black arches, whose caterpillars happily feed on a wide range of tree leaves, but the pine looper or bordered white is a much commoner insect, one whose caterpillar can cause serious defoliation. Another caterpillar that can cause considerable damage does not produce a moth or a butterfly, but a sawfly, the pine sawfly, while the pine weevil is equally damaging, but for a different reason: it eats away the bark of the young wood to reach the sapwood and so destroys it.

Pine looper

Pine hawkmoth

Black grouse

Wood ants' nest

Pine sawfly

Pine hawkmoth

Pine looper

Pine weevil

Black arches

Mushrooms and Toadstools

Just as the flush of flowers is the epitome of the woodland spring, so the autumn brings a different crop —mushrooms and toadstools. True, some fungi can be found all the year round, but the damp of autumn coupled with the great flood of dead leaves, on which they feed, on to the forest floor, brings up the fruiting bodies of the fungi by the score. For the rest of the year the fungus lives as a tangled web (called a mycelium) amongst its food material—dead leaves, dead or living wood, or any other form of organic matter. This mycelium can always be seen simply by turning over the leaf litter on the ground. Many fungi are very specific as to the trees they will grow with, either because they parasitise them, as does the common bracket fungus on birch, or because they form symbiotic associations with them, for example the showy but poisonous fly agaric, again most often found with birch. If you dig up the fine roots of many forest trees, but particularly pine, you will find that they end in white, stubby fingers: these are mantles of fungal material wrapped round the roots and known as mycorrhiza. The fungus obtains energy from the tree and provides it with nutrients from the soil. Particular fungi are associated with the roots of various trees, though any one tree species may have hundreds of fungal partners.

Different woods will then have very different fungi growing in them, but most fungi are not quite so fussy. That most famous of all deadly fungi, the death cap, is most often found under oak, but is equally at home with beech or ash. Very few toadstools are as dangerous to eat as this; most are harmless and a few are culinary delicacies, such as the chanterelle, another common woodlander. Of the fungi growing on the ground, one of the most obvious genera is *Russula*, whose members have widely spaced gills and unmarked, brightly coloured caps— purple in *R. atropurpurea*, yellow-brown in *R. ochroleuca* and so on.

More obvious perhaps are those that grow out of rotting wood, branches on the ground, stumps, or even living trees. The sulphur-tuft forms striking yellow clumps on old stumps, while the larger and browner honey fungus is a dangerous pest, attacking living trees. Three smaller fungi can be seen on dead wood all year round: candle-snuff fungus has little white-tipped black fingers, and coral spot is the name of the fungus that comes out in bright pinkish-orange spots all over dead branches. One of the oddest fungi is the jew's ear whose fleshy, ear-like fruit-bodies have a predilection for elder wood, but are found on many other trees.

Birch polypore

Common yellow
russula

Dark purple
russula

Fly agaric

Death cap

Sulphur tuft

Chanterelle

Candle-snuff
fungus

Coral spot

Honey fungus

HEATH, MOOR
AND MOUNTAIN

What could look wilder or more natural than a 'blasted heath', its gorse and heather lashed by high, cold winds? Indeed, the mountains of Scotland and north Wales, the upland moors of northern and south-west England, and the lowland heaths that stretch across southern England, are among the most inhospitable of all British habitats.

Surprisingly, both lowland heath and upland heather moor are as man-made as any other habitat. These vast wild areas, dominated by *Calluna vulgaris* or ling, only persist if they are managed. Lowland heaths, left alone, would quickly become birch or oak woodland; upland moors too might be colonized by birch if there were fewer sheep on the hills. Most of the heaths and moors of north-western Europe were probably created from neolithic times onwards as man felled the original woodlands to cultivate the land for crops. But in these high rainfall areas, primitive farming techniques could not counteract the fatal loss of nutrients, washed out from the soil. Crops failed, the land was abandoned, and the impoverished soils formed a fine habitat for heathers.

Heather or ling is a long-lived plant, but successful management of a heather moor depends upon keeping the plants permanently youthful. This is mainly achieved by fire. Burning the heather allows regeneration of vigorous new shoots which form a better defence against invasion by other plants, particularly bracken, and provide more nutritious and tender fodder for sheep and red deer. They also provide the ideal habitat for that most characteristic of moorland birds, the red grouse – on whose behalf so much of this vast artificial wilderness is maintained.

93

Heathland Plants

In Britain lowland heath is a common type of habitat, yet in the rest of Europe such heaths are uncommon, being confined largely to the mild, wet Atlantic coastlines of France and northern Spain, and to the North Sea coasts northwards to southern Norway. Some heaths develop on freely draining sands and gravels, particularly in Berkshire, Hampshire and Surrey, but others, mainly in wetter areas, occur on peaty soils and grade progressively to peat bogs—there is no absolute distinction.

What makes heathland quite distinctive among British habitats, is that it is dominated neither by trees nor by grasses or herbaceous plants, but by shrubs, dwarf shrubs, the heaths that give it its name. Heather has woody stems and so is a shrub, but even in the most favourable situations it never exceeds a metre in height, and so it is known as a dwarf shrub, as are several other members of the heather family Ericaceae that grow with it: besides bell heather, there are cross-leaved heath in wetter places and bilberry in dry ones. One of the most prolific and delicious wild fruits in Britain, bilberry in the north of England becomes whortleberry in the south—the fruits are called hurts there—and blaeberry in Scotland. It has rather inconspicuous, but very attractive flowers in spring,

long before the heathers flower. The other heathland shrubs are the three species of gorse: the widespread and often very large common gorse, the much shorter but equally spiny western gorse and dwarf gorse, which is like western gorse but more softly spined. Common gorse flowers almost throughout the year—hence the saying 'kissing's out of season when gorse is out of bloom'—but its main glory comes in April and May in the south, extending to June in the north. The other two flower mainly in late summer and autumn.

Where grazing pressure is light, trees will invade. Birch is the commonest tree of heathland—downy birch in damper spots and silver birch elsewhere. Other common heathland trees are rowan with its brilliant scarlet clusters of berries in autumn, and aspen, which is very susceptible to grazing, but in damp, protected spots suckers and forms dense thickets. Aspen gets its scientific name *Populus tremula* from the way in which its leaves tremble in the slightest breeze. In amongst the trees in these damp spots, shrubs of alder buckthorn are often found.

The flowers of heathland are few, but the quartet of tormentil, slender St John's-wort, heath milkwort, and heath bedstraw are almost invariably found. In bare places sheep's sorrel is common while wetter hollows are usually studded with the

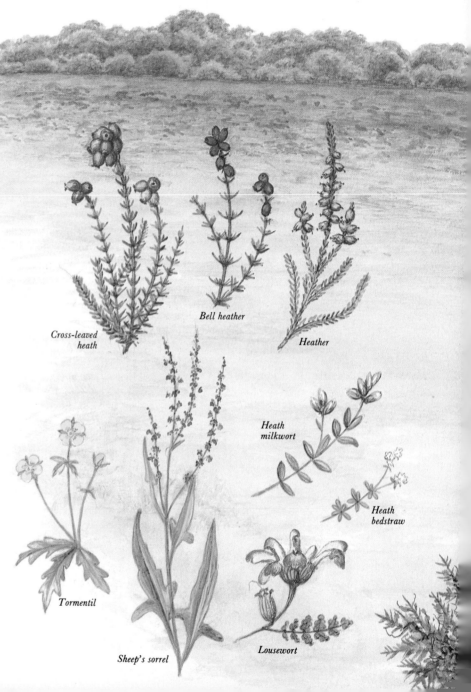

Cross-leaved heath

Bell heather

Heather

Heath milkwort

Heath bedstraw

Tormentil

Sheep's sorrel

Lousewort

Petty whin

Dwarf gorse

Western gorse

Gorse

pink flowers of lousewort, a plant which parasitises the roots of others. One of the most remarkable heathland plants is dodder, a leafless parasite, whose red stems twine in a thick mat over the gorse and heather, and are dotted with clusters of tiny, white, bell-like flowers. In contrast to the lousewort, which has its own leaves, dodder gets all its nutriment from its host.

Really wet heaths, usually on thin peat over infertile sands, were once common in lowland areas, but are now one of the most threatened habitats. They are home to a number of attractive plants, such as marsh gentian and marsh clubmoss, which have become rare along with their habitats. Other species are common in the wet moorlands and bogs of the north-west and so, though rare in the south and east, are scarcely endangered. Bog asphodel, with its yellow flowers and orange fruiting spikes, and grass of Parnassus with its white saxifrage-like flowers are two such, and so are the sundews, which supplement the infertility of the soil by trapping insects. Sundews are perhaps the most familiar of the small group of plants which have turned the tables on insects; but butterwort and bladderwort perform the same trick.

Silver birch

Rowan

Alder buckthorn

Bilberry

Heathland Reptiles and Birds

Sand lizard

Smooth snake

Adder

Common lizard

Natterjack toad

Heathland is a diminishing habitat and sadly many of the characteristic heathland birds are disappearing with it, but the commonest heathland bird is one that is in no danger, for it is common in other habitats too—the linnet. Two of its companions are more conspicuous by sound than sight: the stonechat is easily enough seen, but its presence is often given away by the harsh chacking call, resembling two stones being struck together. The nightjar, on the other hand, is not an easy bird to see since it is nocturnal, but its low persistent churring call may be heard at dusk a quarter of a mile or more away, sounding confusingly like a two-stroke motor-bike. Nightjars feed on moths and other night-flying insects which they catch on the wing; the red-backed shrike does the same in the daytime, and characteristically impales its prey, which may include nestling birds as well as insects, on thorns to make a 'larder'—hence its other name of butcher bird. Both the nightjar and the shrike are summer visitors only, for they feed on larger flying insects and there are too few of those around in winter to support them. The hobby, a small fast-flying falcon that still breeds on a few southern heaths where there are scattered pines to nest in, is also a summer visitor, though it feeds on other birds; but its prey is mainly swallows and martins, and since they feed on insects and fly south in the autumn, the hobby follows them.

The special rarity of the southern heathlands is the Dartford warbler, which was our only resident warbler until the 1970s, when it was joined by the marshland Cetti's warbler. Warblers are insect eaters too, so both are confined to the very south-

Hobby

Swallow

Dartford warbler

Nightjar

Wheatear

Linnet

Stonechat

Red-backed shrike

ern parts of Britain, where the winters are short enough. The Dartford warbler is probably doomed in the long run, for it is confined to heathlands south of the Thames, which are steadily being destroyed. It is doubtful whether the few heaths that survive in nature reserves within its limited range can provide a safe enough refuge, in view of its special requirements for gorse and heather at a certain stage of development. The hard winters of the early 1960s almost exterminated it, and the more recent drought-ridden summer of 1976 showed how vulnerable small stretches of heathland are to uncontrolled fire.

No mammals are confined to heathlands but the heaths make up for that with reptiles and amphibians. The special rarities, found mainly between south-west Surrey and eastern Dorset, are the smooth snake and its preferred prey the sand lizard, and in ponds the natterjack toad. However, much the most likely lizard and snake to be seen on a walk over a southern heath are the common lizard and its predator, our only venomous snake, the adder or viper. Adders are easily told by the striking blackish zigzag mark down the centre of their back, and do not have the pale mark at the base of the head that is the hallmark of the harmless grass snake.

Adders are in no way aggressive, and unless a man approaches them remarkably quietly, have usually heard his footsteps and glided away long before he can see them. Some-

times, however, they can be caught unawares while sun-bathing. Do not touch them, of course; but there is no need whatever to kill an adder if you find one, for it is only by the most extraordinary mischance that a human being is even bitten by an adder, let alone killed by one. If by chance someone is bitten, it is important to keep calm and remember that adder bites are almost never fatal. Do not cut or suck the wound, but obtain medical attention.

Adders are, of course, cold-blooded and are only active on warm days. In winter they gather in communal dens to hibernate. In summer they are most active in warm weather, and their basking in the sun is a device to raise their body temperature.

Upland Moors

Heather

Alpine bearberry

Bearberry

Chickweed wintergreen

On the higher hills and further north, the typical lowland heaths which develop on well-drained, often sandy soils, give way to heather moors on wetter peaty soils. The dominant plants are the same—heather and the two common heaths, cross-leaved heath and bell heather. The most obvious difference is the lack of gorse, so that the upland moors in August have a uniformly purple blanket, not the gold-spangled pattern of the heaths.

These moors are also man-made, prevented from becoming woodland, or even usually from having more than the odd scattered birch or rowan, by recurrent burning. On the highest heather moors the persistent strong winds and frequent frosts also help to prevent tree growth, or lead to extremely stunted specimens. Left to itself, moorland heather lasts about 30 years, but to provide continuing feed for sheep

and, particularly, grouse, it needs to be burned every ten or 15 years or so in the east of Scotland. In the west, where climate and soil are very different, muirburn should only be undertaken at intervals of about 20 years. If heather is burned every four to six years, and ineffectively at that as too often happens, it does not manage to grow more than about 15 cm high, and the moor is taken over by grasses, sedges and bracken. Besides, every time a moor is burned many of the mineral nutrients in the soil either literally go up in smoke or are washed into the nearest burn by the next rainstorm. This treatment over the centuries, coupled with constant overgrazing, has turned most of the Scottish Highlands into a heather desert.

An increasing and very unwelcome phenomenon is the wildfire, an uncontrolled fire started by thoughtless visitors tossing an un-

finished cigarette into dry heather, or even sometimes as a deliberate act of vandalism. In controlled fires, the flames move rapidly and the moist peat stays cool only a few centimetres below the surface, protecting seeds and dormant buds of heather, and insects and other soil animals. Regrowth from such a fire is rapid. Typically wildfires occur in dry spells when the surface peat has dried; then the peat itself may catch fire and continue to burn for days afterwards, slowly smouldering and exterminating all the seeds and animals. Recolonisation from such a catastrophe is a slow process; the peat may be wholly destroyed, leaving behind a sterile layer of infertile subsoil, subject to erosion and hostile to all life.

Upland moors are even more heather-dominated than the lowland heaths; indeed it is possible to find pure heather moors with almost

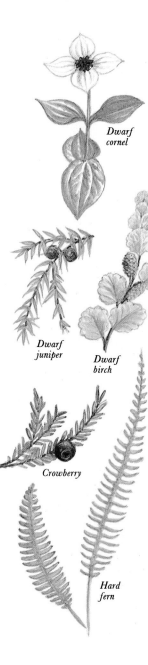

Dwarf cornel

Dwarf juniper

Dwarf birch

Crowberry

Hard fern

no other plants, although heathland plants can be found up to considerable altitudes, particularly where the drainage is good. The moorland habitat is particularly well suited to the swarf shrub growth form—tough and unpalatable to sheep, woody and resistant to extreme climates, and not so tall as to suffer damaging exposure. There are several dwarf shrubs characteristic of upland moors. Bearberry and its smaller, far northern relative alpine bearberry, both somewhat resembling bilberry, along with dwarf birch—a distinct species—and dwarf juniper—a prostrate subspecies of common juniper. Other northern or upland species include chickweed wintergreen (a relative of the primrose), hard fern, dwarf cornel, with its striking white flowers whose 'petals' are really bracts—the actual flowers are tiny—and crowberry, which can be found from sea-level to the summits of the highest hills. The mountain-top crowberry has hermaphrodite flowers which can set seed without the aid of an insect pollinator.

A puzzling group of upland plants is the clubmosses, primitive moss-like relatives of the ferns whose ancestors dominated the coal-measure forests, hundreds of millions of years ago. The surviving species are much smaller than their ancestors, the largest only 20 or 30 cm high.

Common clubmoss

Fir clubmoss

Alpine clubmoss

Upland Mammals and Birds

By contrast with the southern heaths, the moors of the north have the most exciting array of mammals to be found in the British Isles, including both red and roe deer, wild cat, pine marten and blue hare. In Central Wales the polecat also survives, its taste for raiding the henhouse having caused its extermination everywhere else. The red deer, the largest and most conspicuous of our mammals, ranges over all the uplands, feeding as much on grass and young tree shoots as on heather. It is really a woodland animal, which used to inhabit the largely vanished pine forests of the Highlands, but nowadays a deer forest is almost treeless. The flies and midges drive the deer up to the hilltops in summer, just when most visitors come to the Highlands. Deer are constantly on the move, both seasonally, from low ground to high ground, and during each day. During the autumn rut stags may travel several miles to find hinds in another forest. Red deer are only really red in summer, between May and September, their winter pelage being dark brown. Their antlers start growing again as soon as they are cast in March and April, and reach their maximum size again in July.

Roe deer are also red-brown only in summer, and appear grey-brown between October and March or April. Their antlers are shed from late October to December and have grown to maturity again by April. They too are really woodland animals and appear on moorland only where there is tall heather.

Wild cats, which can be very ferocious when cornered, are larger and appear somewhat longer-legged than the domestic tabbies which they strikingly resemble and indeed interbreed with. They are, however, more uniformly striped than tabbies, which often have blotches as well. For most of the past century wild cats have been more or less confined to the Scottish Highlands, but now there are some indications that they are spreading back into the hills of the Border country, and if so may yet reoccupy the English Lake District and the northern Pennines. Pine martens too are spreading southwards from their Highland fastnesses and are already to be found not only in Snowdonia and the Lake District, but in three or four other hill districts of northern England and southern Scotland.

The blue hare is much more tied to heather, which forms about 90 per cent of its diet in winter, and even in summer about half. It feeds heavily on the shoots of heather that has been burned within the previous two or three years. It is squatter than the brown hare, with shorter ears and greyer fur. In winter blue hares turn wholly or partly white.

Red deer

Roe deer

Wild cat

Blue hare

Polecat

Pine marten

Peregrine

Hen harrier
♀
♂

Merlin

Hooded crow

Raven

Carrion crow

Ring
ouzel

Greenshank

Red grouse

Black grouse

The birds of the moorlands differ substantially from those of the lowland heaths, though some, such as the skylark and wheatear, are common to both. The essential moorland bird is the red grouse, which eats heather shoots throughout the year as its predominant diet, and stays on the moor throughout the year except when it is under heavy snow. The leaves, shoots and fruits of the bilberry are also a favourite food, together with other moorland fruits such as bearberry, crowberry and cloudberry. The black grouse, a bird of the moorland edge rather than of the open moor, feeds especially on young tree shoots. It is one of the classic lek species: birds which choose their mates at an assembly where all the males give their courtship display and spar with one another.

The moorland birds of prey are the golden eagle, which also stays there all the year, and the peregrine, merlin and hen harrier, all of which move downhill in winter and are more likely to be found on coastal estuaries. The golden eagle is most likely to be seen soaring high over mountainous moorland in the Scottish Highlands or some of the larger Hebrides, such as Skye. Adult eagles are all dark, but young birds are conspicuously white at the base of the tail. In the white-tailed sea eagle, which is currently the subject of a reintroduction experiment on the Hebridean island of Rum, the reverse is the case, the adults having an all-white tail and the young birds an all-dark tail. The best way of distinguishing between these two eagles is in fact the shape of their tail. The golden eagle has a square-ended tail, whereas the sea eagle's tail is wedge-shaped. Incidentally, golden eagles sometimes nest on cliffs by the sea, which are also the preferred nest site of the sea eagle. A very few golden eagles now nest in south-west Scotland and the English Lake District.

Among the crows both the raven and the carrion crow (hooded crow in the Highlands) are moorland species. Weather on the moors is so harsh in winter that it is not surprising that all other birds are summer visitors, wintering either in the lowlands, like the skylark, meadow pipit and golden plover, or overseas, like the ring ouzel, wheatear and greenshank. The meadow pipit is the commonest and most widespread of all moorland birds, and is confusingly never found in meadows; its other English name, titlark, is equally misleading. Another very frequent moorland bird is the ubiquitous wren, whose loud challenging song comes from every rocky clough whose few scattered rowans or sallows diversify the monotonous uniformity of the moor.

Moorland Insects

Small copper

Oak eggar
and
caterpillar
♂
♀

Small heath

Grayling

♂

♀

Silver studded
blue

Dark green
fritillary

Fox moth
and
caterpillar

Several attractive species of butterflies and moths inhabit the heathlands and moorlands, although they are not, perhaps, as spectacular as those of chalk grassland. Among them are the silver-studded blue, the grayling and the dark green fritillary, as well as such widespread species as the small copper and the small heath. There are also a number of striking species of day-flying moths, notably the emperor moth, the fox moth and the oak eggar. The male moths can be seen careering at a dizzy pace above the heather on sunny days, searching for the females. These sit tight and emit a

scent of astonishing power, which attracts the males from distances of at least a mile. A freshly-emerged female can be used in this way to attract sometimes as many as 40 male moths.

The fox and emperor fly in late spring and early summer. So too does the oak eggar in the north, but in southern England a different race is found, which flies in late summer. The two races also differ in that the caterpillars of the southern race hatch in August, hibernate until the following spring and pupate in June, and the moth appears in July. In the north, however, the caterpillar takes

longer to mature and passes the second winter as a chrysalis, emerging as a moth the following spring.

The fox and oak eggar caterpillars are dark brown and furry, the eggar with black rings, and may be 10 cm long. The emperor has a bright green caterpillar with black stripes, which is remarkably hard to spot on the heather on which it typically feeds; the other two, in contrast, are familiar sights as they cross moorland paths in search of a place to pupate. Perhaps the commonest moorland moth is the antler moth, a small brown insect, whose caterpillars feed on the poor moorland

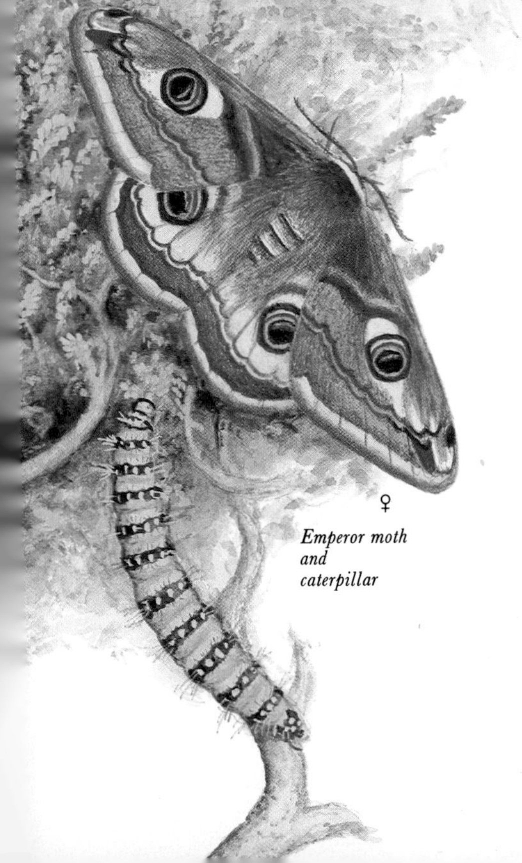

White
beak-sedge

Scotch argus

Blackflies

Emperor
moth ♂

Large heath

Mountain
ringlet

Mosquito

Emperor moth
and
caterpillar
♀

grasses and sometimes occur in huge numbers, devastating vegetation and attracting flocks of rooks and other predators.

The heathland butterflies and moths mostly go some distance up on to the moors – indeed the northern race of the oak eggar is very much a moorland insect – but in Scotland there are a number of butterflies and moths found only on the higher moors. These include the large heath, whose caterpillars feed on purple moor-grass and on white beak-sedge, so that it is found, along with its food-plants on the wetter moors and bogs (see p. 106); and

the Scotch argus, a grass-feeder, whose larva is especially found on blue moor-grass, a plant of very limited distribution.

There are, too, a few truly montane moths and one butterfly, the mountain ringlet, which occurs only on alpine grasslands in the Lake District and in Scotland. Mountain tops proper have little grass and these grass-feeding insects cannot survive there; the mountain moths such as the mountain burnet moth have caterpillars that feed on such dwarf shrubs as crowberry.

In some ways, the most important, and certainly the most noticeable,

insects in the Scottish Highlands are the swarms of midges which, in summer, not only drive the deer up to the high tops but plague the human inhabitants and visitors severely. Their larvae live in fresh water (see p. 128), but the adults pervade most of the terrestrial habitats of Scotland. Blackflies can be equally tiresome. Although only the females actually bite, both sexes have the infuriating habit of hovering in clouds around any human being in sight, sometimes so close to the face that even opening the eyes or breathing deeply can become hazardous operations.

Grass Heath and Moor

Bracken

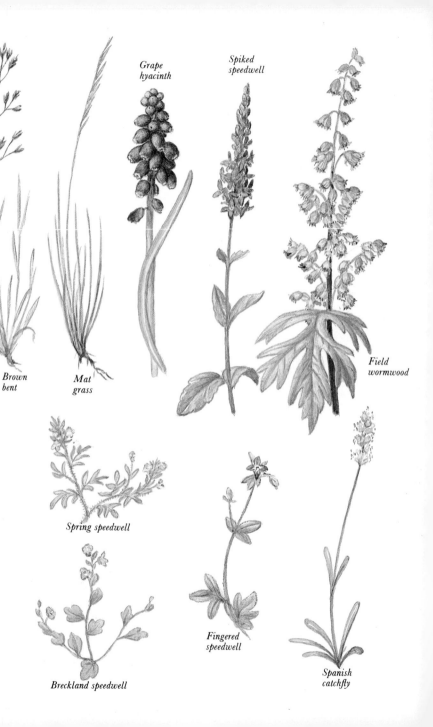

Grape hyacinth

Spiked speedwell

Field wormwood

Sheep's fescue

Brown bent

Mat grass

Spring speedwell

Breckland speedwell

Fingered speedwell

Spanish catchfly

When upland heather moor is heavily grazed, the characteristic dwarf shrubs such as heather are soon killed and replaced by grasses. Grass heath is also found in the lowlands, probably as the result of intensive exploitation of forests in the neolithic and subsequent periods, which on certain light sandy soils caused such a loss of fertility as to inhibit the growth of trees. This appears to be the explanation for the heaths of the East Anglian Breckland, with their unique flora and fauna, including stone curlew, crossbill and ringed plover among the breeding birds. Areas of true heather or ling heath occur in the Breckland, but if sheep are grazed there, grass heath takes over.

As a result of its continental climate—hot summers and cold dry winters—several plants more characteristic of the East European steppes grow there and almost nowhere else in Britain. These include field wormwood, Spanish catchfly, grape hyacinth, and no fewer than four species of speedwell—the magnificent spiked speedwell and the obscure, often quite tiny annual speedwells *Veronica verna*, *V. praecox*, and *V. triphyllos*.

Upland grass heath or moor is

Golden
plover

Stone
curlew

also the result of forest denudation by man, and again intensive grazing kills the dwarf shrubs so that grass moor results. On dry soils these moors are of two types—either a relatively nutritious turf of bent and fescue grasses, or a very poor and unproductive sward dominated by mat-grass. These moors have rather few wild flowers, and most of them are shared with the heather moors— tormentil, heath bedstraw, slender St. John's-wort and the like. Mat-grass is almost totally inedible in summer, although in early spring it is quite palatable, and it has spread greatly on the hills since changing farming practices now mean that sheep are rarely put out on the fell until after its early succulence has passed.

Heavy grazing causes heather to give way to grasses; if the grazing is too severe the grasses may themselves be replaced by such invasive and inedible plants as bracken or, in the south-west, western gorse. The influence of man's management (or mismanagement) on these habitats is profound. Bracken is one of the most important weeds in permanent grassland in Britain, and it is currently increasing in area by about 5–10% each year. The sight of whole hillsides completely covered in bracken is now not unusual. Quite apart from the sterilising effect it has in rendering land completely unproductive for grazing, it can actually poison stock by virtue of a whole arsenal of noxious chemicals that it contains. The only feasible form of control at present is spraying, but this is too expensive to be truly economic and is effective for only a few years. Probably biological control, using an introduced insect that would feed on it, will prove to be the only answer, for bracken has many insect pests in other parts of the world.

Bogs

Where the ground is waterlogged, usually as a result of poor drainage, dead plant material falling to the ground does not rot; instead it is preserved as peat – and ultimately perhaps as coal. If the surrounding rocks are acid, so that no basic minerals such as calcium drain into the peat, a bog is formed. Such bogs are usually dominated by the bog-mosses *Sphagnum*, and indeed in the north of England they are called mosses. There are three main types of bog: valley bogs develop in shallow valleys, where drainage is poor and where acid water seeping in from the surrounding rocks produces waterlogging. Raised bogs are the result of the activity of *Sphagnum*, which has the ability to create waterlogged conditions *above* the water-table; since all the water in such a system must come from rainfall (which is distilled water and contains few minerals), raised bogs are very acid. As the *Sphagnum* grows upwards away from the water-table, it creates a mound of peat, highest in the centre, which is isolated from the effects of the water draining from the surrounding land, and sloping down gradually to end in a sharply defined bank called a lagg. Finally blanket bog occurs where the rainfall is high enough for *Sphagnum* to grow everywhere, even on higher or better drained land; it comprises a blanket of peat

entirely covering the landscape, and is the explanation for the monotonous appearance of parts of Ireland and western Scotland.

Raised and blanket bogs are both usually more acid than valley bogs, for they rely entirely on rainfall and receive none of the dissolved minerals which even the most acid of catchments will supply. The peat produced by bog formation, being simply unrotted plant remains, can be dried and used as a fuel. It was once the main source of domestic fuel in many parts of the country, and still is in the blanket bog areas of Scotland and Ireland. The Norfolk Broads are now known to be the flooded basins left after mediaeval peat extraction.

Sphagnum bogs are probably the most stable habitats in Britain. To an ecologist, the attraction of a peat-bog is that it lays down, in the peat that the growth of *Sphagnum* produces, a complete record of its own history. Where no peat-cutting has taken place, 10–12,000 years of ecological history may be preserved. To examine this record involves sinking a peat borer into the ground. Since peat deposits may be up to 6 m thick and are very wet, extracting a peat core is one of the messiest tasks known to ecologists.

The predominant plants of bogs are the *Sphagnum* mosses and a number of grasses and sedges: com-

mon and harestail cotton-grasses (which are actually sedges), deer grass (another sedge) and purple moor-grass which really is a grass. It is a well-known piece of country lore that it is unsafe to tread where common cotton-grass or bog cotton grows, for this will be a treacherous bog surface; the harestail cotton-grass, however, distinguished by its single white tuft, usually grows on firmer ground. The most colourful plants of these bogs are the vivid yellow bog asphodel, which turns wholly orange in late summer after flowering, cross-leaved heath, and the rather shy-flowering cloudberry. Cloudberry does produce an edible berry, but not usually in sufficient quantity to be worth picking. There is, too, one shrub that may be found in bogs—bog myrtle or sweet gale, a very aromatic plant that has the ability to make its own organic nitrogen from the nitrogen gas in the air, with the aid of a bacterium in its roots; in these very nitrogen-deficient habitats that must be a considerable advantage.

The animal life of bogs is similar to that of moorlands, though the large heath butterfly is commonly found on them. Black-headed gulls will not infrequently choose tufts of sedges sticking out of a wet bog for their nesting colony, as this naturally helps protect them from foxes and the like.

Sphagnum capillifolium

S. palustre

S. cuspidatum

S. papillosum

Cotton-grass

Harestail cotton-grass

Deer-grass

Blue moorgrass

Bog asphodel

Cloudberry

Cross-leaved heath

Large heath

Trailing azalea

Crowberry

Dwarf willow

Golden eagle

Mountains

In the mountains the climate is colder, wetter and windier, and true Arctic conditions prevail, though we have no permanent snow-patches in Britain. Trees peter out far below and only tiny creeping shrubs like crowberry and the minute willow *Salix herbacea* are left. On the high summits and on steep slopes, stones and boulders and patches of gritty soil separate the depauperate clumps of vegetation, often comprising only the moss *Rhacomitrium lanuginosum*, the sedge *Carex bigelowii*, and the rush *Juncus trifidus*. What little does grow must be able to withstand the grazing of the freely roaming sheep, the occasional mountain hare, and the herds of red deer, driven upwards in summer by the biting flies and midges.

Rhacomitrium moss often forms curious striped patterns on high mountain summits, for it grows continuously away from the direction of the prevailing wind, produc-ing a series of waves, consisting of a dying edge on the windward side and a growing edge on the leeward. Here is a whole plant community on the march. Another sign of climatic severity is the stone stripes, often seen in bare areas on mountains, where frost-heaving in winter has forced the smaller stones away, leaving only large stones in stripes. In truly Arctic regions such stripes cover huge areas with polygonal patterns.

The birds of the mountains are largely the same as those of the upland moors (p. 100–1), but a few seek out the summits to breed. These include dotterel, the special rarity of Highland mountain tops, and golden plover and dunlin. There is also a tiny Scottish breeding population of a genuinely Arctic bird, the snow bunting, though you are more likely to see one on the East coast in winter. The one bird that spends the whole year in the moun-tains, snow and wind notwithstand-ing, is that close relative of the red grouse, the ptarmigan. It even moults into white plumage, like the mountain hare, which must aid its survival amidst the snow.

But perhaps the real symbol of the mountains is the golden eagle, our largest breeding bird since its relative the sea eagle became extinct at the beginning of the century. Carefully protected in most areas, though still illegally persecuted in a few, it is slowly increasing and making tentative attempts to re-colonise southern Scotland, north-ern Ireland and northern England. Though it hunts mostly in the glens and on the moors, where most food is, the sight of a golden eagle soaring majestically over a mountain top makes it seem a quintessentially mountain bird. Two golden eagles engaged in a courtship display high over a wild landscape make the birdwatching sight of a lifetime.

Dotterel

Golden plover

Ptarmigan

Snow bunting

Dunlin

Mountain hare
(Blue hare)

Mountain Flowers

For the botanist there are two things wrong with British mountains: it rains too much and there are too many sheep. The objection to rain is not for its effect on the botanist, but because it washes essential bases out of the soil, producing acid soils of little floristic interest; the sheep of course eat anything that does rear its head above the carpets of mat grass. British mountains therefore lack the flower-studded meadows of the Alps. The botanist seeks out two habitats: wet flushes, where base-rich water seeps out, and rock-ledges on basic soils inaccessible to sheep. The flowers of these ledges are all able to avoid both acidity and over-grazing, and are of two kinds: woodland and meadow plants and true mountain plants needing lime. Among the first group are globeflower, red campion, wood cranesbill and primrose. There is some debate as to why so many woodland plants should be found on mountain ledges, but it seems likely that they were left behind when the forests, that once clothed the hills up to at least the 600 or 700 m contour lines, were cleared. Nowadays they survive as isolated populations. The more strictly montane species are represented by purple saxifrage, flowering in April, roseroot, mountain sorrel and alpine saw-wort, to name a few of the commonest. Some of the rarer species, such as mountain avens and alpine gentian, are among our most beautiful wild plants.

It is also worth looking at wet flushes, where springs emerge, and at streamsides, where the action of water creates locally higher fertility, and where two more saxifrages, yellow saxifrage and the white-flowered starry saxifrage with its conspicuous red anthers often grow. On the rocks by mountain streams grow a number of dwarf willow-herbs: alpine and chickweed willow-herbs are native species, particularly fond of the bright green mossy carpets that form around mountain springs. On gravel and damp rocks, however, may be found creeping the curious New Zealand willow-herb, an introduced plant, with inconspicuous rounded leaves and very long seed pods. It is one of the few introduced species to have found an apparently vacant niche in native vegetation—most are weeds of disturbed ground, often in towns.

Exposed mountain summits support an unexpected group of sea-side plants, including thrift and sea campion. Both sea cliffs and mountains are subject to fierce winds and these plants form well adapted cushions, as do the wholly montane species, moss campion and cyphel. Other high mountain plants such as trailing azalea and mountain avens form creeping mats.

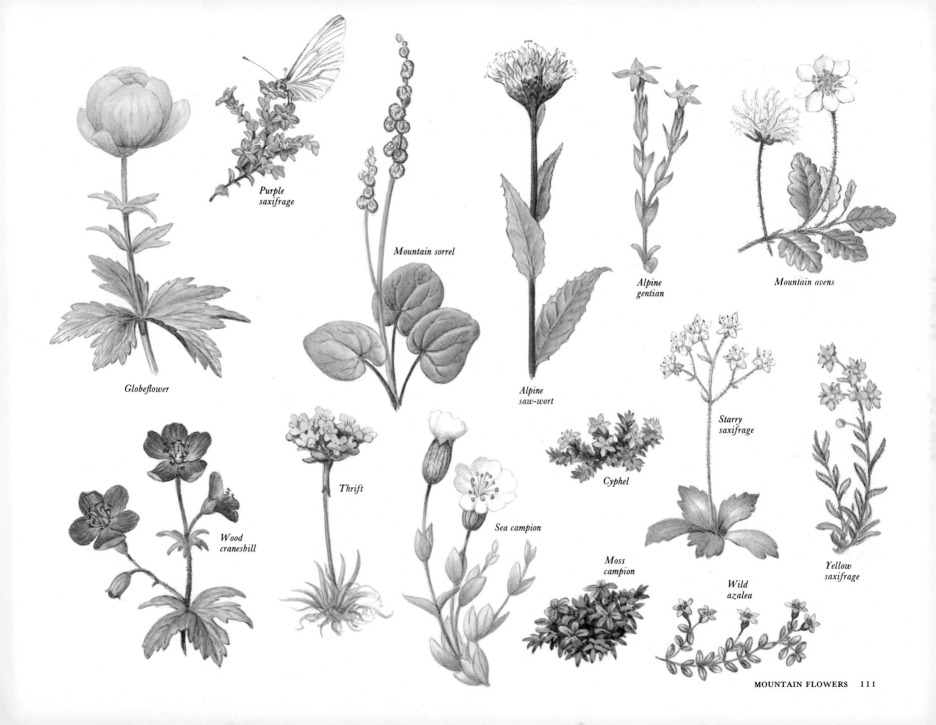

Purple
saxifrage

Mountain sorrel

Alpine
gentian

Mountain avens

Globeflower

Alpine
saw-wort

Starry
saxifrage

Wood
cranesbill

Thrift

Sea campion

Cyphel

Moss
campion

Wild
azalea

Yellow
saxifrage

FRESH WATER

There are stretches of water all over Britain, varying from temporary ponds to large lakes, many man-made as reservoirs. Those in the lowlands differ from their upland counterparts in many ways. They can be larger, since many streams may converge on one lowland lake, and where water flows it will do so more slowly since gradients are less steep. Most importantly, lowland waters are usually much more productive, and are termed *eutrophic* from the Greek meaning "well-fed".

There are several reasons for this. First lowland waters are warmer and plants grow faster, and second they more often contain water that has passed through base-rich rocks, such as limestones, dissolving minerals that promote plant growth. By contrast the hills of upland Britain are mostly made of hard, acidic, base-poor rocks, such as granite, and these give rise to infertile waters. Perhaps most importantly lowland waters tend to be shallower, so that the nutrients that fall to the bottom of the lake can be recycled.

The productivity of any habitat depends on the growth of its plants and in aquatic habitats the most important of these are often algae, which may be single-celled and individually invisible to the naked eye, but can still colour water green in enormous numbers if the fertility of the water has been artificially raised by sewage or the leaching of agricultural fertilisers. This has happened in the Norfolk Broads, where the once crystal-clear water is now green and murky. As the algae die, their decomposition consumes oxygen and renders the water unfit for fish and other animals.

Other algae are larger and visible without a microscope. These algae and the higher plants provide the food for all the animals in the water. Minute floating animals such as rotifers and water-fleas feed on the algae, and then form the prey for many of the larger insect larvae, which in turn feed the fish, and finally large carnivores such as herons and pike, and the whole system forms a complex food-web.

Freshwater Plants

A pond or a lake provides a complete range of aquatic habitats for its denizens, from its damp margins to its deep-water centre. But these habitats are created partly by the plants which grow there – a lake is not a permanent thing, for gradually, over tens, hundreds, or even thousands of years it is filled with soil by the growth and death of its plants, and you can easily see this taking place by looking at the zones of vegetation.

Except for duckweeds and a few oddities such as frogbit, higher plants need to root in the soil and so very deep water has no plants. This is why the sea has so few higher plants – most is too deep and the shores are too wave-battered. In the same way, the shores of lakes with a long wind reach are usually unvegetated. As the water gets shallower towards the edge, however, plants such as white water-lily and its yellow-flowered relative, the brandybottle, appear, rooted in the mud but with floating leaves. Other plants may be rooted here, but have all their leaves submerged, for example the water milfoils and many of the pondweeds, while marestail, arrow-head and the bur-reeds are examples of species whose leaves stick out of the water.

Plants whose leaves are borne underwater have a problem: they need oxygen for respiration and carbon dioxide for photosynthesis. These gases are dissolved in the water but move a hundred thousand times more slowly there than in air. Both water plants and aquatic animals have solved the problem in the same way – very finely divided, finger-like leaves or gills, with a huge surface area to get what little there is of the essential gases in the water. These are beautifully illustrated by the common water crowfoot, which has threadlike underwater leaves but normal ones floating on the surface. Other plants, such as the water milfoil have even more intricate leaf patterns. The gills of fish are hidden behind flaps and hard to see, but more primitive animals have their gills outside, as do very young tadpoles. The water spider has solved this problem quite differently, by taking down an air bubble to its nest.

In flowing water there is less difficulty in getting oxygen, but both plants and animals then have the problem of staying put. There are no floating plants and, if the current is strong, not even rooted plants with floating leaves, and animals that are not bottom dwellers must be strong swimmers, such as fish. Plants growing in water have little need of roots to get water and minerals as on land, but they must be well anchored, and so rocky streams have fewer plants than muddy ones, which are slower-flowing anyway. The animals keep themselves in place either by hiding in vegetation, by crawling on it like the water snail, or by remarkable adaptations of body form, as in the larvae of some mayflies and stone-flies which cling to stones and are flattened to reduce their resistance to water.

Each year plants growing in still water build up the soil level fractionally by trapping silt and depositing dead leaves, and so eventually make it possible for the invasion of plants which can tolerate water-logged soil but must have their leaves in air. There are many of these, notably yellow iris, water plantains, water dock, and water speedwells, all typical lake- and riverside plants. They continue the soil building process until eventually

Frogbit

Duckweed

White waterlily

Spiked water milfoil

Curled pondweed

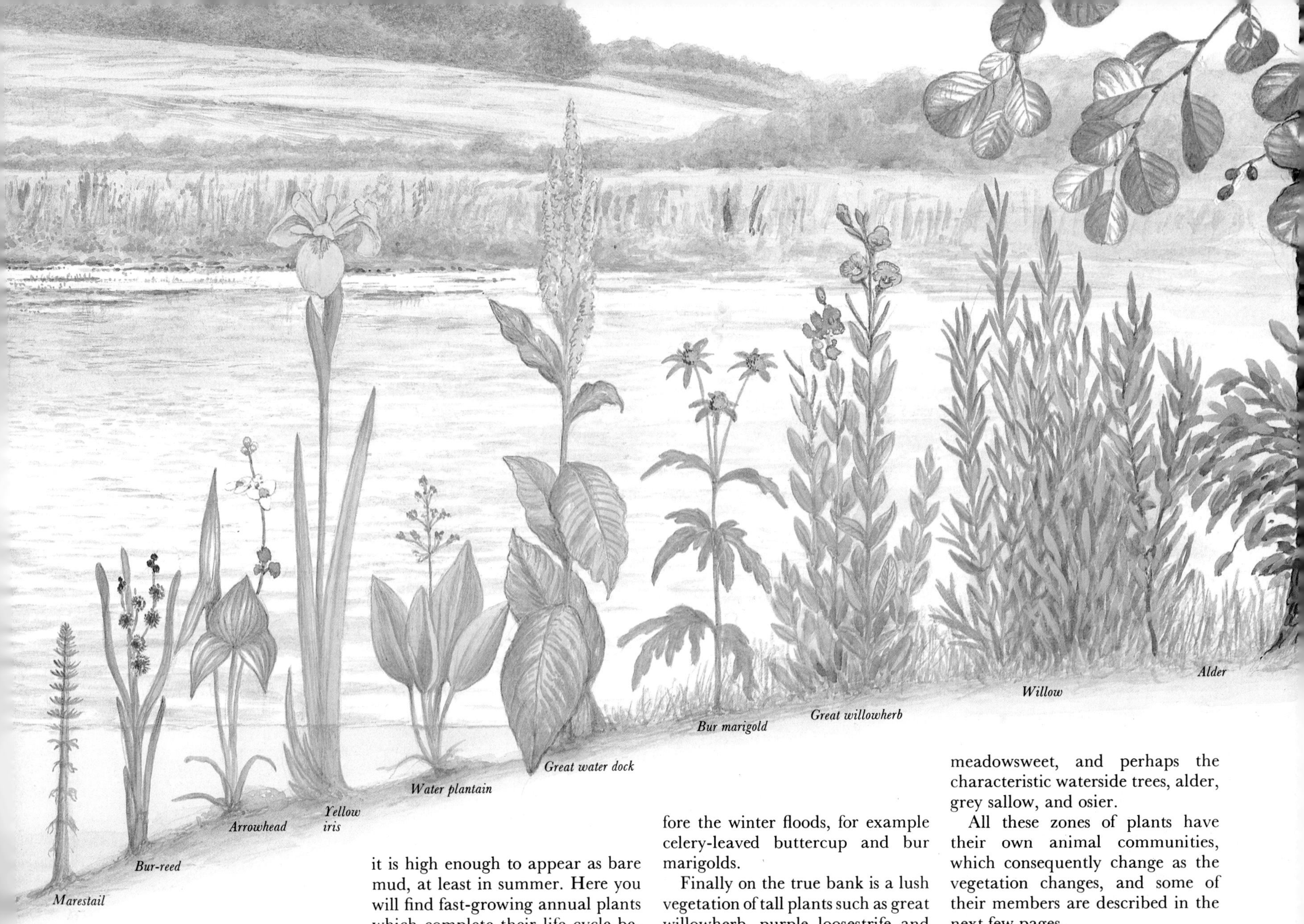

Marestail

Bur-reed

Arrowhead

Yellow iris

Water plantain

Great water dock

Bur marigold

Great willowherb

Willow

Alder

it is high enough to appear as bare mud, at least in summer. Here you will find fast-growing annual plants which complete their life cycle be-fore the winter floods, for example celery-leaved buttercup and bur marigolds.

Finally on the true bank is a lush vegetation of tall plants such as great willowherb, purple loosestrife and meadowsweet, and perhaps the characteristic waterside trees, alder, grey sallow, and osier.

All these zones of plants have their own animal communities, which consequently change as the vegetation changes, and some of their members are described in the next few pages.

Lakes

The distinction between a lake and a pond is arbitrary, and in many ways they present similar habitats, but the greater size of lakes does have a number of important consequences for wildlife. The depth of a lake is one of the main factors determining its productivity. In a deep lake the tiny floating algae that colour green the waters of a fertile lake, sink so far when they die that they carry the nutrients locked up in their bodies out of the lake's circulation. These deep reserves of nutrients may be brought up to the surface by turbulence or the cooling of the surface water in winter if the lake is not too deep, but are almost permanently lost in a very deep lake, reducing its fertility.

Secondly, the larger a lake is the more plants can grow in it, the more animals can feed on those plants, and other animals on them. A pond cannot be a habitat for many carnivores for there is simply not enough food. So the big predators, such as herons, great crested grebe and pike are lake dwellers. For the same reason birds that like to flock together, including coots and many ducks, such as tufted duck and pochard, characteristic diving ducks which eat almost anything they can find on the lake bottom, are found on lakes. Most bottom-feeding birds dive for their food, but the mute swan has a long enough neck to stay

on the surface; if all else fails it will up-end, but never dives. By contrast other birds sift the water surface for food, like the aptly-named shoveler duck.

Thirdly, large stretches of water can generate sizeable waves in windy weather, so that exposed shores are sometimes devoid of vegetation, and floating plants like duckweeds are rarely found, allowing submerged plants to grow better. This is important because if these plants, such as Canadian pondweed and water milfoil flourish, they support a rich community of animals, including water snails and many insect larvae. These in turn supply a myriad of carnivorous animals such as water beetles, dragonfly larvae, and many fish, and the whole complex is one of the most diverse communities to be found in this country, even if hidden from the casual eye.

The evidence of its productivity is to be seen in the huge numbers of birds that either breed on (like the ducks) or come to feed at the lake, as herons and sand martins do.

Great crested grebe

Heron

Tufted duck

Wigeon

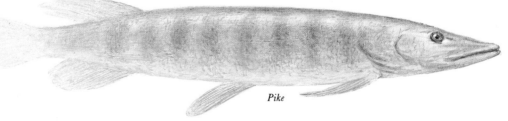

Pike

Great crested grebe

Shoveler

Pochard

Coot

Canada goose

♂
Shelduck

Ponds

Water crowsfoot

Broad-leaved pondweed

Duckweed

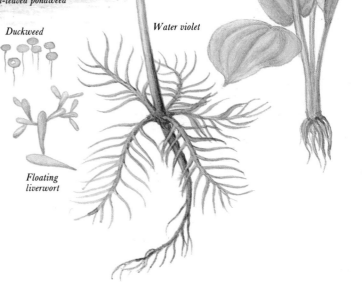

Floating liverwort

Water violet

Water plantain

Ponds are a universal feature of the landscape. In some districts almost every field has a pond and most are man-made. Village ponds were an essential part of farming life until recently, much frequented by cattle and so usually with a muddy bank where house martins collected mud for their nests and celery-leaved buttercup thrived. Field ponds are often old clay-pits, dug to make the local bricks; occasionally one finds a dew-pond on the high waterless downs, cunningly constructed to trap rain and other condensation from the air.

Their size means that the water is calm, particularly when protected by shrubs such as grey sallow, and so plants with floating leaves can thrive. Water crowfoot and broad-leaved pondweed root in the bottom, but duckweed is free-floating and in hot weather grows so fast as to cover the whole surface. Then few plants can survive submerged, generally only algae such as blanketweed, *Spirogyra*, and the curious ivy-leaved

Smooth newt

Common toad

Common frog

House martin

♀ Mallard

♂ Mallard

Coot

Moorhen

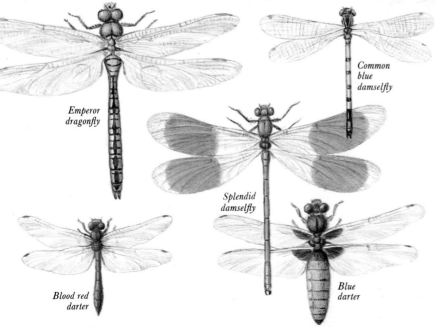

Emperor
dragonfly

Common
blue
damselfly

Splendid
damselfly

Blood red
darter

Blue
darter

duckweed which floats just below the surface, and also those that grow early in the season before the duckweed gets a hold, as does the showy water violet. Otherwise the plants mostly have aerial shoots like water plantain.

Ponds do not usually have streams flowing in or out, so the dead leaves collect each year at the bottom, and in and above this slowly-rotting mass breed millions of insect larvae, particularly chironomids or bloodworms and gnat larvae *Culex*, whose adults make their presence known in great swarms later in the summer. The insect life of ponds is rich. Several species live on the boundary between air and water,

relying on surface tension to keep them afloat. Backswimmers are ferocious predatory bugs, while the closely-related water boatmen feed largely on algae and plant remains. The delicate damselflies and more robust dragonflies are also predators, seizing their prey on the wing.

The rich insect life supports several larger animals. Ponds are characteristic breeding grounds for frogs and toads, which may travel relatively large distances to reach them, and also for newts. Almost every pond in Britain has, too, a resident pair of moorhens, skulking birds who shun large stretches of water, and among the ducks teal and mallard are perhaps commonest.

Reedswamp

Unless the shore of a lake shelves very steeply or is very exposed, it will often be bordered by reedswamp, a dense mass of reeds, whose creeping rhizomes and tall, persistent stems discourage other plants. A small pond may be taken over by reeds in a few years and sometimes its previous existence is only shown by a patch of reeds.

The few other plants that do grow in reedswamp have to be tall and vigorous so as to grow up with the reeds. The reedmace (often incorrectly called bulrush) is a typical example and more colourful plants found in reedbeds include great willowherb, yellow loosestrife, and gipsywort. Sometimes the woody stems of bitterwseet, with its striking red berries, are also found. Eventually the reedbed will itself be invaded by trees, such as sallow and alder, and then develop into alder carr or swamp woodland, described on p. 72. In a few places, however, reedswamp may be cut to make the bundles which form the roof of thatched cottages, and then no trees can establish and the reedbed is maintained. In East Anglia saw sedge or great fen-sedge is cut for thatching too.

The birds of reedbeds form a characteristic and specialised group, the best known of which is perhaps

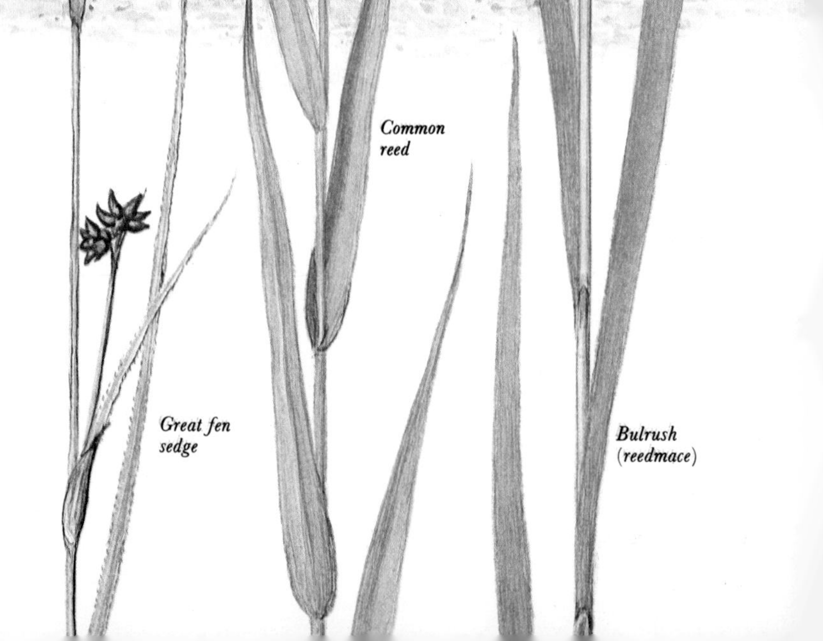

Great fen sedge

Common reed

Bulrush (reedmace)

Sedge warbler

Reed warbler

Bearded tit

Great willowherb

Yellow loosestrife

Sallow

Gypsywort

Bittersweet

Bittern

the bittern, whose booming cry is most frequent in the East Anglian marshes, but breeds in several places in Wales and north-west England too. In autumn and winter, however, bitterns scatter and may turn up in marshes almost anywhere. The other three birds use the reeds as pillars to support their nests, and the commonest are the reed and sedge warblers, which hide in dense reed-beds and are most likely to be detected by their calls. The reed warbler has a rather cross-sounding and fairly uniform "churr" and the sedge a harsher, busier and more varied song. Much rarer than either is the bearded tit, another speciality of the Norfolk Broads and coastal reedbeds.

Upland Lakes

The striking thing about lakes (lochs in Scotland) and tarns in upland areas is usually how little grows in them. The water is cold and poor in plant nutrients, and few species thrive there. Hence they are termed *oligotrophic* (from the Greek meaning poorly fed) in contrast to the eutrophic lowland waters. Most of the plants are found where streams flow in, bringing a little silt and some nutrients, and here there is often a marsh of bottle sedge and water horsetail, giving enough shelter for the floating leaves of bog pondweed, and sometimes for a snipe, probing in the mud with its long bill.

Most upland lakes, however, have largely stony bottoms, supporting a group of three or four plants almost indistinguishable until they flower, when water lobelia is instantly told by its delicate violet-coloured, lobelia-like flowers. When not flowering it is easily mistaken for shoreweed, a relative of the plantains, awlwort, a member of the cabbage family, or even quillwort, a curious fern. These four plants represent a remarkable instance of evolution producing the same solution to an ecological problem from very different starting points. Taxonomically the four species are about as unrelated as they could be. Sometimes the feathery leaves and striking yellow flowers of lesser bladderwort can also be found; on their leaves it has small hollow chambers, each with a trap-door set off by a small animal touching a sensitive hair. When this happens water rushes into the chamber trapping the victim, which is digested at the bladderwort's leisure.

A more obvious predator, if much rarer, is the osprey, which has returned to breed in Britain after being exterminated by hunters and egg-collectors in the last century. Its best known nest-sites are at Loch Garten on Speyside, where the Royal Society for the Protection of Birds mounts a round-the-clock guard in summer, and the Loch of the Lowes in Perthshire, where it is similarly protected by the Scottish Wildlife Trust, but it can sometimes be seen catching a trout or char from many other Scottish lochs.

Two other birds characteristic of upland lakes are the curious saw-billed duck, the red-breasted merganser, and the red-throated diver. Divers breed on often quite small inland lochs but often fly down to the sea to feed, uttering the haunting cry that has earned them the American name "loon" as they fly over. The stony or peaty shores of most lochs and tarns are unattractive to waders, though the redshank is a common enough visitor and common sandpipers are often found, but generally such lakes have an impoverished fauna and flora.

Osprey

Red-throated diver

Snipe

Common sandpiper

Water
lobelia

Redshank

Red-breasted merganser

Water
horsetail

Bottle sedge

Bladderwort

Bog pondweed

Upland streams

For the plants and animals living in a river, its most important feature is its speed. A sluggish lowland river in summer is almost equivalent to a lake and so shares its flora; in contrast the tumbling becks and burns of the hills flow too fast for most plants.

Except in its uppermost reaches, an unmanaged river would look very different from almost any in Britain now, for it would not have a single channel but a complex of small and large ones, weaving an interlocking pattern and shifting from year to year as old channels became blocked. This pattern can be seen in some hill regions, as in the Findhorn valley in Inverness-shire, and in some estuaries.

From an agricultural viewpoint this is wasteful of land, although it provides a free annual dressing of fertiliser in the form of silt, and so rivers have been systematically dredged and embanked since Roman times. The dredging ensures that the main channel is deep enough to take the spate flow and the banks guard against occasional high floods.

The process of eutrophication in a lake occurs also in rivers. Near its source a river will usually be oligotrophic, poor in nutrients and, since its flow here is fast, little will grow in it to increase its fertility. As it flows over the various rocks along its course it will dissolve minerals out of these and slow down, so that more plant life comes in and the food chains build up, until in its lowest reaches it becomes as fertile and productive as most lakes.

Fast-flowing upland streams therefore have few plants. The rocks on the bed of a mountain stream may be covered with the dark green mats of the aquatic moss *Fontinalis antipyretica*, giving shelter to many minute animals. Further down, the banks may be lined with the bay-leaved willow and the shifting gravel banks in the stream bed will be colonised by the brilliant yellow monkey flower, a native of North America, water forgetmenot, and water speedwell.

Very few insects can live in such fast-flowing water and not be washed away and stoneflies are most abundant. Feeding on their larvae and others is the delightful dipper, the only British bird that feeds by running about under water. Another insect-eater typical of these streams is the grey wagtail, and in summer it is hard not to disturb a common sandpiper, with its plaintive call.

Bay willow

Water forgetmenot

Water speedwell

Dipper

Grey wagtail

Common sandpiper

Stoneflies

Monkey flower

Lowland rivers

As the flow slackens the river becomes more hospitable to both plants and animals. Along the waterside a characteristic group of waterside plants develops, including great water dock with its enormous spade-shaped leaves, and the showy purple loosestrife.

In many lowland areas the banks are strengthened with trees, whose roots bind the soil; commonest are alder and white willow which is often pollarded so as to be less liable to be uprooted, damaging the bank.

If the river is dredged regularly, this of course destroys the vegetation in the river and on the bank, but in the dumped mud seeds of many plants germinate producing a curious mix of water plants, weeds, and some typical waterside plants such as wild turnip. In the excavated mud one can often find shells such as the freshwater mussel.

In the shallow water at the edge of an undisturbed river grows a group of plants with emergent foliage, such as arrowhead, unbranched bur-reed, with its spiky football seedheads, and the beautiful flowering rush. Out in the mainstream of the river, where the current is faster, the long trailing stems of river and stream water crowfoots wave in the current along with several pondweeds.

Lowland rivers have a rich fauna. The larvae of mayflies and caddis flies feed on debris on the bottom, the latter weaving for themselves houses of mud, shells and sand grains, and their adults dancing over the river forming the prey for the swallows and martins that skim the surface. The fish range in size from minnows, through tench, dace and roach, up to salmon, which swim through on their way to the ancestral spawning grounds. Each has its predator. The metallic blue flash glimpsed on a summer day is a kingfisher taking minnows to its young in a hole in the bank, and the shy otter will tackle almost any fish. Otters are widespread in the north and west but never common and seldom seen, as they are largely nocturnal and spend the day in a holt in the river bank. The smaller holes that pepper the banks of most rivers are made by water voles.

If the river flows over limestone, crayfish may lurk under the stones, needing the lime in the water for their shells and a stream fast enough to keep the bottom free of mud. The birds are less fussy, and mallard particularly are found on almost every stretch of stream or ditch. Other ducks are more occasional, but a pair of mute swans is almost a *sine qua non* of a good stretch of river.

Mayfly

Caddis flies

Roach

Tench

Dace

Minnow

Salmon trout

White willow

Mute swan

Kingfisher

Alder

Arrowhead

♀
Mallard

Purple
loosestrife

Water crowfoot

Great
water
dock

Bur-reed

Flowering
rush

THE COAST

The overriding factor influencing the terrestrial wildlife of the coast is, not surprisingly, the proximity of the sea. This means especially the presence of salt in the environment, and salt is a mineral that most plants dislike, at least in a 3 per cent solution such as sea-water. Salt may be deposited by the sea directly as on salt-marshes, or may be blown inland as salt-spray. As a result maritime vegetation can be found some way inland on exposed coasts. The second great influence is the wind. Salt and wind combine to inhibit the growth of trees and shrubs, producing the characteristic wind-cut shapes caused by the death of the buds on the windward side. The poor growth of trees means little shade, and the combination of strong winds, salt in the soil (which makes water harder to come by), and no shade means that seaside plants must often be adapted to conserve water; this explains why so many are so fleshy.

Finally the presence of the sea moderates the climate giving cooler summers and milder winters. This has a profound influence on plant distribution and many Mediterranean plants such as sea-heath, sea-holly and wild gladiolus are only found by or near the sea in southern England.

The coast has a number of quite distinct habitats. Nearest to land are cliffs, which may be rounded and vegetated, in which case they have the more salt- and wind-resistant members of the inland grassland, heath and scrub communities; or they may be steep, showing bare rock faces. These cliffs have a quite distinct flora, sharing species with inland walls and rocks. Along cliffless stretches of coast, the shore may be sandy, muddy or shingly, each with its own distinct and specialised flora; those few plants they have in common are also the common plants of bare places inland. At the back of sandy shores may develop the very distinctive plant community of the sand dunes, which may be mobile and sparsely clad in vegetation, or fixed and covered with a short turf rich in species. In between the dunes are the damp hollows termed slacks.

Sea Cliffs

Sea cliffs are of two kinds, grassy and rocky. Either may have an undercliff, a sheltered terrace created by a cliff-fall. Undercliffs rarely have a distinctive maritime flora, but develop scrub or grassland, or sometimes woodland similar to the kinds found a short way inland. True cliff vegetation grows on steep slopes overlooking the sea, and exposed to strong, salt-laden winds. Where the slow, inexorable processes of weathering have rounded off the sharp edges of the rocks and covered them with soil and vegetation, it is only the salt-laden winds that give these plant communities any distinctive character.

Few trees can withstand the full force of the winter gales off the sea, and those few end up bent almost parallel with the ground. The tallest cliff plants are likely to be blackthorn and bracken, though in the west hazel sometimes forms a low dense thicket. Blackthorn is a shrub which can, under these conditions, cover the ground with a thicket as little as twenty or thirty centimetres high; bracken is a fern whose strong rhizomes give it a firm foothold, while its fronds only have to withstand the lesser winds of summer and early autumn. On exposed cliffs bracken is also dwarfed, like the blackthorn, in comparison with the two metre high fronds it can produce in sheltered woodland.

Under the bracken often grow plants, such as bluebell and primrose, which flower in spring and wither by midsummer; to a bluebell there is no difference between the shade of an oakwood and of a bracken stand. Another mainly woodland plant that is often found on cliffs (and on mountain rock-ledges (p. 110) too, another exposed habitat) is red campion, and it illustrates the extra severity of the environment well, for the cliff plants are much hairier than woodland specimens. The hairs presumably help the plant prevent excessive water loss in the strong winds.

Where the wind is too severe to allow plants as tall as bracken to grow, there is a more specialised plant community, only a few centimetres high, that includes buckshorn plantain and sea storksbill, whose pale pink flowers drop almost as soon as they open, leaving only the long, pointed styles at the tip of the young fruit, that give the plant its vernacular name. The more striking plants of this windblown cliff community are thrift, spring squill, whose blue flowers adorn many western cliffs in spring, sea campion, wild thyme, kidney vetch, and the white-flowered English stonecrop whose stubby, fleshy leaves often turn red. Some of these, for example thyme and kidney vetch, are of course common enough inland, but

the others are confined to the coast, except that thrift and sea campion also grow on mountains, another exposed habitat.

The other kind of cliff, where a steep rocky face falls sheer to the sea, shares few of these plants, except where a landslip has created a miniature undercliff with a deeper soil. The plants that grow on the sheer cliffs are those that can survive on a narrow ledge or in a crevice with little or no soil. The constant battering by salty winds ensures that few of the plants of inland cliffs, rocks and walls grow here. Instead you will find such brightly coloured flowers as wild cabbage, which is indeed the parent of all cultivated cabbages, sea stock, rock sea-lavender, scurvy grass and golden samphire, the first two being local plants of the south and west. Two umbellifers are also common on these cliffs, lovage, which is a northern plant, commonest in Scotland, and the more widespread rock samphire. This is the samphire made famous in *King Lear*, where, at the Shakespeare cliff at Dover, 'half-way down hangs one that gathers samphire, dreadful trade'. The 'samphire' offered for sale along the Norfolk coast is glasswort, a saltmarsh plant. At the bottom of the cliff the only plants to survive are lichens, orange *Xanthoria* and grey-green *Ramalina*.

Spring squill

Sea campion

Thrift

Wild thyme

Rock samphire

Sea stock

Rock sea-lavender

Birds of the Cliffs

Herring gull

Lesser black-backed gull

Kittiwake

Storm petrel

Manx shearwater

Fulmar

immature

Gannet

adult

Black
guillemot

Razorbill

Guillemot

Puffin

Peregrine

Buzzard

Cormorant

Shag

Cliffs are especially important for breeding seabirds, since cliff ledges are inaccessible to four-footed predators, such as foxes and stoats, and crevices in cliffs may be difficult even for winged ones, such as crows. Thus cliffs with suitable ledges become the homes of large colonies of seabirds. Herring gulls nest all round our coasts on cliffs, sometimes joined by lesser black-backed gulls, but greater black-backs, being strong enough to beat off most predators, prefer the ground, often in a prominent position on a rocky promontory or cliff stack. Both the other two also nest on the ground, but mainly on islands, which foxes and stoats may be unable to reach. Kittiwakes almost always breed on cliffs, each bird clinging to what appears from above to be a most unsafe little perch. Guillemots, on the other hand, prefer long straight ledges, where they stand in serried ranks, guarding their eggs, which are pear-shaped and so less likely to roll off when disturbed. Razorbills nest singly, and usually in a crevice, or at least under an overhanging rock. Black guillemots, however, nest right in a hole. Cormorants, shags and gannets nest either on a cliff ledge or on flat ground on an island. Fulmars go for ledges, but storm petrels like holes, often in walls overlooking the sea. Puffins and Manx shearwaters use burrows, often old rabbit burrows, in the ground rather than on a cliff.

A few land birds also find holes and ledges in sea cliffs just as good as in inland cliffs. These include the raven, carrion crow, jackdaw and, especially in Ireland, the red-billed chough, with some birds of prey, such as peregrine, buzzard and kestrel. Some of these prey on the eggs and young of the seabirds, others on carrion thrown up by the sea.

Shingle Beaches

Shingle beaches are one of the most specialised habitats of the British coastline. Their material, fragments of rock rounded into pebbles by waves, derives from the cliffs, but while some shingle beaches fringe lines of cliffs, many others lie along flat shores. Tides carry the pebbles along, until a change in the currents causes them to accumulate in a ridge or bar. This is how such famous shingle beaches as Chesil Bank in Dorset, Dungeness in Kent and Blakeney Point in Norfolk have been formed. At Dungeness a whole succession of such ridges have been formed over the years, giving rise to the largest continuous area of shingle in the British Isles, while the 20-mile long Chesil Bank is one of the longest in Europe.

Plants growing on shingle face severe problems. It offers no shelter from wind and salt spray, holds little or no water, and close to the sea the constant movement of pebbles renders survival impossible. Most shingle plants are low growing, which helps them withstand the wind, and long-rooted, well anchored against the shifting stones and better able to reach water supplies underlying the beach. They also tens to grow well spaced, thus eking out the available water.

Only one shrub is at all common on shingle – shrubby seablite – and that rarely exceeds a metre in height. A Mediterranean plant, it is only common in Britain at Blakeney and on the Chesil Bank. Its shelter is greatly welcomed by tired bird migrants making their first landfall across the North Sea. Common wild flowers of the shingle include sea campion, sea sandwort, the large cabbage-like clumps of sea kale, whose shoots were once widely eaten as a vegetable, and yellow horned poppy, whose large yellow flowers produce the longest seed-pods of any British plant, up to 30 cm long.

Some common inland plants grow on shingle in special varieties. For instance, a fleshy-leaved variety of woody nightshade or bittersweet grows on beaches in Sussex, and curled dock also has a maritime variety. Wallpepper, an attractive yellow-flowered stonecrop, is a plant of dry places that finds shingle banks as congenial as the bare chalk, rocks, and even abandoned concrete runways that it favours inland.

Among the special rarities of the British shingle are the sea pea, conspicuous both on the Chesil Bank and around Orfordness in Suffolk, and the oyster plant, a Scottish plant that scarcely penetrates into England, and whose succulent blue-grey leaves are said to taste like oysters.

Large expanses of shingle as at Dungeness develop a quite different vegetation from narrow banks, with grassland, heath and even woodland developing as the sea retreats. A unique feature of Dungeness is a wood consisting almost entirely of holly, but more generally the shingle there is colonised by broom, which is a woody legume and shares with its relatives the clovers the ability to fix nitrogen from the air in its roots with the aid of a symbiotic bacterium, a valuable advantage in such a primitive, infertile soil.

Sea kale

Wall pepper

Sea campion

Sea sandwort

Sea pea

Oyster plant

Yellow horned poppy

Coastal Dunes and Sandy Shores

On sandy shores that are not backed by cliffs, the forces of wind and tide combine with vegetation to form sand dunes. The tide accumulates the sand on the beach, the wind blows it inland, and plants catch it and start the process by which dunes are formed, eventually rising sometimes to as high as 30 m. At the top of the beach, along the strand-line, a very characteristic group of plants is found: sea rocket, a fleshy, radish-like plant, prickly saltwort, spear-leaved orache and sea beet. The last three are all related to spinach and sea beet is in fact the wild sub-species of the plant that in cultivation gives us beetroot, sugar beet and the like.

Just behind this narrow strip of plants the foredunes begin. These are only a few centimetres high, and are formed by sand couch grass and the dune form of the common red fescue, but also sometimes by sea sandwort. Behind this pioneer zone, the real dunes begin, formed almost entirely by one highly specialised plant, marram grass. Marram has an immensely long, tough and complex root system, which holds the whole dune system together. Any interference with it, such as digging a hole in the sand, allows the wind to shift the sand and a blow-out is the result; on a large scale this can be exceedingly dangerous. Whole fields, and in the past whole villages,

have been overwhelmed by sand blow-outs caused by storms, among the most notable of which have created the Culbin Sands in Moray-shire and Newborough Warren on Anglesey.

On the seaward front, exposed to the full blast of the spray-filled winds, few other plants are found, but among them are sea holly, which is actually a somewhat atypical umbellifer; sea bindweed, with its beautiful striped pink and white morning glory flowers flush with the ground; sand sedge, whose under-ground rhizomes advance into areas of bare sand such as blow-outs, sending up shoots at regular intervals; and two spurges, sea spurge and Portland spurge. These plants can grow in the almost pure sand that makes up the 'soil' of the fore-dunes. As they grow and die, they add humus to the soil, which gradually becomes more fertile and better at retaining water. Then inland plants, such as ragwort, spear thistle, scarlet pimpernel, viper's bugloss and wallpepper appear, until eventually the sward becomes continuous, and the dunes are then known as fixed dunes. Since most maritime sand consists largely of crushed shell particles, it is rich in lime and the flora of a fixed dune has much in common with that of a chalk down. They share for example such species as lady's bedstraw, purging flax,

autumn gentian, carline thistle and pyramidal orchid, and where shrubs develop they are very often lime-lovers such as privet. Since the soil is young, it is infertile, and particularly poor in nitrogen, so that nitrogen-fixing legumes are common, including such attractive, if common, species as birdsfoot trefoil. There is one specialised sand dune shrub, sea buckthorn, which forms dense grey-leaved thickets, bright with orange berries in autumn, and though not a legume shares with them the ability to use atmospheric nitrogen. Fixed dunes, and especially those highly calcareous ones in the Hebrides known as machair, which are formed entirely of shell sand, are among the most gaily floriferous habitats in the British Isles.

As dunes age, the lime is leached out of the porous soil which becomes acid, and such old dunes may have a heathland vegetation. Eventually the process of succession should lead to woodland, but this is rarely allowed to occur naturally in Britain. In many places, however, foresters have anticipated the process by planting extensive conifer forests, notably at Newborough Warren in Anglesey and on the Culbin Sands by the Moray Firth.

The most characteristic butterflies of the fixed dunes are grayling, small copper and common blue.

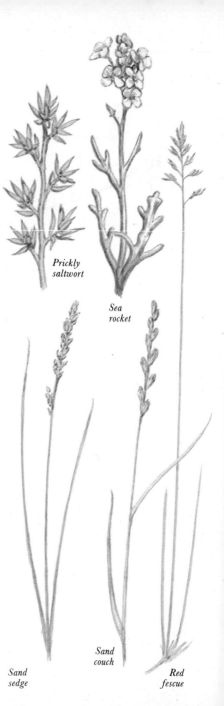

Prickly saltwort

Sea rocket

Sand sedge

Sand couch

Red fescue

Lyme grass

Marram grass

Sea spurge

Sea holly

Spear thistle

Ragwort

Portland spurge

Viper's bugloss

Sea bindweed

Dune Slacks

Dune systems typically consist of several ranks of tall dunes, formed successively with the youngest nearest the sea, grading into old, acid, 'grey' dunes to the landward. In between the ridges are low-lying areas that flood in winter and may remain damp all the summer. These are the dune-slacks. They are the only parts of the dune system where moisture-loving plants may grow and they have a quite different and very rich flora.

The slacks contain species that can all be found growing inland; none of them are exclusively maritime, but it is the richness and concentration of the flora that is striking. Rushes are abundant and the round leaves of marsh pennywort often form an almost continuous cover. Water mint, brookweed, which though not a seaside plant definitely favours brackish water in the soil, and knotted pearlwort are all common, and in very low vegetation the creeping mats of bog pimpernel stud the ground with their exquisite pink flowers. The glory of these slacks, however, is undoubtedly the orchids, Marsh helleborine, its flowers an intricate mixture of crimson, white, purple and brown, is often common, and the marsh orchids are characteristic. The first to flower, in May and June, is the early marsh orchid, whose flowers may range from purple through to salmon-pink. It

is followed in the south by the southern marsh orchid, with rosy-purple flowers and in the north by northern marsh orchid, which has deep purple flowers. Confusingly all three will hybridise and where they grow together a wide range of intermediates is found.

In many slacks creeping willow is found. This may form a wet community or it may start to catch blowing sand and so gradually fill in the slack, forming in its place low dunes through which the young shoots of the willow continually grow, until conditions become too dry for it.

In many respects the wetter dune slacks have more in common with fen than with other dune habitats. Dune soils tend to be very low in humus, until the oldest dunes—the grey dunes—are reached, and then leaching of the lime in the soil has gone so far that the soils are often strongly acid. The low humus content is simply due to the very low productivity of the vegetation on these dry, infertile soils, and to the frequency of wind erosion. In the slacks, by contrast, lime-bearing water running off the dunes accumulates, so that they are rarely acidic, and the wetness permits much more vigorous plant growth and so the more rapid accumulation of humus. Indeed, in very wet slacks the breakdown of humus may be very slow

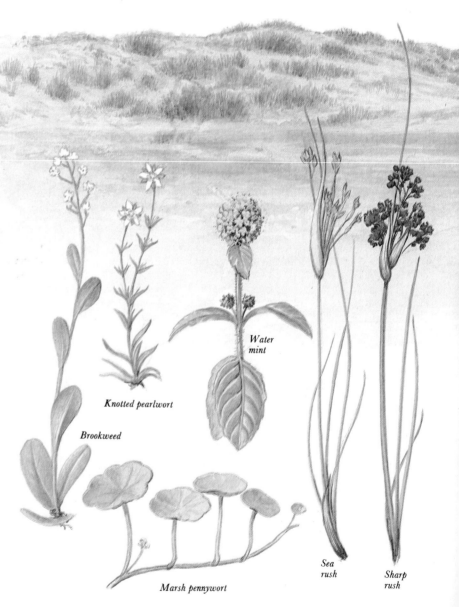

Knotted pearlwort

Water mint

Brookweed

Marsh pennywort

Sea rush

Sharp rush

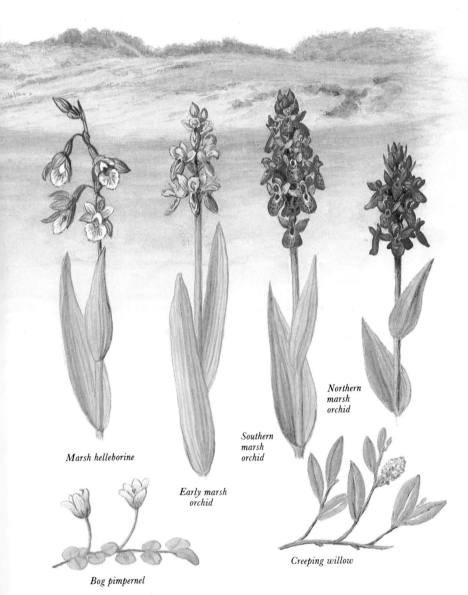

Marsh helleborine

Bog pimpernel

Early marsh
orchid

Southern
marsh
orchid

Northern
marsh
orchid

Creeping willow

indeed, and a thin layer of peat may form, just as in fens and bogs. The waterlogging of the soil brings problems to plants, though, for oxygen from the air does not penetrate the soil well, and the roots cannot obtain enough to respire. What is more, in such conditions several toxic ions are produced by the soil, including those of elements such as iron and manganese, which are normally essential nutrients of plant growth. Plants growing in wet dune slacks may therefore have considerable problems to overcome.

Though such slacks are much wetter than the dune ridges, at the back of old dune systems there are often extensive areas of flat ground, sometimes called dry slacks. Here the water table is 1–2 metres below the surface but the flatness of the ground means that little wind erosion occurs, and a stable and species-rich community develops. Mosses are often particularly well represented along with other low growing plants, such as thyme and self-heal. Sand sedge, so prominent on the open dunes, persists into these mature dry slacks but no longer grows in long lines as when colonising bare sand.

Dune systems are often very un-stable both physically and ecologically and provide considerable problems in their conservation. There are few lowland areas of Britain which would not develop naturally to woodland by the processes of ecological succession if left alone, and the dunes and their slacks are no exception. Two factors keep them free of trees: one is their tendency to erode when the winter storms cause blowouts, creating hollows and moving whole dunes. No tree can withstand such instability. The older dunes, with a complete cover of turf, are much less susceptible to this and are readily colonised by hawthorn, birch, or whatever trees grow nearby.

Normally dune systems only persist as open turf if they are grazed. For many years the animal responsible was the rabbit, but after the advent of myxomatosis in the 1950s, dune systems such as that at Newborough Warren have undergone radical changes, the old, short, species-rich turf being replaced by a rank growth of tall grasses such as false oat, with many invading shrubs. In some places sheep have been used experimentally to control this.

Birds of Sand and Shingle

Gulls, terns and waders all nest in colonies on the remoter and less disturbed sand and shingle beaches around our coasts. The advantage of a large, flat expanse like a sand or shingle beach is that birds have ample warning of the approach of any two- or four-footed predator. Almost all these birds, notably the black-headed gull and the common and arctic terns, gain protection by nesting in a colony, for on the approach of a predator they will rise in a swirling, screaming, confusing and even terrifying mass. Arctic terns will readily attack the top of the head of a man who approaches their nests—and they have very sharp beaks. It also means that the parent birds themselves are likely to escape any attacks; Sandwich terns in particular are noted for flying off *en masse* and breeding elsewhere if disturbed at their first site. Another advantage is that beaches are warm places, the stones and sand absorbing heat from the sun that must help in the incubation of the eggs when the brooding bird is forced off by the approach of a predator; conversely, in cold springs the opposite effect must occur.

The alternative approach to nest protection is that of the oyster-catcher and ringed plover, which nest singly, and of the little tern, which has a very loose colony. Here the survival strategy relies on cam-ouflage, the eggs of all three species bearing an extraordinary resemblance to the pebbles among which they are laid. Even on a pure sand surface, there are usually enough stones lying around for the eggs of a ringed plover to be mistaken for them.

However, this approach is no protection against the human picnicker. Nowadays little tern colonies in particular have to be wardened against disturbance by holiday-makers, who have no idea of the damage they are doing.

Oystercatchers have another technique, once the young are hatched: they make a fearful racket, drawing the predator away. Ringed plovers, on the other hand, use the 'broken wing' trick, fluttering off as if injured, fooling the predator—so the theory goes—into thinking it is an easy catch, until, well out of the way of the flightless chicks, the parent takes wing and flies back.

The skylark is one of those land birds that breed on the larger stretches of sand dunes, especially where the dunes are largely grass-covered. Others include meadow pipits, wheatears, linnets and part-ridges. And with small song-birds there you also get the cuckoo, which is especially fond of laying its own eggs in the nests of the meadow pipit. Skylarks, wheatears and linnets can all also be its victims.

Oystercatcher

Black-headed gull

Sandwich tern

Common tern

Arctic tern

Skylark

Little tern

Ringed plover

Sandwich tern

Common tern

Arctic tern

Little tern

Oystercatcher

Little tern

Ringed plover

Muddy Shores and Estuaries

Nowhere does the sea dominate terrestrial vegetation – as distinct from the seaweeds that grow on rocky shores – more than on muddy shores and estuaries, with their associated saltmarshes. In sheltered bays and estuaries, and in Scotland at the head of sea-lochs, the water is calm enough sufficiently often to allow fine particles of mud, brought down by rivers or created by the erosive force of the sea, to settle out. Gradually these mud particles build up substantial deposits, and once they are thick enough to appear above the tide level for a few hours each day, plants begin to colonise them, slowly converting them to dry land.

The very first higher plants to appear do in fact spend most of their life submerged; these are the eel-grasses which look like seaweeds and whose long ribbon-like leaves grow together with various green seaweeds near the low water mark. The first flowering plant to contribute substantially to the land-building process is glasswort or marsh samphire which occupies a wide range of habitats between high and low water marks. Glassworts are curious plants (there are several very similar species), whose leaves are reduced to fleshy scales and whose flowers consist only of one or two stamens and styles tucked away in the joints of these scales.

Once the glassworts have started trapping the suspended silt particles, the surface begins to rise, and other plants, less adapted to prolonged submersion in seawater, appear. The most successful of these – in fact on many coasts it is the first colonist – is a species which owes its existence to man, common cord-grass. This is the result of a cross between the native small cord-grass and a North American species introduced into Southampton Water early in the last century. At first the new hybrid did little, but after some genetic rearrangements had occurred, it began to spread, at first naturally and slowly, but then, when its capacity for colonising wet marine muds was realised, rapidly by human agency. It is now the most important saltmarsh plant around

Eel grass

Glasswort

Cord grass

Sea purslane

Sea aster

Sea lavender

Annual seablite

most of the British Isles, and may eventually lead to the reclamation for agriculture of many hundreds of acres. Before the advent of cord-grass, the chief agent of reclamation was probably sea purslane which characteristically grows along the edge of the channels and pools, where drainage is better.

Saltmarshes are places where succession is very active. Each set of plants that colonises traps more mud, raises the ground a little, exposes it for a longer period, and so makes the habitat suitable for a new set. There is in fact a clear topographic gradient from the bottom of the marsh of perhaps some 2 metres to the highest point that the tides reach, where true land vege-

tation takes over. After the cord-grass, moving up the marsh, there is typically a belt where sea aster, a relative of the Michaelmas daisy, and sea lavender are abundant; the latter can turn the lower marsh into a sheet of purple in July. Next comes what is known as the 'general salt-marsh community' which is often a close turf with the aster and the sea lavender as well as masses of thrift, saltmarsh grass, sea spurrey and sea plantain and the similar-looking, but quite unrelated sea arrow-grass.

Finally at the top of the marsh the vegetation begins to take on a more 'terrestrial' look, with common grassland plants such as red fescue, albeit in a specially adapted form that can resist salt in the soil. Here

too the mud rush and the much larger sea rush are common. In fact this top end of the marsh is in some ways a more difficult habitat than the bottom: although it is flooded by the sea only rarely, if hot, sunny weather follows such a tide, the salt in the soil can be concentrated many times by evaporation.

Each plant thus has its own place in the saltmarsh, depending on its ability to cope with submergence, with salt in the soil, with the scouring action of the tide, and with the lack of oxygen in the waterlogged soil. The range of habitats in a salt-marsh is as wide as in any strictly terrestrial environment, and the diversity of plants that grow in salt-marshes reflects that.

Birds of Mud and Estuaries

Unlike human holidaymakers, the birds that frequent the seashore are not there because it is a pleasant place for a stroll on a summer afternoon. They are there, like human bait-diggers in a November gale, because they want something that is in the mud. Some birds are after the same prey as the bait-diggers, lugworms *Arenicola marina*, but others are after a great variety of other animals and plants, and their food-seeking equipment, their bill, differs considerably according to their preferred food.

Birds do not normally eat seaweed and indeed a thick covering of green seaweeds may prevent them feeding at all. However the flowering plant eelgrass, of which the commonest species is the large *Zostera marina*, forms extensive beds between the tides (as well as below low water mark) which are relished by two British winter-visiting birds, the brent goose and the wigeon. The great mass of waders scattered over the shore are, however, animal feeders, and are constantly searching for prey that is buried in the sand or mud. On an extensive intertidal sandflat or mudflat, such as the Wash on the east coast of England, if you know what food birds prefer, you can judge the distribution of their invertebrate prey. Thus an area with many feeding oyster-catchers – as distinct from roosting,

which they do on a drier bank – is likely also to have either a bed of mussels *Mytilus edulis* – or to have beneath its muddy surface large numbers of cockles *Cerastoderma edule* or tellins *Macoma balthica*, for all these molluscs are their favourite prey. So much so that human cockle fishers do not like to see oyster-catchers on their fishing grounds, although it has never been proved that they do any substantial damage to cockle stocks. The stout straight bill of the oystercatcher is ideal for opening bivalve molluscs, but the long curved one of the curlew is better for probing for extracting lugworms and other polychaete worms, such as *Lanice conchilega*. Curlews also eat small crabs and molluscs. Polychaete worms are tempting prey for many other wading birds, such as bar-tailed godwit, grey plover and redshank. The redshank is the only common shore wader that commonly feeds up the creeks that dissect the saltmarshes, its diet including small crabs, shrimps and small molluscs, such as the laver spire-shell *Hydrobia ulvae*, which is very common in saltmarshes and feeds on sea lettuce or green laver *Ulva lactuca*. The dunlin, a smaller wader than any of the above, is especially fond of both ragworms and laver spire-shells, but its larger relative the knot prefers larger molluscs, such as tellins.

The laver spire shell is also the favourite food of the shelduck. This large duck, in some ways intermediate between the ducks and the geese, is the only waterfowl that commonly frequents muddy shores, though several other ducks can be seen on the tideway. Shelduck have a remarkable habit of all flying off to moult, leaving a small number of adults to mind the young. These young gather into creches, guarded by a few adults, two or three weeks after they hatch. Meanwhile the main body of adults may fly some hundreds of miles to moult. From almost the whole of Britain the shelduck cross the North Sea in June or July to the great mudflats at the mouth of the Elbe in north-west Germany. Indeed virtually all the shelduck in north-western Europe assemble here in late summer. Some more, mainly from Ireland, gather in Bridgwater Bay, Somerset. The return flight takes place in autumn and early winter.

Gulls of various species, especially black-headed and herring, are also common in estuaries and on muddy shores, but when seen standing along the tideline are usually resting rather than feeding. They normally get their food elsewhere, although being scavengers they will quickly mop up any dead animal of an appropriate size washed up by the sea.

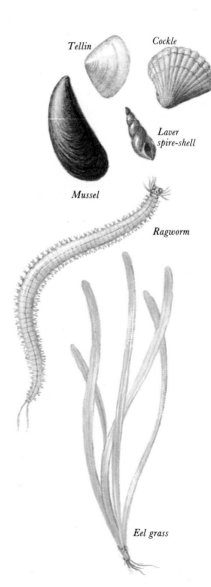

Tellin

Cockle

Mussel

Laver spire-shell

Ragworm

Eel grass

Black-tailed godwit

Bar-tailed godwit

Bar-tailed godwit

Curlew

Oystercatchers

Brent goose

Redshank

Knot

Shelduck

Grey plover

Wigeon

Dunlin

Seashore Mammals

Grey seal

Common seal

Porpoise

Bottle-nose dolphin

Common dolphin

Killer whale

Bottle-nose dolphin

Common dolphin

Porpoise

Killer whale

Bottle-nose
dolphin

Three large mammals occur on British shores, the common and grey seals and the otter. Otters are mainly found in the west of Scotland, where they are now commoner than anywhere else in Europe. They are not infrequent on quiet stretches of coast. Their presence may be given away by fish carcases, often only partly eaten.

Common seals are most frequent on the muddy and sandy shores of eastern England, notably in the Wash, but also in Scotland, the headquarters of the grey seal. There are probably about 46,000 grey seals on our coasts and though characteristic of rocky shores in the north-west, they have a famous colony on the Farne Islands, off Northumberland, and are spreading down the east coast. They are larger than common seals, but otherwise hard to distinguish: the common seal's head is more rounded and dog-like, while the grey seal's is more pointed and horse-like. Young common seals are never seen alone on shore, for they can swim as soon as they are born – may indeed actually be born in the water – and go off with their mothers at once. Young grey seals, however, in their white woolly pelage, can sometimes be found on the rocks in a secluded cove, where they have been left for safety while their mothers go fishing. Seals are all inquisitive and intelligent, and their heads often peer out of the water at a human intruder. Other sea mammals that can sometimes be seen from the beach are porpoises, dolphins and killer whales swimming offshore.

Rock Pools

Rock pools represent an outpost of the sea on the border between sea and land. If a rockpool remains full of water from one high tide to the next, it provides a habitat for sublittoral species that cannot withstand desiccation and so are rarely otherwise seen. Even sheltered gullies on shore may remain moist and hide unusual seaweeds and animals.

Typical rock pools are lined with encrusting red algae that turn the rocks pink, and many other feathery red algae are found, collapsing when out of water but beautiful if preserved on paper. The larger brown seaweeds, wracks and kelps sometimes occur too providing good cover for fish such as the 15-spined stickleback. Shore crabs scuttle around sideways on the bottom and pugnacious hermit crabs move more boldly, secure in their ability to retreat into the shell which they have taken over as home. Occasionally a sea anemone will settle on the hermit crab's borrowed shell. The beadlet anemone is the commonest in pools, but on the lower shore the irridescent purple snakelocks anemone is common on kelps; unable to retract its tentacles, it cannot tolerate exposure to the air. In the water, transparent opossum shrimps flick back and forth, avoiding the anemones' waving tentacles.

Pools too are havens for shells. The periwinkles are usually the commonest, but topshells are often abundant too. Whelks are found mainly on exposed shores, where their favoured prey—mussels and barnacles—flourish. Whelks are carnivorous molluscs, unlike the grazing limpets, which stick immensely tightly to the rock, and move around slowly when the tide is up, rasping tiny algae off the surface, and often returning to the same spot at low tide.

On very exposed shores, few of the large seaweeds can gain a foothold, and it is the barnacles and mussels which take over the rocks, feeding on minute floating plants and animals, by filtering them out of the water.

The seashore is one of the richest environments of all, for the predictable comings and goings of the tides make a whole series of habitats, graded down the shore, and each subtly different from that above. The topmost region, subjected only to spray from waves and never actually under water, is inhabited by lichens, the odd plant of thrift, by channelled wrack, a seaweed that can withstand extreme desiccation, and tiny small periwinkle shells. Below that, where the highest tides just reach, this wrack and periwinkle are more abundant; and then, going down the shore, come zones successively dominated by spiral wrack, bladder wrack, saw wrack and at low tide by kelps. Each seaweed is able to tolerate a certain degree of desiccation and so finds its niche along this gradient.

It is because the tides are so predictable that so many different habitats are found in a small space and that so many species can live together on the shore. The only comparable situation on land is where different predators, such as owls and kestrels, feed by day and by night. Although both eat small mammals, the predictability of day and night allows them to co-exist.

There are three main groups of seaweeds, divided by their colour, the greens, reds and browns. The broad-leaved, translucent sea lettuce that grows on most rocky shores is the best known green seaweed. The wracks and kelps are brown seaweeds. Edible dulse is a red seaweed.

The aspect of the seashore that we are most familiar with is that when the tide is out, but this is when least is happening there. At high tide the big seaweeds, the kelps and the wracks, no longer lie limply on the rocks, but stand up in the water, forming a canopy like a forest and cutting out much of the light. Underneath this canopy the real life of the seashore goes on, and our only glimpse of that is in rock pools, where the tide is always high.

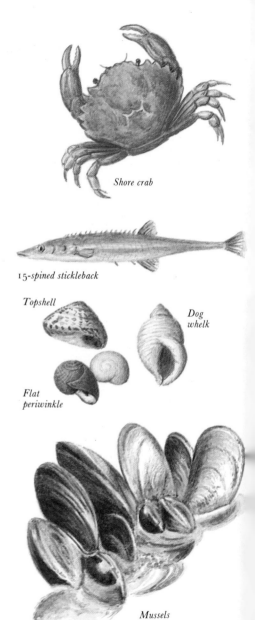

Shore crab

15-spined stickleback

Topshell

Dog whelk

Flat periwinkle

Mussels

Limpets

Key to the Calendar

Trees and shrubs, flowers, grasses, sedges, rushes, ferns and horsetails

The dog rose comes into leaf in spring, flowers in June and produces fruits 'hips' in early autumn that last into the winter, after the leaves have all fallen in late autumn.

Fungi

The field mushroom starts appearing in late summer, is at its most prolific in autumn and has disappeared before the approach of winter.

Mammals

The hedgehog begins to stir in early spring, becomes fully active from spring to early autumn and does not enter into its quiescent period (it does not actually hibernate) until winter has really started.

The grey squirrel assumes its summer pelage, which is browner than in winter, until late spring, and this lasts until early autumn.

The fallow deer casts its antlers in spring, and starts growing them again almost at once, so that it has a head of antlers from late spring until early the following spring.

(dog rose)

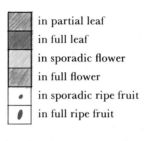

in partial leaf
in full leaf
in sporadic flower
in full flower
in sporadic ripe fruit
in full ripe fruit

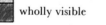
(field mushroom)

partially visible
wholly visible

(hedgehog)

semi active
fully active

(grey squirrel)

summer pelage

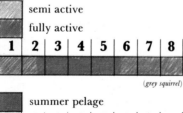
(fallow deer)

 full antlers

Reptiles and amphibians

The smooth newt becomes active in late winter or early spring, spawns in spring, is a tadpole from late spring to the end of the summer and goes into hibernation again in autumn.

Birds

The golden plover moves to its winter quarters in early autumn; at the end of the winter, it begins to return to the moors, where its mellifluous song can be heard until early summer.

The black-headed gull arrives from its winter quarters in early autumn and returns to its breeding grounds at the end of winter. The brown hood develops towards the winter, and lasts until the summer.

Butterflies and moths

The small skipper butterfly flies in summer, producing caterpillars that hibernate until the following spring, when they quickly feed up, pupating in late spring.

The herald moth emerges in late summer and goes into hibernation from early autumn to spring, reappears to lay its eggs, and caterpillars emerge in late spring.

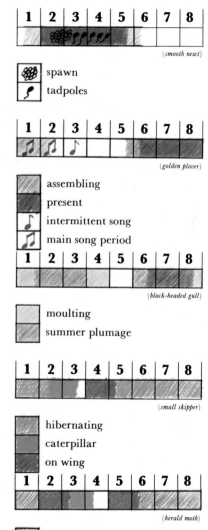

(smooth newt)

spawn
tadpoles

(golden plover)

assembling
present
intermittent song
main song period

(black-headed gull)

moulting
summer plumage

(small skipper)

hibernating
caterpillar
on wing

(herald moth)

 hibernating

COUNTRYSIDE CALENDAR

The Calendar aims to tell readers what kinds of wildlife they may expect to find in the countryside at each season. Our normal monthly calendar does not, however, match the seasons very well. The turn of the year between December and January, for instance, does not mark the turn of any season; it is part of midwinter. So the seasons are defined here to start the year most appropriately around St. Valentine's Day, February 14. This is the day when, according to our medieval forebears, the birds begin their courtship. We need to take into account the eleven days "lost" by our ancestors in 1752, when Britain's Julian Calendar, which had prevailed for nearly 2000 years, was brought into line with the Gregorian Calendar, which Pope Gregory XIII had introduced on the Continent 170 years previously. Then "Old St. Valentine's Day" falls about February 25, which is just about the time many of our resident birds are starting to sing, pair and search for nest sites.

We have therefore broken the year up into eight periods, covering the four main seasons and their respective overlaps with each other. So the year starts with late winter's overlap into early spring and ends with the true winter period that begins just before Christmas and ends in early February, when already daylight is nearly two hours longer than in the depths about Christmas and New Year's Day. In some years spring is well advanced by late February; in others it has hardly got going by the end of March, so we can never be quite sure of spring until April. Much the same applies to all the seasons through the year; hence these overlapping periods.

The Calendar itself seeks to give information such as when trees and shrubs are in leaf, in flower or in fruit; when wild flowers have leaves, flowers and conspicuous fruits; when ferns appear in leaf; and when fungi appear at all. For mammals hibernation, summer or winter pelage, such as the white coat of the mountain hare, and for deer the presence of antlers are the features indicated. Similarly, for reptiles and amphibians we have hibernation, spawning times and tadpoles; for birds migration times, summer and winter plumages and song periods; and for butterflies and moths hibernation, caterpillar periods and when they are actually on the wing.

Thus you will find that in the late winter woods the green hellebore is already in flower, by early spring the small tortoiseshell, peacock and brimstone butterflies can be seen, as well as primroses and wood anemones, and the red deer of the Highland moors shed their antlers in early spring and start growing them again in late spring and early summer. Likewise the onset of autumn sees dormice and herald moths beginning to hibernate and winter visitors like fieldfares and redwings appearing in the fields.

Using the Calendar
The key on the facing page gives an explanation of the different shades, colours, and symbols that have been used. In order to give the reader a better idea of how to interpret the information, we have given, for each category, one or more actual examples drawn from the pages that follow. Each of these examples has a written resumé alongside it, showing how to convert the calendar information into words. An explanation of the time periods used is given below.

Calendar Periods

1	Late winter/early spring	:	*mid Feb–Mar*
2	Spring	:	*April–mid May*
3	Late spring/early summer	:	*end May–June*
4	Summer	:	*July–early Aug*
5	Late summer/early autumn	:	*mid Aug–Sept*
6	Autumn	:	*Oct–mid Nov*
7	Late autumn/early winter	:	*late Nov–mid Dec*
8	Winter	:	*end Dec–early Feb*

Farmland

Trees and Shrubs	1	2	3	4	5	6	7	8
Hazel	█	█	█	█	█	█		
Oak		█	█	█	█	●	●●●	
English elm		█	█	█	█	●	●●●	
Bramble		█	█	█	█	●●●●	●●●	●
Dog rose	●	█	█	█	█	●	●●●●	●●● ●●● ●
Hawthorn		█	█	█	█	● ●●●	●●● ●● ●	
Blackthorn		█	█	█	█	● ●● ●●●	●●● ●	
Field maple		█	█	█	█	●● ●● ●●	●	
Spindle tree		█	█	█	█	● ●●●●	●	
Buckthorn		█	█	█	█	● ●● ●●		
Dogwood		█	█	█	█	● ●●●		
Ash		█	█	█	█	● ●●●	●●● ●●●	
Privet		█	█	█	█	●● ●●●	●●● ●●●	
Elder		█	█	█	█ ●	●●● ●		
Wayfaring tree		█	█	█	█ ● ●	●●●● ●●		
Wild Flowers								
Nettle		█	█	█	█	█	█	
Annual nettle		█	█	█	█	█	█	
Knotgrass		█	█	█	█	█	█	
Redshank		█	█	█	█	█	█	
Black bindweed		█	█	█	█	█	█	
Common sorrel		█	█	█	█	█	█	
Curled dock		█	█	█	█	█	█	
Broad-leaved dock		█	█	█	█	█	█	
Clustered dock		█	█	█	█	█	█	
Fat hen		█	█	█	█	█	█	
Common chickweed	█	█	█	█	█	█	█	█

Wild flowers (cont.)	1	2	3	4	5	6	7	8
Greater stitchwort	█	█	█	█	█	█		
Common mouse-ear	█	█	█	█	█	█	█	
Corn spurrey		█	█	█	█	█	█	
Bladder campion		█	█	█	█	█	█	
Red campion		█	█	█	█	█	█	█
White campion	█	█	█	█	█	█	█	█
Ragged robin		█	█	█	█	█	█	
Wood anemone	█	█	█	█	█			
Pasque flower		█	█	█	█			
Traveller's joy	●●	█	█	█	█	●● ●●●	●●● ●●●	●●●
Creeping buttercup		█	█	█	█	█	█	█
Meadow buttercup		█	█	█	█	█	█	█
Bulbous buttercup		█	█	█	█	█	█	
Field poppy		█	█	█	█	█	█	█
Common fumitory		█	█	█	█	█	█	█
Garlic mustard		█	█	█	█	█	█	
Cuckoo flower		█	█	█	█	█	█	
Shepherd's purse	█	█	█	█	█	█	█	█
Field pennycress		█	█	█	█	█	█	█
Wild candytuft		█	█	█	█	█	█	█
Charlock		█	█	█	█	█	█	█
Wild mignonette		█	█	█	█	█	█	█
Dropwort		█	█	█	█	█	█	
Agrimony		█	█	█	█	█	█	█
Great burnet		█	█	█	█	█	█	
Salad burnet		█	█	█	█	█	█	
Herb bennet		█	█	█	█	█	█	█
Silverweed	█	█	█	█	█	█	█	█

Farmland

Wild flowers (cont.)	1	2	3	4	5	6	7	8
Creeping cinquefoil								
Barren strawberry								
Wild strawberry								
Lady's mantle								
Dyer's greenweed								
Tufted vetch								
Common vetch								
Meadow vetchling								
Rest-harrow								
Black medick								
Lucerne								
White clover								
Hop trefoil								
Lesser trefoil								
Red clover								
Birdsfoot trefoil								
Horseshoe vetch								
Sainfoin								
Meadow cranesbill								
Wood cranesbill								
Dovesfoot cranesbill								
Purging flax								
Common milkwort								
Common mallow								
Musk mallow								
Common St. John's wort								
Sweet violet								
Hairy violet								

Wild flowers (cont.)	1	2	3	4	5	6	7	8
Field pansy								
Common rock-rose								
White bryony								
Great willowherb								
Ivy								
Cow parsley								
Rough chervil								
Shepherd's needle								
Burnet saxifrage								
Hemlock								
Pepper saxifrage								
Wild parsnip								
Hogweed								
Upright hedge parsley								
Wild carrot								
Primrose								
Cowslip								
Scarlet pimpernel								
Yellow-wort								
Common centaury								
Autumn gentian								
Chiltern gentian								
Squinancywort								
Lady's bedstraw								
Hedge bedstraw								
Common cleavers								
Crosswort								
Hedge bindweed								

Farmland

Wild flowers (cont.)	1	2	3	4	5	6	7	8
Field bindweed								
Viper's bugloss								
Field forgetmenot								
Houndstongue								
White dead-nettle								
Red dead-nettle								
Black horehound								
Hedge woundwort								
Self-heal								
Wild basil								
Marjoram								
Wild thyme								
Corn mint								
Wild clary								
Black nightshade								
Bittersweet								
Great mullein								
Sharp-leaved fluellen								
Germander speedwell								
Common field speedwell								
Eyebright								
Red bartsia								
Common broomrape (no leaves)								
Greater plantain								
Hoary plantain								
Ribwort plantain								
Cornsalad								
Field scabious								

Wild flowers (cont.)	1	2	3	4	5	6	7	8
Devil's bit scabious								
Small scabious								
Clustered bellflower								
Harebell								
Venus's looking glass								
Sheep's scabious								
Common fleabane								
Yarrow								
Sneezewort								
Scentless mayweed								
Pineapple weed								
Mugwort								
Ox-eye daisy								
Corn marigold								
Butterbur								
Winter heliotrope								
Ploughman's spikenard								
Ragwort								
Groundsel								
Carline thistle								
Burdock								
Spear thistle								
Meadow thistle								
Dwarf thistle								
Melancholy thistle								
Marsh thistle								
Creeping thistle								
Musk thistle								

Farmland

Wild flowers (cont.)	1	2	3	4	5	6	7	8
Greater knapweed								
Black knapweed								
Cornflower								
Chicory								
Common catsear								
Rough hawkbit								
Goatsbeard								
Smooth sow-thistle								
Perennial sow-thistle								
Dandelion								
Smooth hawksbeard								
Mouse-ear hawkweed								
Bluebell								
Crow garlic								
Wild daffodil								
Black bryony								
Lords and ladies								
Autumn lady's tresses								
Fragrant orchid								
Frog orchid								
Common spotted orchid								
Green-winged orchid								
Early purple orchid								
Man orchid								
Pyramidal orchid								
Lizard orchid								
Early spider orchid								
Bee orchid								

Grasses, Sedges, Rushes	1	2	3	4	5	6	7	8
Meadow fescue								
Tall fescue								
Red fescue								
Sheep's fescue								
Perennial rye-grass								
Annual meadow-grass								
Rough meadow-grass								
Smooth meadow-grass								
Cocksfoot								
Crested dogstail								
Quaking grass								
Blue moor-grass								
Barren brome								
Upright brome								
Soft brome								
Tor grass								
Common couch								
Wall barley								
Meadow barley								
Wild oat								
Meadow oat-grass								
False oat-grass								
Crested hairgrass								
Yellow oat-grass								
Tufted hairgrass								
Sweet vernal grass								
Yorkshire fog								

Farmland

Grasses (cont.)	1	2	3	4	5	6	7	8
Common bent								
Creeping bent								
Timothy								
Meadow foxtail								
Black grass								
Brown sedge								
Hairy sedge								
Glaucous sedge								
Spring sedge								
Hard rush								
Soft rush								
Toad rush								
Field woodrush								
Ferns, Horsetails etc.								
Field horsetail								
Adderstongue								
Bracken								
Fungi								
Field mushroom								
Common puff-ball								
Mammals								
Hedgehog								
Mole								
Common shrew								
Noctule bat								
Pipistrelle								
Long-eared bat								
Rabbit								

Mammals (cont.)	1	2	3	4	5	6	7	8
Brown hare								
Field vole								
Wood mouse								
Harvest mouse								
Common/Brown rat								
Fox								
Stoat								
Weasel								
Badger								
Birds								
Kestrel								
Red-legged partridge								
Grey partridge								
Pheasant								
Golden plover								
Lapwing								
Curlew								
Redshank								
Black-headed gull								
Stock dove								
Woodpigeon								
Collared dove								
Cuckoo								
Barn owl								
Little owl								
Swift								
Skylark								
Swallow								

Farmland

Birds (cont.)	1	2	3	4	5	6	7	8
House martin								
Pied wagtail								
Wren								
Hedgesparrow								
Robin								
Blackbird								
Fieldfare								
Redwing								
Song thrush								
Mistle thrush								
Whitethroat								
Willow warbler								
Great tit								
Blue tit								
Corn bunting								
Yellowhammer								
Chaffinch								
Greenfinch								
Goldfinch								
House sparrow								
Tree sparrow								
Starling								
Magpie								
Jackdaw								
Rook								
Carrion crow								
Butterflies								
Small skipper								

Butterflies (cont.)	1	2	3	4	5	6	7	8
Large skipper								
Dingy skipper								
Grizzled skipper								
Brimstone								
Large white								
Small white								
Green-veined white								
Orange-tip								
Small copper								
Brown argus								
Common blue								
Chalkhill blue								
Adonis blue								
Red admiral								
Painted lady								
Small tortoiseshell								
Peacock								
Comma								
Dark green fritillary								
Wall								
Marbled white								
Gatekeeper								
Meadow brown								
Small heath								
Moths								
Drinker								
Cinnabar								
Herald								

Towns and Gardens

Trees and Shrubs

	1	2	3	4	5	6	7	8
Goat willow/sallow								
Mistletoe								
London plane								
Hawthorn								
Sycamore								
Horse chestnut								
Lime								
Butterfly-bush/Buddleia								

Wild Flowers

	1	2	3	4	5	6	7	8
Nettle								
Annual nettle								
Pellitory of wall								
Redshank								
Japanese knotweed								
Curled dock								
Broad-leaved dock								
Common Orache								
Thyme-leaved sandwort								
Common chickweed								
Common mouse-ear								
Procumbent pearlwort								
Creeping buttercup								
Greater celandine								
Hedge mustard								
Thale cress								
Wallflower								
Common wintercress								

Wild flowers (cont.)

	1	2	3	4	5	6	7	8
Hairy bittercress								
Shepherd's purse								
Weld								
Wall pennywort								
Creeping cinquefoil								
Goat's rue								
White melilot								
Ribbed melilot								
Black medick								
Sun spurge								
Petty spurge								
Himalayan balsam								
Large-flowered evening primrose								
Rosebay willowherb								
Broad-leaved willowherb								
American willowherb								
Ground elder								
Fool's parsley								
Giant hogweed								
Hedge bindweed								
Field bindweed								
White dead-nettle								
Red dead-nettle								
Black horehound								
Self-heal								
Snapdragon								
Common toadflax								
Ivy-leaved toadflax								

Wild flowers (cont.)	1	2	3	4	5	6	7	8
Thyme-leaved speedwell	■	■	■	■	■	■	■	
Ivy-leaved speedwell	■	■	■	■	■	■		
Wall speedwell	■	■	■	■	■	■		
Greater plantain			■	■	■	■		
Ribwort plantain	■	■	■	■	■	■		
Red valerian	■	■	■	■	■	■		
Teasel	■					■	■	
Canadian golden-rod						■	■	■
Daisy	■	■	■	■	■	■	■	■
Michaelmas daisy							■	■
Canadian fleabane						■	■	■
Gallant soldier					■	■	■	■
Tansy	■	■				■	■	■
Mugwort	■	■				■	■	■
Coltsfoot		■	■	■				
Oxford ragwort	■	■	■	■	■	■	■	■
Groundsel	■	■	■	■	■	■	■	■
Burdock						■	■	■
Spear thistle				■	■	■	■	
Creeping thistle				■	■	■	■	
Common catsear					■	■	■	
Smooth sow-thistle	■	■	■	■	■	■	■	■
Prickly lettuce						■	■	■
Dandelion	■	■	■	■	■	■	■	■
Nipplewort			■	■	■	■	■	
Smooth hawksbeard	■	■	■	■	■	■		
Grasses, Sedges, Rushes								
Red fescue	■	■	■	■	■	■	■	■

Wild flowers (cont.)	1	2	3	4	5	6	7	8
Perennial rye-grass	■	■	■	■	■	■	■	■
Annual meadow-grass	■	■	■	■	■	■	■	■
Smooth meadow-grass	■	■	■	■	■	■	■	■
Cocksfoot	■	■	■	■	■	■	■	■
Barren brome	■	■	■	■	■	■		■
Soft brome	■	■	■	■	■	■	■	■
Common couch	■	■	■	■	■	■	■	■
Wall barley	■	■	■	■	■	■	■	■
False oat-grass	■	■	■	■	■	■	■	■
Yorkshire fog	■	■	■	■	■	■	■	■
Common bent	■	■	■	■		■	■	■
Ferns, Horsetails etc.								
Field horsetail	■	■	■	■	■			
Maidenhair spleenwort	■	■	■	■	■	■	■	■
Wall-rue	■	■	■	■	■	■	■	■
Rusty-back	■	■	■	■		■	■	■
Fungi								
Honey fungus					■	■	■	
Stinkhorn					■	■	■	
Mammals								
Hedgehog		■	■	■	■	■	■	
Grey squirrel	■	■	■	■	■	■	■	■
House mouse	■	■	■	■	■	■	■	■
Common/Brown rat	■	■	■	■	■	■	■	■
Fox	■	■	■	■	■	■	■	■
Red deer (parks)	■		■	■	■	■	■	■
Fallow deer	■		■	■	■	■	■	■
Pipistrelle			■	■	■	■	■	

Towns and Gardens

Birds	1	2	3	4	5	6	7	8
Mute swan	■	■	■	■	■	■	■	■
Mallard	■	■	■	■	■	■	■	■
Pochard	■	■	■	■	■	■	■	■
Tufted duck	■	■	■	■	■	■	■	■
Kestrel	■	■	■	■	■	■	■	■
Moorhen	■	■	■	■	■	■	■	■
Coot	■	■	■	■	■	■	■	■
Black-headed gull	■	■			■	■	■	■
Common gull	■	■			■	■	■	■
Herring gull	■	■	■		■	■	■	■
Feral pigeon	♪	♪	♪	♪	♪	♪	♪	♪
Woodpigeon	♪	♪	♪	♪	♪	♪	♪	♪
Collared dove	♪	♪	♪	♪	♪	♪	♪	♪
Tawny owl	♪	♪	♪	♪	♪	♪	♪	♪
Swift			■	■	■	■		
Swallow		■	■	■	■	■	■	
House martin			■	■	■	■	■	
Wren	♪	♪	♪	♪	♪	♪	♪	♪
Hedgesparrow	♪	♪	♪	♪	♪	♪	♪	♪
Robin	♪	♪	♪	♪	♪	♪	♪	♪
Black redstart	♪	♪	♪	♪		■	■	■
Blackbird	■	♪	♪	♪	■	■	■	■
Fieldfare	■	■				■	■	■
Redwing	♪	■				■	■	■
Song thrush	♪	♪	♪	♪	■	♪	♪	■
Mistle thrush	♪	♪	♪	■	■	♪	♪	♪
Spotted flycatcher		♪	♪		■	■		
	1	2	3	4	5	6	7	8

Birds (cont.)	1	2	3	4	5	6	7	8
Coal tit	♪	♪	♪	♪	♪	♪	♪	♪
Great tit	♪	♪	♪	♪	♪	♪	♪	♪
Blue tit	♪	♪	♪	♪	♪	♪	♪	♪
Chaffinch	♪	♪	♪	♪	♪	♪	♪	♪
Greenfinch	♪	♪	♪	♪	♪	♪	♪	♪
Goldfinch	♪	♪	♪	♪	♪	♪	♪	♪
Redpoll	♪	♪	♪	♪	♪	♪	♪	♪
House sparrow	♪	♪	♪	♪	♪	♪	♪	♪
Starling	♪	♪	♪	♪	♪	♪	♪	♪
Jay	■	■	■	■	■	■	■	■
Magpie	■	■	■	■	■	■	■	■
Jackdaw	■	■	■	■	■	■	■	■
Carrion crow	■	■	■	■	■	■	■	■
Butterflies								
Large white			■	■	■	■		
Small white			■	■	■	■		
Holly blue			■	■	■	■		
Red admiral			■	■	■	■		
Painted lady			■	■	■	■		
Small tortoiseshell	■	■	■	■	■	■	■	■
Peacock	■	■	■	■	■	■		
Moths								
Elephant hawk-moth			■	■				
Garden tiger			■	■	■	■		
Large yellow underwing	■		■	■	■	■	■	
Cabbage moth			■	■	■	■		
Old lady	■		■	■	■			
Peppered moth			■	■				
	1	2	3	4	5	6	7	8

Woodland

Trees and Shrubs	1	2	3	4	5	6	7	8
Douglas fir								
Norway spruce								
Sitka spruce								
Larch								
Scots pine								
Corsican pine								
Juniper								
Yew								
Crack willow								
White willow								
Goat willow/sallow								
Grey willow/sallow								
Grey poplar								
Aspen								
Black poplar								
Silver birch								
Downy birch								
Alder								
Hornbeam								
Hazel								
Beech								
Sweet chestnut								
Oak								
Wych elm								
English elm								
Mistletoe								
Bramble								

Trees (cont.)	1	2	3	4	5	6	7	8
Dog rose								
Crab apple								
Rowan								
Whitebeam								
Hawthorn								
Midland hawthorn								
Blackthorn								
Wild cherry								
Bird cherry								
Field maple								
Sycamore								
Holly								
Spindle-tree								
Box								
Buckthorn								
Alder buckthorn								
Small-leaved lime								
Dogwood								
Ash								
Privet								
Elder								
Guelder-rose								
Wayfaring tree								
Butcher's broom								
Wild Flowers								
Nettle								
Water pepper								
Wood dock								

Woodland

<table>
<tr><td>Wild flowers (cont.)</td><td>1</td><td>2</td><td>3</td><td>4</td><td>5</td><td>6</td><td>7</td><td>8</td></tr>
<tr><td>Greater stitchwort</td><td></td><td></td><td></td><td></td><td></td><td></td><td></td><td></td></tr>
<tr><td>Red campion</td><td></td><td></td><td></td><td></td><td></td><td></td><td></td><td></td></tr>
<tr><td>Ragged robin</td><td></td><td></td><td></td><td></td><td></td><td></td><td></td><td></td></tr>
<tr><td>Stinking hellebore</td><td></td><td></td><td></td><td></td><td></td><td></td><td></td><td></td></tr>
<tr><td>Green hellebore</td><td></td><td></td><td></td><td></td><td></td><td></td><td></td><td></td></tr>
<tr><td>Globe flower</td><td></td><td></td><td></td><td></td><td></td><td></td><td></td><td></td></tr>
<tr><td>Baneberry</td><td></td><td></td><td></td><td></td><td></td><td></td><td></td><td></td></tr>
<tr><td>Wood anemone</td><td></td><td></td><td></td><td></td><td></td><td></td><td></td><td></td></tr>
<tr><td>Marsh marigold</td><td></td><td></td><td></td><td></td><td></td><td></td><td></td><td></td></tr>
<tr><td>Traveller's joy</td><td></td><td></td><td></td><td></td><td></td><td></td><td></td><td></td></tr>
<tr><td>Creeping buttercup</td><td></td><td></td><td></td><td></td><td></td><td></td><td></td><td></td></tr>
<tr><td>Wood goldilocks</td><td></td><td></td><td></td><td></td><td></td><td></td><td></td><td></td></tr>
<tr><td>Lesser celandine</td><td></td><td></td><td></td><td></td><td></td><td></td><td></td><td></td></tr>
<tr><td>Columbine</td><td></td><td></td><td></td><td></td><td></td><td></td><td></td><td></td></tr>
<tr><td>Cuckoo flower</td><td></td><td></td><td></td><td></td><td></td><td></td><td></td><td></td></tr>
<tr><td>Garlic mustard</td><td></td><td></td><td></td><td></td><td></td><td></td><td></td><td></td></tr>
<tr><td>Golden saxifrage</td><td></td><td></td><td></td><td></td><td></td><td></td><td></td><td></td></tr>
<tr><td>Meadowsweet</td><td></td><td></td><td></td><td></td><td></td><td></td><td></td><td></td></tr>
<tr><td>Raspberry</td><td></td><td></td><td></td><td></td><td></td><td></td><td></td><td></td></tr>
<tr><td>Water avens</td><td></td><td></td><td></td><td></td><td></td><td></td><td></td><td></td></tr>
<tr><td>Herb bennet</td><td></td><td></td><td></td><td></td><td></td><td></td><td></td><td></td></tr>
<tr><td>Barren strawberry</td><td></td><td></td><td></td><td></td><td></td><td></td><td></td><td></td></tr>
<tr><td>Wild strawberry</td><td></td><td></td><td></td><td></td><td></td><td></td><td></td><td></td></tr>
<tr><td>Lady's mantle</td><td></td><td></td><td></td><td></td><td></td><td></td><td></td><td></td></tr>
<tr><td>Wood vetch</td><td></td><td></td><td></td><td></td><td></td><td></td><td></td><td></td></tr>
<tr><td>Bush vetch</td><td></td><td></td><td></td><td></td><td></td><td></td><td></td><td></td></tr>
<tr><td>Bitter vetchling</td><td></td><td></td><td></td><td></td><td></td><td></td><td></td><td></td></tr>
<tr><td>Wood sorrel</td><td></td><td></td><td></td><td></td><td></td><td></td><td></td><td></td></tr>
<tr><td></td><td>1</td><td>2</td><td>3</td><td>4</td><td>5</td><td>6</td><td>7</td><td>8</td></tr>
</table>

<table>
<tr><td>Wild flowers (cont.)</td><td>1</td><td>2</td><td>3</td><td>4</td><td>5</td><td>6</td><td>7</td><td>8</td></tr>
<tr><td>Wood cranesbill</td><td></td><td></td><td></td><td></td><td></td><td></td><td></td><td></td></tr>
<tr><td>Herb robert</td><td></td><td></td><td></td><td></td><td></td><td></td><td></td><td></td></tr>
<tr><td>Dog's mercury</td><td></td><td></td><td></td><td></td><td></td><td></td><td></td><td></td></tr>
<tr><td>Wood spurge</td><td></td><td></td><td></td><td></td><td></td><td></td><td></td><td></td></tr>
<tr><td>Mezereon</td><td></td><td></td><td></td><td></td><td></td><td></td><td></td><td></td></tr>
<tr><td>Spurge-laurel</td><td></td><td></td><td></td><td></td><td></td><td></td><td></td><td></td></tr>
<tr><td>Hairy St. John's wort</td><td></td><td></td><td></td><td></td><td></td><td></td><td></td><td></td></tr>
<tr><td>Sweet violet</td><td></td><td></td><td></td><td></td><td></td><td></td><td></td><td></td></tr>
<tr><td>Early dog violet</td><td></td><td></td><td></td><td></td><td></td><td></td><td></td><td></td></tr>
<tr><td>Common dog violet</td><td></td><td></td><td></td><td></td><td></td><td></td><td></td><td></td></tr>
<tr><td>White bryony</td><td></td><td></td><td></td><td></td><td></td><td></td><td></td><td></td></tr>
<tr><td>Enchanter's nightshade</td><td></td><td></td><td></td><td></td><td></td><td></td><td></td><td></td></tr>
<tr><td>Rosebay willowherb</td><td></td><td></td><td></td><td></td><td></td><td></td><td></td><td></td></tr>
<tr><td>Broad-leaved willowherb</td><td></td><td></td><td></td><td></td><td></td><td></td><td></td><td></td></tr>
<tr><td>Ivy</td><td></td><td></td><td></td><td></td><td></td><td></td><td></td><td></td></tr>
<tr><td>Sanicle</td><td></td><td></td><td></td><td></td><td></td><td></td><td></td><td></td></tr>
<tr><td>Pig-nut</td><td></td><td></td><td></td><td></td><td></td><td></td><td></td><td></td></tr>
<tr><td>Angelica</td><td></td><td></td><td></td><td></td><td></td><td></td><td></td><td></td></tr>
<tr><td>Upright hedge parsley</td><td></td><td></td><td></td><td></td><td></td><td></td><td></td><td></td></tr>
<tr><td>Common wintergreen</td><td></td><td></td><td></td><td></td><td></td><td></td><td></td><td></td></tr>
<tr><td>Toothed wintergreen</td><td></td><td></td><td></td><td></td><td></td><td></td><td></td><td></td></tr>
<tr><td>One-flowered wintergreen</td><td></td><td></td><td></td><td></td><td></td><td></td><td></td><td></td></tr>
<tr><td>Yellow birdsnest
(no green leaves)</td><td></td><td></td><td></td><td></td><td></td><td></td><td></td><td></td></tr>
<tr><td>Cowberry</td><td></td><td></td><td></td><td></td><td></td><td></td><td></td><td></td></tr>
<tr><td>Bilberry</td><td></td><td></td><td></td><td></td><td></td><td></td><td></td><td></td></tr>
<tr><td>Primrose</td><td></td><td></td><td></td><td></td><td></td><td></td><td></td><td></td></tr>
<tr><td>Oxlip</td><td></td><td></td><td></td><td></td><td></td><td></td><td></td><td></td></tr>
<tr><td></td><td>1</td><td>2</td><td>3</td><td>4</td><td>5</td><td>6</td><td>7</td><td>8</td></tr>
</table>

Woodland

Wild flowers (cont.)

	1	2	3	4	5	6	7	8
Yellow loosestrife								
Yellow pimpernel								
Chickweed wintergreen								
Woodruff								
Common cleavers								
Jacob's ladder								
Field forgetmenot								
Wood forgetmenot								
Bugle								
Wood-sage								
Skullcap								
Common hemp-nettle								
Yellow archangel								
Ground ivy								
Self-heal								
Bittersweet								
Common figwort								
Foxglove								
Common cow-wheat								
Toothwort (no leaves)								
Honeysuckle								
Twinflower								
Moschatel								
Common valerian								
Giant bellflower								
Nettle-leaved bellflower								
Hemp agrimony								
Golden-rod								

Wild flowers (cont.)

	1	2	3	4	5	6	7	8
Marsh thistle								
Burdock								
Wall lettuce								
Nipplewort								
Bluebell								
Ramsons								
Lily of the valley								
Common solomon's seal								
Angular solomon's seal								
Herb paris								
Black bryony								
Lords and ladies								
Broad-leaved helleborine								
Narrow-lipped helleborine								
Violet helleborine								
Dark red helleborine								
White helleborine								
Narrow-leaved helleborine								
Red helleborine								
Ghost orchid (no leaves)								
Birdsnest orchid (no leaves)								
Common twayblade								
Lesser twayblade								
Creeping lady's tresses								
Greater butterfly orchid								
Military orchid								
Early purple orchid								
Fly orchid								

Woodland

Grasses, Sedges, Rushes	1	2	3	4	5	6	7	8
Rough meadow-grass								
Giant fescue								
Red fescue								
Hairy brome								
Wood barley								
Tufted hairgrass								
Wavy hair-grass								
Sweet vernal grass								
Yorkshire fog								
Soft grass								
Brown bent								
Common bent								
Creeping bent								
Wood small-reed								
Wood millet								
False brome								
Wood meadow-grass								
Wood melick								
Greater tussock sedge								
False fox sedge								
Hairy sedge								
Pendulous sedge								
Wood sedge								
Great woodrush								
Hard rush								
Hairy woodrush								
Compact rush								

Ferns, Horsetails etc.	1	2	3	4	5	6	7	8
Wood horsetail								
Great horsetail								
Tunbridge filmy fern								
Royal fern								
Bracken								
Marsh fern								
Hartstongue								
Lady fern								
Male fern								
Broad buckler fern								
Hay-scented buckler fern								
Hard fern								
Common polypody								

Fungi	1	2	3	4	5	6	7	8
Fly agaric								
Death cap								
Honey fungus								
Jew's ear								
Chanterelle								
Sulphurtuft								
Parasol mushroom								
Coral-spot fungus								
Common bracket fungus								
Purple russula								
Yellow russula								
Candle-snuff fungus								
Stinkhorn								

Woodland

Mammals	1	2	3	4	5	6	7	8
Hedgehog								
Mole								
Common shrew								
Noctule								
Pipistrelle								
Long-eared bat								
Red squirrel								
Grey squirrel								
Rabbit								
Bank vole								
Wood mouse								
Dormouse								
Fox								
Pine marten								
Stoat								
Weasel								
Polecat								
Badger								
Red deer								
Sika deer								
Fallow deer								
Roe deer								
Muntjac								

Birds	1	2	3	4	5	6	7	8
Sparrowhawk								
Buzzard								
Hobby								

Birds (cont.)	1	2	3	4	5	6	7	8
Black grouse								
Capercaillie								
Pheasant								
Woodcock								
Stockdove								
Woodpigeon								
Turtle dove								
Cuckoo								
Tawny owl								
Long eared owl								
Nightjar								
Green woodpecker								
Great spotted woodpecker								
Lesser spotted woodpecker								
Wren								
Hedgesparrow								
Robin								
Redstart								
Nightingale								
Blackbird								
Song thrush								
Mistle thrush								
Grasshopper warbler								
Garden warbler								
Blackcap								
Lesser whitethroat								
Willow warbler								
Chiffchaff								

Woodland

Birds (cont.)	1	2	3	4	5	6	7	8
Wood warbler								
Goldcrest								
Pied flycatcher								
Spotted flycatcher								
Long-tailed tit								
Marsh tit								
Coal tit								
Crested tit								
Great tit								
Blue tit								
Nuthatch								
Treecreeper								
Chaffinch								
Brambling								
Greenfinch								
Siskin								
Redpoll								
Crossbill								
Bullfinch								
Hawfinch								
Starling								
Jay								
Magpie								
Common crow								
Butterflies								
Large skipper								
Wood white								
Brimstone								

Butterflies (cont.)	1	2	3	4	5	6	7	8
Green-veined white								
Orange-tip								
Green hairstreak								
Purple hairstreak								
Holly blue								
Duke of Burgundy fritillary								
White admiral								
Purple emperor								
Comma								
Pearl-bordered fritillary								
Silver-washed fritillary								
Speckled wood								
Gatekeeper								
Ringlet								
Moths								
Pine hawk-moth								
Eyed hawk-moth								
Poplar hawk-moth								
Buff tip								
Puss moth								
Black arches								
Red underwing								
Peppered moth								
Winter moth								
Mottled umber								
Mottled beauty								
Pine looper								
Green oak moth								

Heath, Moor and Mountain

Trees and Shrubs	1	2	3	4	5	6	7	8
Juniper					●	●	●	●
Grey willow/sallow		●						
Dwarf willow				●				
Aspen		●						
Silver birch				●				
Dwarf birch				●				
Sweet gale				●	●			
Alder						●	●	
Oak								
Rowan					●	●		
Broom					●	●		
Gorse					●	●		
Dwarf gorse						●	●	
Western gorse						●	●	
Alder buckthorn					●	●		
Wild Flowers								
Mountain sorrel								
Sheep's sorrel								
Spring sandwort								
Moss campion								
Red campion								
Globe flower								
Alpine Meadowrue								
Whitlow-grass								
Sundew								
English stonecrop								
Rose-root								

Wild flowers (cont.)	1	2	3	4	5	6	7	8
Starry saxifrage								
Yellow saxifrage								
Purple saxifrage								
Cloudberry					●	●		
Mountain avens								
Tormentil								
Alpine lady's mantle								
Petty whin								
Common storksbill								
Heath milkwort								
Slender St. John's wort								
Heath dog violet								
Wild pansy								
Alpine willowherb								
New Zealand willowherb								
Dwarf cornel								
Cross-leaved heath								
Bell heather								
Heather								
Alpine bearberry					●			
Wild azalea								
Cowberry					●	●		
Bilberry					●			
Crowberry					●			
Chickweed wintergreen								
Bog pimpernel								
Thrift								
Alpine gentian								

Heath, Moor and Mountain

Wild flowers (cont.)

	1	2	3	4	5	6	7	8
Heath bedstraw								
Common dodder (no leaves)								
Betony								
Spring speedwell								
Fingered speedwell								
Spiked speedwell								
Lousewort								
Pale butterwort								
Buckshorn plantain								
Harebell								
Sheep's scabious								
Mountain everlasting								
Field wormwood								
Bog asphodel								
Grape hyacinth					●●			
Heath spotted orchid								

Grasses, Rushes, Sedges

	1	2	3	4	5	6	7	8
Sheep's fescue								
Wavy hair-grass								
Early hair-grass								
Brown bent								
Common bent								
Purple moor-grass								
Mat grass								
Deer-grass			●●●●					
Common cotton-grass			●●●●					
Harestail cotton-grass			●●●					
Green-ribbed sedge				●●●●				

Wild flowers (cont.)

	1	2	3	4	5	6	7	8
Pill sedge			●●					
Stiff sedge				●●●				
Compact rush				●●●				
Three-leaved rush					●●			
Heath rush				●●●				
Heath woodrush								

Ferns, Horsetails etc.

	1	2	3	4	5	6	7	8
Stagshorn clubmoss								
Alpine clubmoss								
Bracken								
Hard fern								

Mammals

	1	2	3	4	5	6	7	8
Rabbit								
Mountain hare								
Field vole								
Fox								
Pine marten								
Stoat								
Weasel								
Polecat								
Wild cat								
Red deer								
Roe deer								

Reptiles

	1	2	3	4	5	6	7	8
Slow worm								
Common lizard								
Grass snake								
Adder								

Heath, Moor and Mountain

Birds	1	2	3	4	5	6	7	8
Hen harrier								
Buzzard								
Golden eagle								
Kestrel								
Merlin								
Hobby								
Peregrine								
Red grouse								
Ptarmigan								
Black grouse								
Stone curlew								
Dotterel								
Golden plover	♪		♪					
Lapwing	♪	♪	♪					♪
Curlew	♪	♪	♪	♪	♪			♪
Greenshank		♪		♪				
Black-headed gull								
Common gull								
Cuckoo		♪	♪	♪				
Short-eared owl								
Nightjar		♪	♪	♪				
Skylark	♪	♪	♪	♪	♪	♪	♪	♪
Sand martin	♪	♪						
Swallow								
Tree pipit		♪	♪	♪				
Meadow pipit	♪	♪	♪	♪	♪	♪	♪	♪
Wren	♪	♪	♪	♪	♪	♪	♪	♪

Birds (cont.)	1	2	3	4	5	6	7	8
Whinchat		♪	♪	♪				
Stonechat		♪	♪	♪				
Wheatear	♪	♪	♪	♪				
Ring ouzel	♪	♪	♪					
Blackbird	♪	♪	♪					♪
Grasshopper warbler		♪						
Dartford warbler	♪	♪	♪	♪	♪	♪	♪	♪
Linnet	♪	♪	♪		♪	♪		♪
Twite	♪	♪	♪					
Carrion/Hooded crow								
Raven								

Butterflies	1	2	3	4	5	6	7	8
Small copper								
Silver-studded blue								
Common blue								
Dark green fritillary								
Small mountain ringlet								
Scotch argus								
Grayling								
Meadow brown								
Small heath								
Large heath								

Moths	1	2	3	4	5	6	7	8
Oak eggar								
Fox moth								
Emperor								
Antler moth								
Mountain burnet								

Freshwater

Trees and Shrubs	1	2	3	4	5	6	7	8
Bay willow		▓	▓	▓●●●				
Crack willow			▓	▓●●●				
White willow			▓	▓●●●				
Goat willow/sallow		▓●●●						
Grey willow/sallow		▓●●●						
Osier		▓●●●						
Alder	▓	▓				●●●	●●●	
Wild Flowers	1	2	3	4	5	6	7	8
Amphibious bistort		▓	▓	▓	▓	▓		
Redshank			▓	▓	▓	▓		
Water-pepper				▓	▓	▓		
Water dock				▓	▓	▓		
Clustered dock				▓	▓	▓		
Water chickweed		▓	▓	▓	▓	▓		
White water-lily			▓	▓	▓	▓		
Yellow water-lily			▓	▓	▓	▓		
Marsh marigold	▓	▓	▓	▓				
Celery-leaved buttercup			▓	▓	▓	▓		
Lesser spearwort	▓	▓	▓	▓	▓	▓	▓	
Ivy-leaved crowfoot		▓	▓	▓	▓			
Stream water crowfoot		▓	▓	▓	▓			
Common water crowfoot	▓	▓	▓	▓				
Common meadow-rue			▓	▓	▓	▓		
Great yellow-cress			▓	▓	▓	▓		
Water-cress	▓	▓	▓	▓	▓	▓	▓	
Awlwort	▓	▓	▓	▓	▓	▓		
Wild turnip	▓	▓	▓	▓	▓	▓	▓	

Wild flowers (cont.)	1	2	3	4	5	6	7	8
Golden saxifrage	▓	▓	▓	▓	▓			
Sundew					▓	▓	▓	
Grass of parnassus						▓	▓	▓
Meadow sweet				▓	▓	▓	▓	
Water avens	▓	▓	▓	▓	▓			
Jewel-weed					▓	▓	▓	▓
Himalayan balsam						▓	▓	▓
Marsh violet	▓	▓	▓	▓	▓			
Great willowherb				▓	▓	▓	▓	
Marsh willowherb				▓	▓	▓	▓	
New Zealand willowherb				▓	▓	▓	▓	
Purple loosestrife					▓	▓	▓	
Spiked water milfoil				▓	▓	▓	▓	
Marestail				▓	▓	▓		
Marsh pennywort				▓	▓	▓	▓	
Fool's watercress	▓	▓	▓	▓	▓	▓		
Yellow loosestrife				▓	▓	▓	▓	
Water violet				▓	▓			
Marsh gentian						▓	▓	▓
Bogbean	▓	▓	▓	▓	▓			
Common comfrey	▓	▓	▓	▓	▓	▓		
Water forgetmenot			▓	▓	▓	▓		
Skullcap				▓	▓	▓	▓	
Marsh woundwort				▓	▓	▓	▓	
Gipsywort				▓	▓	▓	▓	
Water mint					▓	▓	▓	▓
Bittersweet					▓●●●	●●●		
Water figwort			▓	▓	▓	▓	▓	

Freshwater

Wild flowers (cont.)	1	2	3	4	5	6	7	8
Monkey flower								
Brooklime								
Water speedwell								
Marsh lousewort								
Common butterwort								
Marsh valerian								
Water lobelia								
Hemp agrimony								
Trifid bur marigold								
Marsh ragwort								
Arrowhead								
Common water plantain								
Flowering rush								
Frogbit								
Water soldier								
Mudwort								
Greater bladderwort								
Shoreweed								
Canadian waterweed								
Broad-leaved pondweed								
Bog pondweed								
Curled pondweed								
Yellow iris								
Ivy-leaved duckweed								
Common duckweed								
Branched bur-reed								
Unbranched bur-reed								
Bulrush								

	1	2	3	4	5	6	7	8
Grasses, Sedges, Rushes								
Reed sweet-grass								
Floating sweet-grass								
Reed canary grass								
Marsh foxtail								
Common reed								
Common clubrush								
Great fen sedge								
Greater tussock sedge								
Lesser pond sedge								
Greater pond sedge								
Bottle sedge								
Sharp-flowered rush								
Jointed rush								
Ferns, Horsetails etc.								
Water horsetail								
Marsh horsetail								
Quillwort								
Marsh fern								
Mammals								
Water shrew								
Pipistrelle								
Daubenton's bat								
Water vole								
Mink								
Otter								
Amphibians								
Smooth newt								

Freshwater

Amphibians (cont.)	1	2	3	4	5	6	7	8
Common frog								
Common toad								
Birds								
Red-throated diver								
Great crested grebe								
Dabchick/little grebe								
Cormorant								
Bittern								
Heron								
Mute swan								
Bewick's swan								
Whooper swan								
Greylag goose								
Pink-footed goose								
White-fronted goose								
Canada goose								
Wigeon								
Teal								
Mallard								
Pintail								
Shoveler								
Pochard								
Tufted duck								
Goldeneye								
Goosander								
Osprey								
Moorhen								
Coot								
	1	2	3	4	5	6	7	8

Birds (cont.)	1	2	3	4	5	6	7	8
Little ringed plover								
Lapwing								
Ruff								
Snipe								
Common sandpiper								
Black-headed gull								
Herring gull								
Swift								
Kingfisher								
Sand martin								
Swallow								
House martin								
Yellow wagtail								
Grey wagtail								
Pied wagtail								
Dipper								
Cetti's warbler								
Sedge warbler								
Reed warbler								
Bearded tit								
Reed bunting								
Dragonflies								
Common aeshna								
Emperor dragonfly								
Blue darter								
Blood red darter								
Splendid damsel-fly								
Common blue damsel-fly								
	1	2	3	4	5	6	7	8

The Coast

Trees and Shrubs	1	2	3	4	5	6	7	8
Corsican pine								
Creeping willow								
Shrubby seablite								
Burnet rose								
Blackthorn								
Broom								
Tree lupin								
Sea buckthorn								
Privet								
Wild Flowers								
Curled dock								
Sea beet								
Spear-leaved orache								
Sea Purslane								
Glasswort								
Annual seablite								
Prickly saltwort								
Sea sandwort								
Knotted pearlwort								
Greater sea spurrey								
Lesser sea spurrey								
Sea campion								
Red campion								
Yellow horned poppy								
Hoary stock								
Early scurvy-grass								
Common scurvy-grass								

Wild flowers (cont.)	1	2	3	4	5	6	7	8
Wild cabbage								
Sea rocket								
Sea kale								
Sea radish								
Wall-pepper								
English stonecrop								
Sea pea								
Birdsfoot trefoil								
Kidney vetch								
Sea storksbill								
Sea spurge								
Portland spurge								
Purging flax								
Marsh pennywort								
Sea holly								
Alexanders								
Rock samphire								
Fennel								
Wild celery								
Scots lovage								
Primrose								
Scarlet pimpernel								
Brookweed								
Thrift								
Common sea-lavender								
Rock sea-lavender								
Yellow-wort								
Common centaury								

The Coast

Wild flowers (cont.)	1	2	3	4	5	6	7	8
Autumn gentian								
Lady's bedstraw								
Sea bindweed								
Viper's bugloss								
Oyster plant								
Wild thyme								
Water mint								
Bittersweet								
Buckshorn plantain								
Sea plantain								
Sheep's scabious								
Golden samphire								
Sea mayweed								
Sea aster								
Sea wormwood								
Ragwort								
Carline thistle								
Spear thistle								
Sea arrow-grass								
Eel-grass								
Spring squill								
Bluebell								
Gladiolus								
Marsh helleborine								
Early marsh orchid								
Southern marsh orchid								
Northern marsh orchid								
Pyramidal orchid								

	1	2	3	4	5	6	7	8
Grasses, Sedges, Rushes								
Red fescue								
Common saltmarsh grass								
Lyme grass								
Sea couch								
Sand couch								
Marram								
Common cord-grass								
Sand sedge								
Sea club rush								
Saltmarsh rush								
Sea rush								
Ferns, Horsetails etc.								
Bracken								
Sea spleenwort								
Mammals								
Common porpoise								
Killer whale								
Bottle-nosed dolphin								
Common dolphin								
Otter								
Common seal								
Grey seal								
Birds								
Red-throated diver								
Great northern diver								
Fulmar								
Manx shearwater								

The Coast

Birds (cont.)	1	2	3	4	5	6	7	8
Storm petrel		♪			♫			
Gannet								
Cormorant								
Shag								
Barnacle goose								
Brent goose								
Shelduck								
Scaup								
Eider								
Common scoter								
Red-breasted merganser								
Buzzard								
Kestrel								
Peregrine								
Oystercatcher								
Avocet								
Ringed plover								
Grey plover								
Knot								
Sanderling								
Dunlin								
Black-tailed godwit								
Bar-tailed godwit								
Whimbrel								
Curlew	♪		♫	♪	♪			
Redshank	♪				♪			♪
Turnstone								
Arctic skua								

Birds (cont.)	1	2	3	4	5	6	7	8
Great skua								
Black-headed gull								
Common gull								
Herring gull								
Lesser blackback								
Greater blackback								
Kittiwake								
Sandwich tern								
Common tern								
Arctic tern								
Little tern								
Guillemot								
Razorbill								
Black guillemot								
Puffin								
Rock dove								
Skylark						♫	♪	♪
Rock pipit								
Stonechat								
Snow bunting								
Linnet								
Jackdaw								
Carrion crow								
Raven								
Butterflies								
Small copper								
Common blue								
Grayling								

Key to the Maps

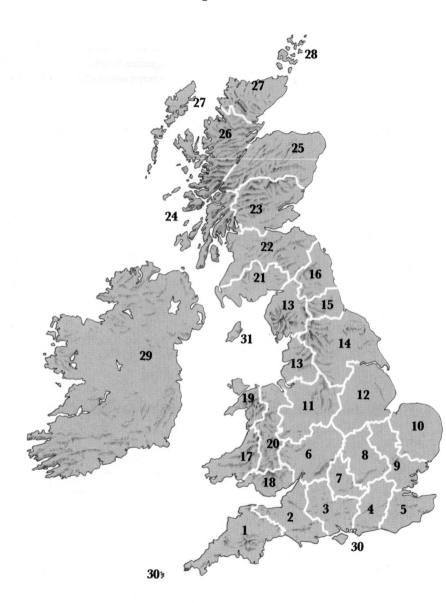

GAZETTEER

The Gazetteer lists, county by county, the most interesting places in the countryside where people can see wildlife, especially birds and wild flowers. Ireland, the Isle of Man and the Channel Isles are covered, but not in such detail as England, Scotland and Wales. A number of places that would otherwise qualify cannot be shown, because the especially rare creatures that live or grow there would suffer if people tried to find them. The magnificent lady's slipper orchid in its single site and the golden orioles that nest in a closely guarded locality within the Four Seas are examples. So are many colonies of the little tern, which have to be wardened to prevent holidaymakers trampling on their eggs and young.

Access is always a problem, for there are many places which can only be visited by permit. We must stress that mention of a locality here does not by any means guarantee that you can walk straight into it. The principal organisations that own or manage nature reserves and stretches of countryside with a wildlife interest, and can issue permits to visit them, are the Nature Conservancy Council, the National Trust, the Royal Society for the Protection of Birds and the county trusts for nature conservation; addresses are given below.

The Nature Conservancy Council is the official body that is responsible for the conservation of wildlife in Britain – there are corresponding bodies for both parts of Ireland. The NCC owns, leases or manages by agreement 189 national nature reserves, covering nearly 150,000 hectares. Most of these require a permit for visits by members of the public.

The National Trust, with over a million members – its slogan is "I'm one in a million" – is the largest conservation membership body in Britain. Most of its land of wildlife interest is open moorland, downland or coast, for which no permit is needed. It also has a few strict nature reserves, such as the famous Wicken Fen in Cambridgeshire, which are generally open when the warden is on duty.

The Royal Society for the Protection of Birds, with its membership driving towards 400,000, is much the largest voluntary conservation body primarily devoted to wildlife, in this case, of course, birds. Its nearly 100 reserves and bird sanctuaries cover some 20,000 hectares, and its most important single achievements have been the restoration as British breeding birds of the osprey, on Speyside in the Highlands, and the avocet, at Minsmere and Havergate Island on the coast of Suffolk. All these sites are listed here.

The 44 county trusts for nature conservation, which use the Royal Society for Nature Conservation as their umbrella body, have 1400 reserves, covering nearly 20,000 hectares. Many of these are open to members only, except by permit. There is now one such trust in each English county, and separate trusts for the whole of Scotland, for Northern Ireland, and for the Isle of Man. Some trusts cover more than one county. For instance, the Yorkshire Naturalists' Trust covers four new counties, the Berkshire, Buckinghamshire and Oxfordshire Naturalists' Trust (BBONT) covers three, and the North Wales Naturalists' Trust covers both Clwyd and Gwynedd.

Other bodies which own significant numbers of nature reserves or sites of wildlife interest include the National Trust for Scotland, the counterpart of the National Trust north of the Border, and the Woodland Trust, which, of course, specialises in woodlands.

Users of the gazetteer must bear in mind that there is at present, despite the best efforts of the conservation bodies, a steady attrition of valuable wildlife sites by farmers and foresters. Marshes are being drained, old meadows ploughed, downland converted to arable, ancient woodlands felled and replanted with conifers or not replanted at all. Unless the site is actually owned by a conservation body, you may therefore find on your visit to any site listed here, that economic pressures have beaten you to it, and the site is no more. The best way to combat this is to join a conservation body yourself.

National Trust, 42 Queen Anne's Gate, London, SW1H 9AS
National Trust for Scotland, 5 Charlotte Square, Edinburgh
Nature Conservancy Council, 20 Belgrave Square, London, SW1X 8PY
Royal Society for Nature Conservation, The Green, Nettleham, Lincoln
Royal Society for the Protection of Birds, The Lodge, Sandy,
  Bedfordshire, SG19 2DL
Woodland Trust, Westgate, Grantham, Lincolnshire

Cornwall, Devon

CORNWALL

The mild wet climate, together with the long coastline, bleak moorland spine and predominantly acid soils, mean that the main wildlife interest is on the coast, most of which is an AONB and much also has a long distance footpath.

West Cornwall (Penwith)

The Land's End peninsula has very fine coastal cliffs and heathland, especially round **Cape Cornwall**.
Marazion Marsh: extensive reedbeds; good for migrant waders.
Hayle Estuary: also good for waders.
Gwithian Towans: an extensive tract of sand dunes.

Lizard Peninsula

The southernmost part of the British mainland and the only part that extends south of the 50th parallel; plateau heathland with some dramatic coastal scenery, as at Kynance Cove.
Goonhilly and Predannack Downs: heathland with extensive tracts of Cornish heath *Erica vagans*, the most conspicuous of the rare plants, many of them associated with outcrops of serpentine rock, that make this one of the best known botanical areas in Britain.
Helford River: a drowned valley with many wooded creeks and mudflats and interesting tidal alderwoods.
Loe Pool: a large freshwater lake created by a shingle bar that blocks the River Cober's exit to the sea.

North Coast

A beautiful and largely unspoilt coastline with fine cliffs and coastal heath, especially from Tintagel to Cambeak and around Morwenstow.

Reskajeage Downs: a good coastal heath.
St Agnes Head: good coastal heath and seabirds.
Perranporth Dunes: a fine stretch of sand dunes.
Camel estuary: good waders and a flock of wintering white-fronted geese.
Newquay has a well known roof-nesting colony of herring gulls, which also nest on roofs in Helston, St Ives, Newlyn and Mousehole.

Bodmin Moor

A stretch of fairly bleak heather moor with an interesting natural feature in **Dozmary Pool**.

South Cornwall

The coast is less exciting than in the north, but there are some good stretches, e.g. around **the Dodman**.
Dunmere Wood, near Bodmin: oakwood with some rare plants.
Glynn Valley, woodlands between Liskeard and Bodmin: oakwood with good birds.
Retire Common, Withiel: a fine damp heath.
Tamar estuary, including St German's and St John's Lakes: good for waders and wildfowl, including wintering avocets. N.B. Tamar Lake is near Bude (see Devon; Dartmoor).

DEVON

Like Cornwall, Devon has a mild wet climate and is largely covered with acid soils. The two chief hill areas, Dartmoor and Exmoor, have more wildlife interest than the Cornish moors, and the wildlife of the coast is very rich, especially in the few areas with basic or calcareous soils.
Westward Ho!, named after Charles Kingsley's famous picaresque tale, has a fine shingle bank.

Taw and Torridge estuaries, the Two Rivers of Henry Williamson's *Tarka the Otter*, both have good mudflats.
Braunton Burrows NNR: one of the largest dune systems in Britain, and a fine botanizing ground, with several rarities, including round-headed club-rush *Scirpus holoschoenus*.
Lundy: an unspoilt island in the Bristol Channel, with fine cliffs, nesting puffins and a plant found nowhere else in the world, the Lundy cabbage *Rhynchosinapis wrightii*, named after its discoverer, Dr Elliston Wright of Braunton. Now owned by the National Trust, it is reached by boat from Ilfracombe. The Lundy Field Society runs a bird observatory.

Exmoor

With its National Park continues the coastline eastwards across the Somerset border, but with wooded slopes descending steeply to the sea. Notable among its rich oakwoods hanging over the valleys are those of Watersmeet, a National Trust property along the East Lyn River, scene of a flood disaster following a cloudburst in 1953; several rare whitebeams grow here. The moorland is fast vanishing, due to state-subsidised agricultural development, but still has a notable herd of several hundred wild red deer, and such moorland birds as ring ouzel, red grouse and merlin.

Dartmoor

The largest tract of wild country in southern England, and a National Park, though still suffering from military use. Largely heather moor with extensive peat bogs and characteristic granite hill-tops called tors, it still has several old and important oakwoods.

Wistman's Wood: best known of the Dartmoor oakwoods and the highest oakwood in England, its gnarled and stunted pedunculate oaks *Quercus robur* are covered with ferns, mosses and other epiphytic plants.
Black Tor Copse: a better developed wood of sessile oak *Q. petraea*, also with many epiphytes.
Bovey Valley and Yarner Woods: much the largest and richest oakwoods, with rare plants and good birds, including pied flycatcher. Both NNRs.
Dunsford in the Teign valley has a well known colony of wild daffodils.
Endsleigh on the eastern edge of the moor, near Tavistock, has the tallest wellingtonia *Sequoiadendron giganteum* in Britain.
Higher Kiln Quarry, Buckfastleigh, has the William Pengelly Cave Studies Centre.
Tamar Lake, a reservoir, is good for winter wildfowl.

South Coast

The western section is noted for its steep-sided fjord-like estuaries, which are river valleys that were flooded when the sea level rose after the last glaciation, some 8–10,000 years ago.
Tamar estuary: see under Cornwall.
Prawle Point: the southernmost point of England east of Cornwall. The cliffs from here to **Start Point** are studded blue with spring squill *Scilla verna* in April.
Dart and Teign estuaries: good for winter wildfowl and waders.
Slapton Ley: the largest natural freshwater lake in Devon, formed, like Loe Pool in Cornwall, by a shingle bar, which is rich in uncommon plants. The Ley is eutrophic and fringed with reeds, and has a field studies centre.
Berry Head: a limestone headland on the south side of Torbay, noted for its

nesting seabirds and several very rare plants.

Paignton has its own zoo and botanic garden, run by the Herbert Whitley Trust, which also owns Slapton Ley.

Exe estuary: noted for its brent geese, eiders and other waterfowl and waders; the sand bar across its mouth,

Dawlish Warren, now largely a golf course, has a special and very charming rarity, the sand crocus *Romulea columnae*, whose flowers open in April only when the sun shines.

Woodbury Common: one of a group of heaths resembling those of Dorset and the New Forest.

Beer Head: the westernmost outcrop of chalk in England and the south-western terminus of the great prehistoric trackway that leads via the Ridge Way and the Icknield Way to northern Norfolk.

Axmouth-Lyme Regis Undercliffs NNR: a remarkable area, shared with Dorset, the result of a landslip on Christmas Day, 1839, when nearly 800 million tons of rock collapsed; it has now developed into an ashwood, with unusual plants and insects.

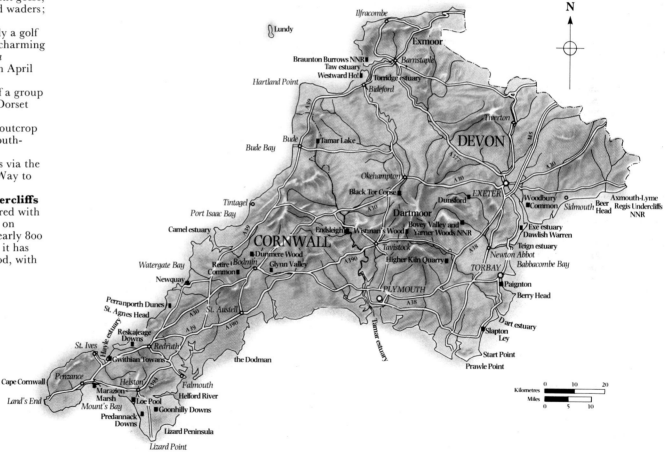

Somerset and South Avon, Dorset

SOMERSET AND SOUTH AVON

This area has an eastern block of limestone hills, a western block of uplands with acid soils, with the peatlands of the Somerset Levels between, a mainly muddy coastline in the north and a belt of fertile farming country in the south.

Brendon, Quantock and Blackdown Hills: AONBs stretching north and east from Exmoor (see Devon), largely unspoilt with heathy tops and wooded valleys, the Brendons and Quantocks coming close to the sea at Dunster and West Quantoxhead respectively. Coleridge's Nether Stowey is on the northern slopes of the Quantocks, with Wordsworth's Alfoxton a few miles off.
Bridgwater Bay: one of the outstanding wetlands of Europe, with extensive mudflats. **Steart Island** at the mouth of the Parret is noted for wildfowl and waders.
Brean Down: a promontory in the Bristol Channel with several rare lime-loving plants, such as white rock-rose *Helianthemum apenninum*, some of which also occur on **Crook Peak** and other limestone outcrops further east.
Steep Holm: a small rocky island in the Bristol Channel off Weston-super-Mare, covered with a 'forest' of alexanders *Smyrnium olusatrum* and breeding herring gulls. It is the only British locality for the peony *Paeonia mascula*, supposedly introduced by medieval monks; the rare leek *Allium babingtonii* also grows here.

Somerset Levels

A once extensive area of fenland and raised mires, now sadly mostly drained, with a long and fascinating history. Once part of the sea, with the Quantocks and Mendips as its cliffs, and later an extensive marshland, it still has prehistoric wooden trackways and lake villages and a Christian tradition dating back to the 1st century A.D. – nobody has ever explained just how the early-flowering Glastonbury thorn came to grow nearby. It was the site of the last pitched battle on English soil, Sedgemoor in 1685.
Tealham and Tadham Moors, West Sedgemoor and Shapwick Heath NNR are among the most important surviving sites. Unusual plants survive in many ditches, but Shapwick is the best peatland, with sundews, butterworts and other characteristic bog plants.
The M5 near Wellington has the first tunnel ever built under a motorway especially for badgers.

Mendip Hills: a range of Carboniferous limestone hills, whose summits show remains of Roman and later lead mines, with a distinctive flora, including alpine pennycress *Thlaspi alpestre* and spring sandwort *Minuartia verna*, e.g. at **Ubley Warren** near Charterhouse. The limestone gorges along their southern face are famous for rare plants, most notably Cheddar pink *Dianthus gratianopolitanus*, and hanging ashwoods.
Cheddar Gorge with its stalagmitic caves is far the best known gorge, with botanical delights that include Welsh poppy *Meconopsis cambrica* and lesser meadow rue *Thalictrum minus*.
Ebbor Gorge NNR terminates in the celebrated prehistoric site, **Wookey Hole**.
Rodney Stoke NNR: the best of the Mendip ashwoods.
Barrow Gurney and Blagdon Reservoirs, and **Chew Valley Lake:** all good for waterfowl, Chew Valley being the headquarters in the south-west for the now well acclimatised ruddy duck *Oxyura jamaicensis* from North America.
Leigh Woods: a fine woodland with many small-leaved limes *Tilia cordata* on the south side of the **Avon Gorge** (see Gloucestershire) and sharing many of its rare limestone plants.

DORSET

A rich mixture of calcareous and acid soils, especially in Purbeck, makes it an epitome of southern England. Much of the south of the county, which mercifully still lacks a coast road, is an AONB.

The Coast
Axmouth–Lyme Regis Landslip: see Devon. Not far inland lies one of our only two native colonies of spring snowflake *Leucojum vernum*.
Abbotsbury Swannery: one of the very few places – Radipole Lake (below) is another – where mute swans breed colonially in Britain. There are sub-tropical gardens nearby.
Chesil Bank: one of the longest shingle banks in Europe, its shingle grades from very fine at the western (Bridport) end to coarse pebbles about 3 in. across at the eastern (Portland) end, some 15 miles away. From Abbotsbury eastwards it is separated from the mainland by the Fleet, a good winter wildfowl resort. Three species of tern nest on the main shingle bank, which also has two uncommon plants, sea pea *Lathyrus japonicus* and shrubby seablite *Suaeda vera*, together with good stands of sea kale *Crambe maritima*.
Isle of Portland: fine limestone cliffs, with some rare plants, abundant ivy broomrape *Orobanche hederae* and a good bird migration watchpoint and observatory on **Portland Bill**.
Radipole Lake and Lodmoor: two good sites for breeding, migrating and wintering birds, including bearded tits.
Cliffs from Weymouth to Purbeck: a fine stretch of varied cliffed coast, with many remarkable features, including the Burning Cliff at **Ringstead Bay**, where oil shales burned for four years in the 1820s; **Durdle Door**, a striking rock arch at Lulworth; the only British habitat of the Lulworth skipper butterfly *Thymelaea actaeon* along the grassy cliffs on either side of **Lulworth Cove**; the best place to see early spider orchid *Ophrys sphegodes* and scattered seabird colonies at **Durlston Head** and elsewhere. The great stone globe at Durlston Head is an interesting man-made feature.
Purbeck Marine Wildlife Reserve: one of the first such reserves to be set up in Britain.
Poole Harbour: an almost land-locked tidal lagoon, good for bird-watching all the year round, but especially in winter, for waders, ducks and grebes.
Brownsea Island: a Dorset Trust reserve, with a large heronry and a good ternery.

The Heathlands
The Dorset heaths, a fast diminishing wildlife resource, used to be continuous with the New Forest, but are now only scattered fragments around Wareham. The best are the NNR's of **Decoy Heath** north of Wareham and in Purbeck **Hartland Moor** together with the RSPB's **Arne**. Their specialities include Dartford warbler, smooth snake, sand lizard, Dorset heath *Erica ciliaris* and some fine colonies of marsh gentian *Gentiana pneumonanthe*. On Decoy Heath many of the pines are naturalised maritime pines *Pinus pinaster* from the

Mediterranean. A few woods in this area have the native lungwort *Pulmonaria longifolia*.

Cranborne Chase and the Downs:
Dorset has as fine a stretch of chalk downs as anywhere in England, but their flora and fauna do not differ significantly from those further north and east, apart from the soaring buzzards and the many roe deer in the woods. **Hambledon Hill** north-west of Blandford is one of the finest and there are two nationally famous archaeological features: Maiden Castle a mile or two south-west of Dorchester and the Cerne Giant in the valley leading north from Cerne Abbas.

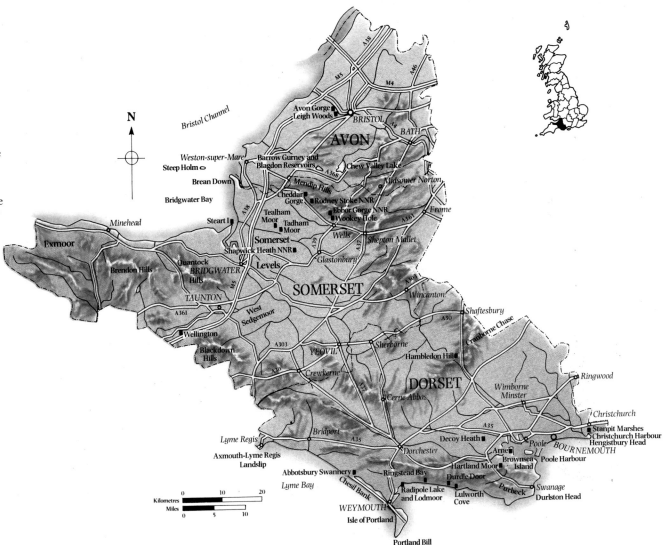

N

Bristol Channel

Avon Gorge
Leigh Woods
BRISTOL
BATH
AVON

Weston-super-Mare
Steep Holm
Barrow Gurney and
Blagdon Reservoirs
Chew Valley Lake
Midsomer Norton

Brean Down
Mendip Hills
Cheddar Gorge
Rodney Stoke NNR
Ebbor Gorge NNR
Frome
Wookey Hole

Bridgwater Bay
Tealham Moor
Tadham Moor

Minehead
Steart I
Somerset
Wells
Shepton Mallet
Shapwick Heath NNR

Exmoor
Quantock Hills
Bridgwater
Levels
Glastonbury

Brendon Hills
BRIDGWATER
SOMERSET
Wincanton

TAUNTON
West Sedgemoor
Shaftesbury

A361
A30
Cranborne Chase

Wellington
A303
YEOVIL
Sherborne
Ringwood

Blackdown Hills
Crewkerne
Hambledon Hill

DORSET
Wimborne Minster
Christchurch

Cerne Abbas
Stanpit Marshes
Christchurch Harbour
Hengistbury Head

Lyme Regis
Bridport
A35
Decoy Heath
Poole
BOURNEMOUTH

Axmouth-Lyme Regis Landslip
Dorchester
Hartland Moor
Arne
Brownsea Island
Poole Harbour

Abbotsbury Swannery
Ringstead Bay
Durdle Door
Purbeck
Swanage

Lyme Bay
Chesil Bank
Radipole Lake and Lodmoor
Lulworth Cove
Durlston Head

WEYMOUTH
Isle of Portland

Portland Bill

Kilometres
0   10   20
Miles
0   5   10

Hampshire, Wiltshire

HAMPSHIRE

The central county of southern England, with elements of both eastern and western floras and other wildlife: divided into four parts: the coast, the New Forest, the chalk and a small area of heathland in the north east, adjoining the much larger area in south-west Surrey and south Berkshire.

The Coast

Christchurch Harbour, with **Stanpit Marshes**: good for wildfowl and waders.

Hengistbury Head: interesting flora, especially small spring annuals, of the sort that make botanists go down on their hands and knees.

Solent Marshes from Hurst Castle to Calshot: good saltmarshes and shingle beaches, with important breeding colonies of little terns and, at **Needsoar Point**, black-headed gulls.

Southampton Water: much industrialised, but the birthplace of common cordgrass *Spartina anglica* (a wholly new and fertile species which arose from a hybrid between the European *S. stricta* and the North American *S. alterniflora*) which during the present century has colonised, with some human aid, the estuarine mud along almost the whole British coastline.

Farlington Marshes: good for both birds and saltmarsh plants.

Langstone Harbour: an almost landlocked estuary on the east side of Portsmouth, once noted for the hulks in which convicts bound for Van Diemen's Land (now Tasmania) were housed, now one of the finest winter waterfowl and wader haunts in southern England, especially for brent geese and both godwits.

Hayling Island: still has an interesting flora on its few unbuilt-on dunes.

The New Forest: in many ways the premier wildlife site south of the Thames, this former royal forest is partly wooded and partly heathland. **The oak and beech woods** have many rare and unusual animals and plants, including red, roe, fallow and sika deer, common and honey buzzards, hobbies, Lady Amherst's pheasants and unequalled butterflies and beetles, among them the rare silver-grey form of the silver-washed fritillary *Argynnis paphia*.

The heathlands cover extensive areas, grading in the shallow valleys into valley bogs. Their flora and fauna includes Dartford warbler, wild gladiolus *Gladiolus illyricus* and pale butterwort *Pinguicula lusitanica* almost at its eastern limit, but summer lady's tresses *Spiranthes aestivalis* is now extinct.

Beaulieu Abbey has more than a motor museum; on its ancient walls are Canterbury bell *Campanula medium*, winter savory *Satureja montana* and other unusual plants.

Hatchet Pond, Beaulieu, has a remarkable number of scarce and rare plants.

Sowley Pond: a place to see Hampshire purslane *Ludwigia palustris*, now confined to this area, but, it must be admitted, a rather dull plant.

The Hampshire Downs still have many good sites with typical chalk downland and beechwoods. In the south-east they are an extension of the South Downs of Sussex; in the south-west they run into the Dorset downs and Salisbury Plain; and in the north the border with Berkshire runs along the crest of the escarpment.

Old Winchester Hill: a NNR with a fine Iron Age camp. Rich chalk grassland, juniper scrub and woodland with yews.

Butser Hill: now a country park and the site of an interesting experiment on how Iron Age people actually lived.

Catherington Down: another interesting site north-west of Havant.

Steep: the woodlands around here are good for narrow-leaved helleborine *Cephalanthera longifolia*.

Martin Down: the best chalk site in the west of the county.

Selborne Hanger: a fine hanging beechwood made famous by its association with Gilbert White, the founder of the English tradition of field natural history, whose book 'The Natural History of Selborne' was first published in 1789. Some of the plants he mentioned are still growing in the same spots that he knew them.

Test and Itchen Valleys: many water meadows with their rich flora still survive in these famous (to fly fishermen) chalk-stream valleys.

Marwell Park: has a notable zoo, specialising in endangered species.

The Northern Heaths: the Greensand area of the north-east is continuous with the more famous Surrey heaths.

Alice Holt Forest: an ancient woodland, the site of the Forestry Commission's research station.

Frensham Great Pond: see Surrey.

Woolmer Forest: an area of heath, birchwoods and valley bogs surrounding Woolmer Pond and extending to the neighbourhood of White's Selborne.

WILTSHIRE

The county is substantially a large block of chalk, divided into three by the Vale of Pewsey and the upper Kennet valley, which carries the A4. Non-calcareous habitats occur only on the fringes. In the south it merges with the Hampshire and Dorset chalk; in the north with the Berkshire Downs.

The Chalk

Salisbury Plain: the largest stretch of undulating chalk country in England, mostly farmed or under military occupation, but wherever the plough has left a corner or a bank untouched and the tanks have not churned up the turf, a good chalk flora survives, e.g. around **Great Ridge Wood** and **White Sheet Hill**. Stone curlews and quail are among the interesting birds, and the Great Bustard Trust hopes to release great bustards into their ancient breeding haunts on the Plain before long.

Yarnbury Camp alongside the A303 west of Stonehenge, still has a very rich flora, including burnt-tip orchid *Orchis ustulata* and the local south-western dwarf sedge *Carex humilis*, which flowers in March.

Pewsey Downs: the steep chalk escarpment north of the Vale of Pewsey also supports a rich flora of lime-loving plants. Rising to 294m, the second highest altitude in the south-east half of England, at Milk Hill and Tan Hill, they are now partly a NNR.

Marlborough Downs: an extensive plateau with a good chalk flora and notable for the sarsen stones or grey wethers (wethers are male sheep, which at a distance they resemble), large chunks of siliceous sandstone from Tertiary deposits that have otherwise all weathered away; the best groups are in **Clatford Bottom**, where there are 25,000, and at **Fyfield Down NNR**. Many sarsens were used in the stone circles at Stonehenge and Avebury. The local round-headed rampion *Phyteuma orbiculare* grows on the chalky Avebury banks.

The Fringes

Fonthill Abbey: besides echoes of the eccentric William Beckford, has one of the tallest wellingtonias *Sequoiadendron giganteum* in England, at 165 ft.

Landford Common: one of the few remaining patches of heathland south-east of Salisbury, which used to form a northward extension of the New Forest.

Savernake Forest, south-east of Marlborough: an extensive ancient oakwood noted for its fine old trees and rich insect fauna.

Stourhead: perhaps the finest landscape garden in England, just west of Mere; many fine old trees and an ornamental lake.

Thames Valley: the floristically rich meadows of the upper Thames – most of which have long been agriculturally 'improved' – are the finest surviving localities for the handsome spring-flowering snakeshead fritillary *Fritillaria meleagris*, most notably at **Cricklade** (the North Meadow is a NNR) and **Minety**. **Coate Water** just outside Swindon (sorry, Thamesdown) was the favoured youthful haunt of the great Victorian writer and naturalist, Richard Jefferies.

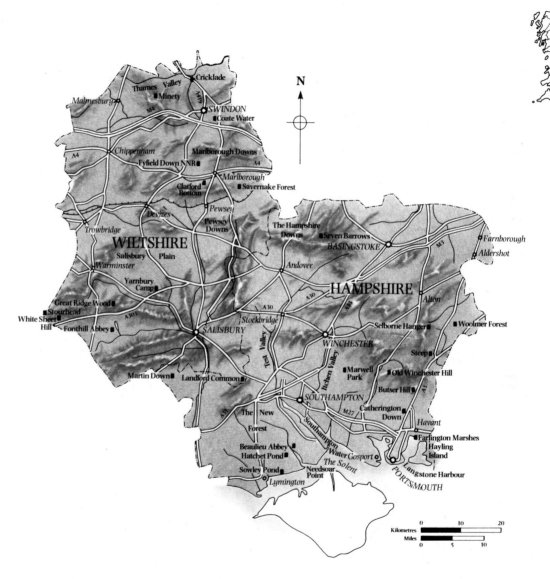

Surrey, Middlesex & Greater London, West Sussex

SURREY

As in Kent the chalk of the North Downs is sandwiched between the Wealden clays and sands in the south and the London Clay basin in the north. Much of what used to be Surrey is now in Greater London, but in return the county has received the Staines district of Middlesex.

The Weald

Leith Hill, at 294m the highest point in south east England, lies on the Greensand ridge, which provides much of the wildlife interest of the Surrey Weald; its extensive tracts of heath, bog and woodland have much heather *Calluna* and a good deal of bilberry *Vaccinium myrtillus,* whose fruits, known locally as 'hurts', name the great Hurtwood which once occupied most of the hills west of Leith Hill. The garden shrub Juneberry *Amelanchier lamarckii* is well naturalised in parts of the Hurtwood, e.g. near Peaslake.

Frensham Great Pond: an attractive natural water, with one corner in Hampshire, on the western edge of a fine range of heathlands that includes **Frensham, Hankley, Ockley and Thursley Commons** and the Devil's Jump at Churt. Frensham Little Pond is not much smaller. Smooth snakes, sand lizards, hobbies, nightjars, and in some years Dartford warblers occur. Cranberry *Vaccinium oxycoccos* is one of the many interesting bog plants to be found.

Haslemere Natural History Museum: one of the best natural history museums in Britain.

Holmwood Common: an extensive and well wooded Wealden common.

The North Downs

Quite narrow in Surrey, especially along the ridge of the **Hog's Back**

west of Guildford. They are extensively wooded and have numerous patches of good chalk turf, especially on the escarpment.

Newlands Corner: a well known beauty spot at the west end of the fine block of wooded hills between the Mole and the Wey, at the east end of which is **Ranmore Common.**

Box Hill: probably the best botanical site in Surrey, with its fine native boxwood on the cliff overlooking the River Mole – one of fewer than half a dozen such woods in Britain. The chalk turf has many good plants, which support a rich butterfly fauna, including chalkhill blue *Lysandra coridon* and silver-spotted skipper *Hesperia comma.* It was at Juniper Top at the back of Box Hill that the National Conservation Corps, forerunner of the British Trust for Conservation Volunteers, performed its first task, the clearing of dogwood, on February 29, 1960.

Juniper Hall: one of the first four field centres of the Field Studies Council.

Nower Wood: an educational centre of the Surrey Trust.

Headley and Walton Heaths: a fine stretch of acid heathland on the clay-with-flints that overlies the chalk, with breeding nightjars.

The London Basin

The London Clay itself always has rather dull wildlife, but the sandy deposits that overlie it, such as the Thanet Sands, produce a fine range of acid heaths and commons.

Bookham Common: one of the best of these commons – others are at Effingham, Ashtead and Epsom – which belongs to the National Trust. It has been studied for many years by members of the London Natural

History Society, and is one of the nearest places to London to hear a nightingale singing or a woodcock roding.

Staines Reservoirs: the most accessible of a group of reservoirs around Staines and Ashford much frequented by London birdwatchers. They have a public causeway, whereas most of the rest need a permit.

Staines Moor: one of the few stretches of meadow grassland in this part of the Thames valley that have not been dug for gravel, and so a continual Naboth's vineyard for the gravel companies.

Windsor Great Park and Virginia Water: see Berkshire, but the large heronry at Fort Belvedere is in Surrey.

Chobham Common: one of a group of acid heaths in north-west Surrey, now traversed by the M3, that share much of the interesting flora of the Greensand heaths in the south west.

Wisley: the Royal Horticultural Society's Gardens are among the finest in Britain. Close by are **Wisley and Ockham Commons,** acid heathland, and the Hut Pond, alongside the A3, all of some natural history interest.

MIDDLESEX & GREATER LONDON

London is surrounded by wooded, heathy and grassy open spaces, of which only a few of the more outstanding and relatively rural can be mentioned here.

Brent Reservoir: formerly, from its shape, called the Welsh Harp; still good for winter bird-watching and some unusual plants.

Bushy Park has a famous avenue of horse chestnuts; Chestnut Sunday is fixed on the mid-May day when they can be visited at their best.

Hampstead Heath and Ken Wood: the outstanding North London open space, with still some fine old beeches from the ancient Forest of Middlesex in Ken Wood.

Harrow Weald Common: a woodland open space with interesting birds and plants. Two more are **Scratch Wood** and **Stanmore Common.**

Inner London Parks, such as Hyde, Regent's and St. James's Park are essentially urban lungs, but their lakes are often good for birds, especially the Serpentine in Hyde Park and Kensington Gardens (where it is called the Long Water). On town park lakes many of the ornamental waterfowl are pinioned and so cannot fly.

Lea Valley Reservoirs: a string of artificial waters, Walthamstow, King George V and William Girling Reservoirs, much watched by London bird-watchers for winter wildfowl.

Walthamstow has a well known heronry, with 80–90 breeding pairs, which has now almost supplanted the ancient heronry in Wanstead Park; and a winter roost of over 100 cormorants.

Ruislip Reservoir: good for water birds. Much of the wildlife interest of the adjoining Poor's Field was recently destroyed by an insensitive local authority. **Park Wood** to the east and **Copse, Mad Bess and Bayhurst Woods** west of the reservoir are all good London clay oakwoods. Bayhurst Wood is a country park.

Ecological Park, Hays Wharf, London Bridge: a fascinating experiment in bringing nature to the people.

Mitcham Common: though much used by people, still has a good deal of botanical and other wildlife interest.

Richmond Park with its herds of red

and fallow deer and its Pen Ponds, and the adjacent **Wimbledon Common** and **Putney Heath** form the best block of wildlife habitat within ten miles of Central London.

Selsdon Wood: a good oakwood belonging to the National Trust.

WEST SUSSEX

The chalk of the South Downs is sandwiched between the varied parallel geological formations of the Weald, most of them forming acid or neutral soils, and the coastal plain, much of which is now built up.

The Coast: the beaches are shingle, with a few saltmarshes.

Chichester Harbour shares many of the characteristics of Langstone Harbour across the Hampshire border. Together with **Pagham Harbour** it is one of the best south-coast sites for brent geese and other wildfowl and waders, as well as saltmarsh plants.

The South Downs: the southern chalk still has many fine stretches of chalk grassland, with good orchids and other wild flowers, including in a few places early spider orchid *Ophrys sphegodes* and round-headed rampion *Phyteuma orbiculare*; also many excellent beechwoods.

Kingley Vale NNR: all stages in the development of woodland on chalk are represented, including open chalk grassland, scrub and the finest yew-wood in Europe.

Arundel Park: fine beechwoods, Swanbourne Lake with its 'blue pools' (the white chalk bottom seen through very clear blue water) and in the Arun valley close by one of the Wildfowl Trust's collections of exotic ducks, geese and swans.

Amberley Wild Brooks: a complex of low-lying water meadows and marshes in the floodplain of the Arun, with a number of scarce plants, including cut-grass *Leersia oryzoides*, which only flowers in hot summers.

Chanctonbury Ring: a clump of planted beeches that is a landmark over a wide area of the Weald.

The Weald: there are still so many fine oakwoods and heaths in the Weald that it is hard to pick out individual sites.

Ashdown Forest: see under East Sussex.

The Mens: a magnificent old oakwood, now a reserve of the Sussex Trust.

St Leonard's and Tilgate Forests: several good fragments of these once extensive Wealden oakwoods survive, one with a fine display of lily of the valley *Convallaria majalis*.

Wakehurst Place: an interesting arboretum and woodland garden run by the Royal Botanic Gardens, Kew.

Weirwood Reservoir, south of East Grinstead, shared with East Sussex: perhaps the best of the many small Sussex reservoirs and ornamental lakes for winter wildfowl.

Key to Greater London sites
1 Copse, Mad Bess and Bayhurst Woods
2 Park Wood
3 Ruislip Reservoir
4 Harrow Weald Common
5 Stanmore Common
6 Scratch Wood
7 Brent Reservoir
8 Hampstead Heath and Ken Wood
9 Inner London Parks
10 Bushy Park
11 Richmond Park
12 Putney Heath
13 Wimbledon Common
14 Lea Valley Reservoirs
15 Ecological Park
16 Mitcham Common
17 Selsdon Wood
18 Cuckoo Wood
19 Darwin's Orchid Bank, Downe

East Sussex, Kent

EAST SUSSEX

Unlike West Sussex both the Downs and the Weald come down to the sea, and there is much less coastal plain.

The Coast: the beaches are still shingle, but backed by chalk cliffs from Brighton to Eastbourne and by sand and clay cliffs at Hastings and Fairlight.

Cliffs from Brighton to Beachy Head: the longest stretch of chalk cliffs in Britain, backed by downs with a good chalk flora and a few rarities; the wildest part is from Seaford Head along the Seven Sisters to Beltout. Herring gulls and cormorants are the only nesting seabirds.

Cuckmere Haven: the only break in the chalk cliffs, with a few saltmarsh plants.

The Crumbles and Langney Point: a now somewhat degraded stretch of shingle east of Eastbourne.

Rye Harbour: an important stretch of shingle, with good plants and breeding terns, together with flooded gravel pits which are good for winter wildfowl; a local nature reserve.

Broomhill Level and the Midrips: the Sussex portion of Romney Marsh and Dungeness, for which see Kent.

The South Downs: see under West Sussex.

Devil's Dyke: a spectacular deep and steep ravine in the chalk escarpment north of Brighton.

Ditchling Beacon: another good stretch of downland at the back of Brighton.

Mount Caburn: one of the finest remaining sites for chalk plants; around here grows the scarce wild rose *Rosa agrestis*.

Lullington Heath NNR: one of the best examples of acid heath forming over the chalk, as a result of rain leaching the lime out of the soil. This 'chalk heath' has lime-hating plants like heather *Calluna* growing mixed with the typical chalk down plants.

The Weald: in the eastern Weald there are ghylls (small wooded ravines) where the microclimate is so warm and wet that several western plants, among them Cornish moneywort *Sibthorpia europaea* and ivy-leaved bellflower *Wahlenbergia hederacea* grow here at their eastern limit in Britain. So also do two ferns, hay-scented buckler fern *Dryopteris aemula* and Tunbridge filmy fern *Hymenophyllum tunbrigense*. Nightingales are fairly frequent.

Ashdown Forest, shared with West Sussex: a still quite extensive complex of oak and birch woodland and wet and dry heaths, with a herd of fallow deer.

Chailey Warren: a good wet heath with marsh gentian *Gentiana pneumonanthe*.

Eridge Park: a fine old park with ancient trees for hole-nesting birds, such as jackdaw, stockdove and redstart.

Heathfield: according to local tradition, the cuckoo is let out of a cage every year on the date of Heathfield Fair, April 14.

Weirwood reservoir: see under West Sussex.

KENT

In contrast to Sussex, in Kent chalk (the North Downs) provides the filling of the sandwich, whose outer layers are formed by the varied geology of the Weald in the south and the London Clay of the Thames and Medway marshes in the north, both layers having more acid soils. Kent is the most continental part of the British Isles and its chalk flora, in particular, is closely related to that of France, scarcely 20 miles east across the Strait of Dover.

The East Coast: the stretch of coast from Dungeness to the North Foreland has a remarkable wealth of wildlife, especially plants and insects.

Dungeness: an extensive shingle headland, unique in the British Isles and now sadly marred by two nuclear power stations. The shingle is bare in places, but its gradual build-up over the millennia can still be demonstrated and the whole range of vegetation succession up to a unique patch of holly scrub woodland still survives. The many rare and local plants include Nottingham catchfly *Silene nutans*. The breeding birds include terns and stone curlews, but no longer the Kentish plover. The **Open Pits** are excellent for migrant and winter water birds. There is a bird observatory at the point, which is good for both winter sea-watching and migration. In the west the area overlaps into Sussex, where the **Midrips** are shallow pools well known to bird-watchers.

Romney Marsh: to men of Kent this is the fifth continent– Europe, Asia, Africa, America and Romney Marsh – the vast expanse of marshland with its own breed of sheep is now almost all cultivated, but the many rhines and marsh drains, together with the Royal Military Canal, which separates it from the 'mainland' of Kent, are still rich in wildlife, including the introduced marsh frog *Rana ridibunda*.

Folkestone Warren: an area of landslipped cliffs, classical ground for butterfly and moth buffs, and with many local and interesting plants.

The Chalk Cliffs between Folkestone and Dover – the symbolic white cliffs of Albion visible from the Pas de Calais – together with those between the North and South Forelands: their chief wildlife interest is in the plants growing on their undercliffs, e.g. at St Margaret's Bay, such as ivy and carrot broomrapes *Orobanche hederae* and *O. maritima*, and in the excellent chalk flora on the cliff-tops, which represent the seaward end of the North Downs. Wild cabbage *Brassica oleracea* grows on the Dover Cliffs.

Sandwich Bay: the finest stretch of dunes in south-east England, with many special plants, such as bedstraw broomrape *Orobanche caryophyllacea* and good birds. A bird observatory is located here.

The Weald: a rich mixture of woods and heaths on often acid soils, with many interesting plants, such as Coralroot *Cardamine bulbifera* and often with nightingales.

Sevenoaks has two famous water-bird sites, **Sevenoaks Gravel Pit Reserve,** created by the late Jeffery Harrison and turned into one of the finest water-bird breeding sites in the south of England, and **Bough Beech Reservoir,** the best of the Kentish reservoirs for winter wildfowl.

Bedgebury Pinetum, run by the Royal Botanic Gardens, Kew, is the national collection of conifers.

Hothfield Common LNR: a good heathland reserve.

Ham Street Woods NNR: one of the first NNR's, renowned for its entomological interest.

The North Downs: much narrower in Kent than in Surrey, but broaden out eastwards where they meet the sea. Chalk flora very good, including many unusual orchids: both spider orchids, *Ophrys sphegodes* and *O. fuciflora*, grow in the grassland, together with man orchid *Aceras anthropophorum* commoner than anywhere else in Britain, and in one or two secret localities the once almost extinct monkey orchid *Orchis simia*. The beechwoods have lady orchid *O. purpurea*, almost confined to Kent, and often in abundance. The best chalk grassland lies on the Surrey border, from Wrotham to Halling, between Wouldham to Hollingbourne, around Wye, and along the coastal cliffs.

Boxley: the box grove may be native.

Darwin's Orchid Bank, Downe: where the great man studied orchid pollination, now a reserve of the Kent Trust. **Cuckoo Wood** nearby is a fine beechwood.

Queendown Warren: very rich in chalk flora.

Wye and Crundale Downs NNR: another splendid site, where the rare milkwort *Polygala amarella* grows among many other good chalk plants.

Yockletts Bank: good for both chalk grassland and beechwood flora, including lady orchid.

Thanet and the Blean
This north-east corner of Kent is crammed with wildlife interest, and was the last known location of the now extinct black-veined white butterfly *Aporia crataegi*.

Stodmarsh and the lower Stour valley: the only area in south-east England that can challenge the best East Anglian sites for its birds: breeding bearded tits, bitterns and Savi's warblers and the largest population of the new invader, Cetti's warbler. It was originally a mining subsidence.

Blean Woods: a remarkable group of oakwoods, including a NNR and a RSPB reserve, noted for its unusual combination of sessile oak and

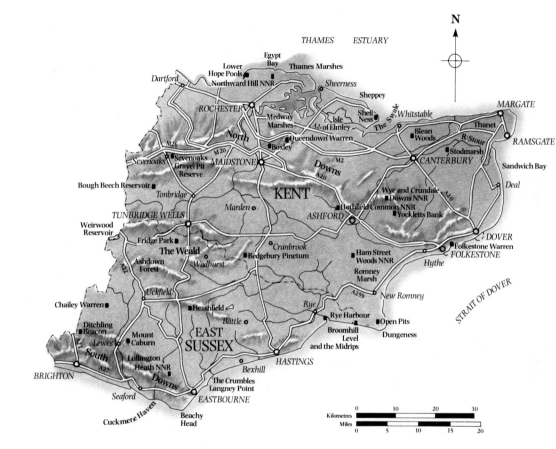

hornbeam, and several rare insects, among them the heath fritillary butterfly *Mellicta athalia*.

Thames and Medway Marshes, Sheppey and the Swale
The whole coastline, one of the few north-facing ones in England is good both for saltmarsh plants and for breeding and wintering birds,

especially at the **Lower Hope Pools, Egypt Bay** and the **Isle of Elmley** in Sheppey.

Northward Hill NNR, High Halstow: the grey heronry here is the largest in Europe.

Shell Ness: at the east end of Sheppey, the gathering point of waders when the mudflats are covered at high tide.

Gloucestershire & North Avon, Hereford & Worcester, Warwicks

GLOUCESTERSHIRE & NORTH AVON

A county that is neatly divided in two by the Cotswold escarpment, east of which all is oolitic limestone, with more acid rocks, except for the Carboniferous limestone of the Avon Gorge and Wye valley lying to the west.

Cotswolds

Comparatively little remains of the vast open sheepwalks that helped to make England the main source of wool for Europe in the Middle Ages, but on the escarpment are still some open stretches of limestone grassland, as at **Crickley Hill**, Birdlip, **Dover's Hill**, Chipping Campden; and **Haresfield** and **Painswick Beacons**, the first three all belonging to the National Trust, which also has the commons of **Littleworth, Minchinhampton** and **Rodborough** up the valleys around Stroud.

Beechwoods are also largely confined to the escarpment, the best being **Buckholt, Cranham** and **Witcombe Woods**, south of Cheltenham, and some further east around the **Chedworth** Roman villa. Both woods and grassland still have an excellent flora, including some rarities, such as angular Solomon's seal *Polygonatum odoratum* in the woods.

Boxwell has a possibly native boxwood.

The **Cotswold Farm Park**, Guiting Power, specialises in rare breeds of domestic animals.

The **Cotswold Water Park**, near Kemble, is too heavily used for recreation to be really good for waterfowl.

Westonbirt Arboretum has the best collection of temperate trees in the world.

Avon Gorge

Really a part of the Mendips (see Somerset) this spectacular viewpoint and famous botanical site has four plants found nowhere else in Britain, round-headed leek *Allium sphaero-cephalon*, Bristol rock-cress *Arabis stricta* and two white beams *Sorbus*, together with a number of other rare and local species.

Durdham Down: the best individual site.

Severn estuary and Vale of Berkeley

The **Severn estuary** has the second largest tidal range in the world, after the Bay of Fundy in eastern Canada, and the resultant bore is a magnificent sight at spring tides at Quedgeley and other places below Gloucester. Some interesting saltmarshes still border the estuary's extensive mudflats.

Ashleworth Ham, Tewkesbury: a fine water meadow with some unusual plants.

Badgeworth nature reserve consists largely of a small pond, one of only two British sites for the rare buttercup *Ranunculus ophioglossifolius*.

Slimbridge, where Sir Peter Scott founded his Wildfowl Trust in 1946, is now the home of the most famous of all wildfowl collections. Besides the almost complete collection of the ducks, geese and swans of the world, there are also in winter the old-established flock of wild white-fronted geese and the newly acquired assembly of Bewick's swans. The **Tortworth Chestnut** is a relic of a giant tree mentioned in Domesday Book.

Forest of Dean

West of the Severn the ground rises nearly 1000 ft to May Hill and to the Dean Forest, one of the great medieval forests of England that still survives, despite many conifers, as fine stretches of durmast oakwood. Here too individual coal mines still survive from the days when 'sea coal' was regarded as a dangerous innovation in cities such as London and Bristol, whose citizens justifiably resented its smoke.

Nagshead Plantation: one of the many Dean woodlands where pied flycatchers can be found nesting, along with the two other characteristic western woodland species, redstart and wood warbler.

Dymock and **Newent** are the centre of an area where wild daffodils *Narcissus pseudonarcissus* grow more abundantly than anywhere else in Britain, except perhaps North Yorkshire. They have also been imaginatively planted on the banks of the Ross Spur motorway.

Symonds Yat: a well known viewpoint in the Wye valley, where the Carboniferous limestone reappears and supports an interesting flora, including several rare white beams *Sorbus*. See also Herefordshire.

HEREFORD & WORCESTER

Two ancient counties, now joined together, consisting mainly of the lower reaches of the rivers Severn, Avon, Wye, Teme, Lugg and a few others, and verging in the west on the hills of Wales.

Herefordshire

In the west includes part of the **Black Mountains,** the eastern extension of the Welsh hills, whose moorlands hold red grouse and ring ouzels, and in the east the main part of the grassy and heathy **Malvern Hills,** whose distinctive outline heralds the West Country for those descending the Cotswold escarpment. Buzzards often soar over the hills west of Hereford. The **Wye Valley,** shared with Gloucestershire, has important outcrops of limestone, especially at **Great and Little Dowards,** with an interesting flora that includes both green and stinking hellebores *Helleborus viridis* and *H. foetidus,* columbine *Aquilegia vulgaris* and several uncommon sedges. Many of the great old Border oakwoods have now been replanted with conifers. In the south-east the wild daffodil area of Gloucestershire overlaps into the county.

Worcestershire

In the north-west is the fine old oakwood of **Wyre Forest,** shared with Shropshire, and further east are many sandy commons and grassy hilltops, such as **Castlemorton** and **Hartlebury Commons, Kinver Edge** and **Clent, Lickey and Walton Hills.**

In the south-east the county just reaches the Cotswolds at **Broadway Hill** and the outlying mass of **Bredon Hill,** where elements of the Cotswold limestone flora may be found.

Parts of the **Severn valley** still hold marsh warblers and good old meadows with a rich natural flora, including meadow saffron *Colchicum autumnale.* Brackish springs and pools, especially in the **Salwarpe valley** and around **Droitwich,** which has a well known spa, provide a surprising maritime element to the flora, including wild celery *Apium graveolens* and lesser sea spurrey *Spergularia marina.*

In the fringe of Birmingham are some reservoirs noted for winter wildfowl, such as **Bartley, Bittell and Cofton.** The **Wren's Nest** at Dudley, a NNR with famous fossil exposures, is now well engulfed in the West Midland conurbation.

Whitty pear or service tree *Sorbus domestica*: a famous tree grew for many years in the Wyre Forest, and a direct descendant, now more than 40 ft high, now grows on the same site.

WARWICKSHIRE

Another lowland county, almost entirely agricultural away from Birmingham and Coventry, but with contrasts north/south instead of Worcestershire's east/west.

Sutton Park: perhaps the outstanding area, in the north, where northern flora begins to appear among the heaths and woodlands.

In the south, around **Shipston-on-Stour** on the edge of the Cotswolds, the limy grassland brings southern forms.

The most notable freshwater sites are **Alvecote Pools, Coleshill Pool, Earlswood Lakes, Shustoke Reservoir** and **Wootton Pool.**

Charlecote Park, near Stratford on Avon, where the youthful Shakespeare poached deer, still has more than a hundred of both red and fallow deer.

Edge Hill: a noted wooded escarpment, the site of a famous Civil War battle.

Tile Hill Wood, Coventry: a good urban nature reserve.

Berkshire, Oxfordshire

BERKSHIRE
A county which has recently lost its north west portion to Oxfordshire; the remainder divides fairly neatly into a mainly calcareous west with the chalk downs, and a mainly sandy or gravelly east with acid soils. As with the other Home Counties, a substantial proportion is either cultivated or built on.

The Thames Valley
Cock Marsh (National Trust), north of Cookham: the best remaining site for valley grassland, overlooked by **Winter Hill** (largely a golf course) and various other NT properties, stretching as far west as **Maidenhead Thicket**, which has now lost most of its former wildlife interest.
Windsor Great Park, partly in Surrey, still has many fine old oaks.
Virginia Water and **Great Meadow and Obelisk Ponds** are all good for waterfowl, including the introduced mandarin duck from China, which nests in tree-holes around ponds and lakes in woodland.

East Berks Heaths and Commons
Burghfield or Wokefield Common: probably the best of a group of pine and heather heaths south of Reading. Good for birds, such as nightjar and tree pipit.
Englemere Pond, Ascot: interesting plants and freshwater invertebrates.
Finchampstead Ridges: an attractive pine and heather area belonging to the National Trust.
Heath Pond nearby is an interesting acid pool.
The Loddon Valley still has a number of sites for the local speciality summer snowflake *Leucojum aestivum* as well as the Loddon pondweed *Potamogeton nodosus*.

Padworth Gully: well known for rare sedges and other interesting plants.

Kennet Valley
Marshes and reedbeds along the valley, notably at **Thatcham, Theale and Aldermaston,** are very rich entomologically, and also good for birds, such as reed, sedge and Cetti's warbler's.
Bucklebury Commons: a group of heathy commons.
Inkpen Common: an interesting common in the extreme south of Berks, with the easternmost pale dog violets *Viola lactea* in Britain.
Snelsmore Common, north of Newbury has many good bog and wet heath plants, such as sundews *Drosera*, bogbean *Menyanthes trifoliata* and bog asphodel *Narthecium ossifragum*. It is now a country park.

Berkshire Downs
Now partly in Oxfordshire: very largely ploughed, but some chalk grassland remains on the escarpment, where the **Ridge Way** and the **Fair Mile** have some good chalk plants along their verges.
White Horse Hill, Uffington: perhaps the best remaining stretch of chalk turf that is readily accessible to the public (some others in private ownership are managed by BBONT). The famous hill figure is visible for miles around; some of the best plants are in the steep-sided 'manger' at its foot.
Inkpen Beacon and Walbury Hill: really a part of the Hampshire chalk, right on the county boundary; at 297m Walbury is the highest point in Berks.
Sarsens (see under Wilts) occur only in Ashdown Park and on Parkfarm Downs.
Seven Barrows, near Lambourn, has some good chalk turf.

OXFORDSHIRE
One of the most calcareous counties in England, with the largely basic Oxford clay and associated formations filling the sandwich between the chalk of the Chilterns and the oolitic limestone of the Cotswolds. Heather *Calluna* is a rare plant in Oxfordshire and bell heather *Erica cinerea* almost unknown.

The Oxfordshire Chilterns
As usual in the Chilterns, chalk grassland is found only on the steeper slopes, unsuitable for ploughing, and most of these are on the escarpment, which flattens out considerably south of Ewelme. The plateau is largely covered with clay-with-flints and wooded, mainly with beech planted in the 18th and 19th centuries for the High Wycombe chair trade. Many sites, both woodland and grassland, have good flora and insect fauna, and with the adjoining part of Bucks the area is noted for its three nationally rare orchids: military, monkey and ghost, *Orchis militaris*, *O. simia* and *Epipogium aphyllum*.
Chinnor Hill: a BBONT reserve, with a fine view out over the Vale of Aylesbury; still with some good juniper.
Beacon Hill: part of the Aston Rowant NNR, with a good nature trail through chalk grassland and scrub; marred only by the M40, which is the only motorway ever allowed to be driven through the middle of a national nature reserve.
Watlington Hill: a National Trust property with some fine old yews and good chalk plants.
Swyncombe Down: perhaps the best site in Oxfordshire for the plants of chalk turf, especially on the old earthwork.

The Thames Valley
The meadows by the Thames above Oxford, and especially above New Bridge, still have a wonderful air of remoteness, since mercifully the Thames floods have always prevented major roads following the line of the river. Below Oxford Loddon lily *Leucojum aestivum* grows in several places, e.g. at Nuneham Courtenay.
Buscot Park: a National Trust property with a heronry.
Wytham Woods, overlooking the wide curve of the river above Oxford, have a remarkable mosaic of woodland and limestone grassland habitats, and thanks to the pioneer work of Charles Elton have probably been studied more intensively (by Oxford University biologists) than any other area in Britain of comparable size.
Magdalen Meadow, Oxford: famous for its fritillaries *Fritillaria meleagris*; by the Cherwell, in the grounds of Magdalen College, which also has a park with fallow deer. Another well known fritillary meadow at **Iffley** is now a BBONT reserve.
Shotover Plain: a wooded escarpment east of Oxford.
Dorchester Gravel Pits: good for winter bird watching; another good group is at **Stanton Harcourt** and the best of all is **Farmoor Reservoir**, south-west of Oxford.
Hartslock Woods: a fine hanging woodland above the river between Whitchurch and Goring, with some good yews; next door is a small BBONT reserve with very good chalk plants and butterflies.

The Vales of Oxford and White Horse
Waterperry Wood: an interesting oak-wood with much wild service tree *Sorbus torminalis*, partly a forest nature reserve.

Otmoor: formerly an extensive marsh, now largely drained, but around the edges are still some meadows with good sedges and other plants, as well as butterflies.

Port Meadow and the Meads: two grassland areas north-west of Oxford, which have been managed in the same way for a millennium or more. Port Meadow is grazed, but the Meads (Oxey, Pixey and Yarnton) are cut for hay on an ancient system in which strips are reallocated each year. When a visiting American asked Oxford historian F. W. Maitland to show him the oldest thing in Oxford, Maitland took him down to Port Meadow.

Cothill Fen and Parsonage Moor: a famous wetland site, part of which forms the Ruskin Memorial Reserve, with many interesting orchids and other plants; world famous for the population of scarlet tiger moths *Panaxia dominula*, by studying which E. B. Ford was able to pioneer the science of ecological genetics.

Dry Sandford Pit: a disused sandpit with some limestone grassland and an incipient fen which supports an abundance of orchids and variegated horsetail *Equisetum variegatum*, which is rare in the south.

The Cotswolds

Oxfordshire has only a small corner of the Cotswolds proper, around Burford, but similar soils and vegetation extend north to Banbury, in the few places where they have not been ploughed.

Blenheim Park has some fine old oaks, and good water birds on its lake, which is the dammed steep-sided valley of the R. Glyme.

Cherwell Valley: near Somerton are some water meadows with interesting flora and, when they flood in winter, water birds, often including wild swans.

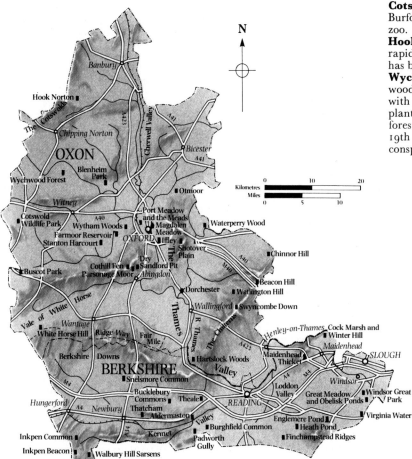

Cotswold Wildlife Park, south of Burford: an interesting small open-air zoo.

Hook Norton: a disused railway line, rapidly growing into a small oakwood, has become a BBONT reserve.

Wychwood Forest: one of the richest woodland areas in southern England, with good birds and many uncommon plants; all that is left of an extensive forest that was disafforested in the mid 19th century, leaving Leafield church conspicuous on its windswept hilltop.

Buckinghamshire, Bedfordshire, Hertfordshire, Northamptonshire

BUCKINGHAMSHIRE
Like so many English counties, Bucks divides into three: the chalk of the Chilterns in the south, the varied soils of the Vale of Aylesbury in the middle and the limestone of north Bucks. Again like Oxfordshire, it is almost entirely calcareous.

The Chilterns
Bucks forms the core of the Chilterns and is especially noted for its many fine beechwoods, with some good patches and even stretches of chalk turf surviving, mainly on the escarpment. In the south some acid soils overlie the chalk, notably around Burnham Beeches.

Wraysbury Gravel Pits: winter wildfowl, including one-fifth of the British wintering smew, a large flock of Canada geese and a cormorant roost.

Burnham Beeches and East Burnham Common: saved for the public by the City of London Corporation, and noted for fine old pollard beeches; some of the best acid-soil flora remaining in Bucks.

Black Park and the RSPB's **Church Wood**, Hedgerley, are outliers.

Hodgemoor Wood, Seer Green: an oak/birch wood with some acid-loving plants.

The Chiltern Open Air Museum, Newland Park, Chalfont St. Giles, mainly covers architecture, crafts and history.

Hog and Hollow Wood between Marlow and Medmenham: one of a group of excellent beechwoods on the edge of the Thames valley, with some very interesting plants. The others are Davenport and Pullingshill Woods.

Moorend Common between Frieth and Lane End: interesting plants of neutral and slightly acid soils.

Lodge Hill: good for wild candytuft

Iberis amara and other chalk plants.

Grange Lands: good chalk scrub and grassland above Monks Risborough, adjoining the Chequers estate, which has one of our very few native boxwoods in two steep-sided coombes above Great Kimble.

Coombe Hill: a very popular National Trust property, good for juniper and other scrub, chalk turf and heathy habitat on the clay-with-flints.

Pitstone to Ivinghoe: the most extensive series of chalk hills in the Chilterns that have been neither afforested nor ploughed; includes Pitstone Hill, Steps Hill and **Ivinghoe Beacon**, and adjoins the Ashridge estate in Herts.

The Vale of Aylesbury
A fine stretch of largely unspoiled traditional English farming countryside.

Bernwood Forest: an oakwood with an extremely rich butterfly fauna and good for plants, including wild service tree *Sorbus torminalis*.

Weston Turville Reservoir: an outlier of the Tring group (see Herts), sometimes with good winter wildfowl and migrant birds.

Boarstall Decoy: one of three or four remaining working duck decoys in Britain, now run for research purposes by BBONT.

Calvert Jubilee Pit: a flooded claypit close to the Calvert brickworks; good for wildfowl, a winter gull roost.

Brickhills Greensand Area: still has patches of heathy vegetation; muntjac and Lady Amherst's pheasants, escaped from Woburn Park next door in Beds, are not uncommon in the woods.

The Northern Limestone
The Bucks sector of the oolitic band that crosses England from the Humber to the Severn is now mostly under

cultivation. The new city of Milton Keynes also occupies a substantial slice, but the old market town of Olney, made famous by the poet Cowper, remains one of the gems of the southern Midlands.

Great Linford Gravel Pits: an interesting group between Stony Stratford and Newport Pagnell, the home of a colony of feral greylag geese and with a winter gull roost.

Stony Stratford Conservation Area: an interesting experiment in the creation of an urban wetland nature reserve, managed by BBONT for the Milton Keynes New Town Corporation.

Foxcote Reservoir: good for winter wildfowl, which can be seen from the public road; also has a gull roost.

Salcey Forest: see Northants.

BEDFORDSHIRE
Another largely calcareous county, continuing the pattern of Bucks, with chalk downs in the south, limestone in the north (almost all under cultivation) and only a strip of Greensand in between to diversify the flora with acid-loving plants.

Dunstable Downs: one of the best remaining stretches of chalk grassland; others are Totternhoe Knolls, Sharpenhoe Clappers, Barton Hills, Galley and Warden Hills and Deacon Hill.

Woburn Park lies on the Greensand and in the woods in and around it muntjac deer and both golden and Lady Amherst's pheasants may sometimes be seen. Chinese water deer roam the open grasslands of the park, but are not often seen outside.

Heath and Reach: a very large sand martin colony, 375 nests, in a sandpit.

Flitwick Moor: an interesting valley fen, ranging from birch and alder carr to oakwood.

Stewartby Claypits: perhaps the best wildfowl resort in the county; others are the gravel pits at Felmersham and in the Ouse valley between Sandy and Wyboston. Feral greylag geese breed at several pits in north Beds.

Sandy Warren: the RSPB headquarters on the Greensand lies in the middle of an interesting wooded and heathy area, with some excellent nature trails.

Zoos
Bedfordshire is lucky in having two of Britain's most outstanding outdoor wildlife collections: Whipsnade Zoo and Woburn Safari Park, the one noted for its herd of white rhinos, the other for its Père David's deer, a species which has long been extinct in the wild.

HERTFORDSHIRE
Except in the south, where it dips under the London clay, chalk underlies most of Hertfordshire. In the south west, which is a continuation of the Chilterns of Bucks and Oxon, the chalk is largely covered by clay-with-flints, but to the east of Hitchin this is replaced by a thick layer of chalky boulder-clay.

Tring Reservoirs NNR: a classic site for breeding and migrating water birds, with a small heronry; being canal reservoirs, not for drinking water, they do not have all-concrete banks.

Ashridge estate and Berkhamsted Common: the wildest piece of the Hertfordshire Chilterns, with good oak and beech woodland, including **Frithsden Beeches** and some heathy patches.

Oughtonhead Common: an interesting area of fen and marshy grassland west of Hitchin.

Royston and Therfield Heaths: the

best surviving patch of chalk grassland, noted for pasque flower *Pulsatilla vulgaris* and spotted catsear *Hypochaeris maculata*.

Wormley and Broxbourne Woods: the best of a group of oak-hornbeam woods, the oaks being sessile or durmast oaks *Quercus petraea*, more usually found in the west, and the hornbeams coppiced, rare elsewhere except in Essex and east Kent. **Blackfan Wood,** Baybury, is another of the group.

Northaw Great Wood: an interesting piece of deciduous woodland, where woodcock still rode.

Bricket Wood Scrubs: an unusually large patch of scrub woodland, with an interesting insect fauna.

Rothamsted Experimental Station, Harpenden: a patch of the Broadbalk Field was left unploughed in the mid 19th century and has now grown into an oakwood, in a classic demonstration of ecological succession.

Stockers Lake: the largest of a group of flooded gravelpits in the Colne valley that stretch north to **Hamper Mill** and are good for winter bird-watching. In this area the normally maritime dittander *Lepidium latifolium* is established in several places.

Oxhey Woods: an interesting oakwood sandwiched between Watford and Northwood.

NORTHAMPTONSHIRE

Another county whose main botanical interest lies in its limestone soils, being a north-eastward extension of the Cotswolds, linking them to the Lincolnshire limestone, but which is predominantly agricultural, with some outliers of the old industrial Midlands. The stone villages are mostly built of a warmer brown limestone than those of the Cotswolds; Aynho in the extreme

south-west is noted for the apricot trees trained up many house walls.

Woodlands: once almost entirely forested, the county now has only fragments of the great oak forests of Rockingham in the north and Salcey, Whittlewood and Yardley Chase in the south. **Salcey Forest** has a small nature reserve. Where old blackthorn bushes survive there is still a good chance of seeing the very local black hairstreak butterfly.

Fresh Water: the numerous reservoirs and flooded gravel pits give good sport for the winter bird-watcher. **Pitsford** and **Stanford Reservoirs** and **Thrapston** gravel pits are a somewhat arbitrary selection.

Country Parks: Barnwell, Daventry, Irchester.

Cambridgeshire & Huntingdonshire, Essex

CAMBRIDGESHIRE AND HUNTINGDONSHIRE

Modern Cambridgeshire is an amalgam of four small old counties (Cambridgeshire, Huntingdonshire, Isle of Ely and Soke of Peterborough) and comprises the bulk of the ancient fenland with its western and south-eastern fringes of low uplands. The rich soils of the drained peat fens make this one of the most cultivated parts of Britain.

The Western Fringe

Along the western 'shore' of the fenland runs the 'seaward end' of the scarplands of south central England, from the Greensand at Gamlingay, north through the Oxford clay in Huntingdonshire to the oolitic limestones of the Soke of Peterborough, the north-eastern terminus of the Cotswolds.

Ailsworth Heath and Castor Hanglands NNR: in the heart of the John Clare country, the most important remaining patch of semi-natural vegetation in the oolite north and east of the Cotswolds, until recently a well known habitat of the chequered skipper butterfly *Carterocephalus palaemon*. The nearby **Hills and Holes** at Barnack, a NNR, are the grassy spoil heaps of an old limestone quarry, with good calcareous plants. **Bedford Purlieus** is a good ash/oak wood on the oolite.

Grafham Water: now the best waterfowl site on the west side of the county.

Monks Wood, Abbots Ripton: a famous ancient oakwood on the Oxford clay, exceptionally rich in both flora and insects. Has a well known research station, which is the head-quarters of the Institute for Terrestrial Ecology.

The Fenland

Once almost an inland sea, especially during the winter floods, the Fens were drained for agriculture between the mid 17th and mid 19th centuries, and now only a few carefully cherished fragments remain of the plant, fish and bird communities that once provided a good living for numerous thatchers, fishermen and fowlers.

Borough Fen Decoy: one of three or four remaining active duck decoys in Britain, now run by the Wildfowl Trust for scientific instead of, as formerly, commercial purposes. The Trust also has a good collection of captive wildfowl at **Peakirk** nearby.

Chippenham Fen NNR: an important site on the eastern fringe of the Fens.

Holme Fen NNR: now largely grown up to birchwood (crossed by the main King's Cross to Scotland railway) and containing a post which shows that the peat surface has shrunk by 12 ft, due to oxidation of the wholly organic soil, since Whittlesey Mere, five miles to the north, was drained in 1851. The post was an iron column from the old Crystal Palace.

Ouse Washes: marshy meadows between the Old and New Bedford Rivers (the main device for draining the Fens), which have become a top-class bird reserve both in the breeding season and in winter. The best viewpoint is from the Wildfowl Trust's reserve at Welney, just inside Norfolk.

Wicken Fen: the best known remaining fragment of the undrained fen, the first nature reserve owned by the National Trust.

Woodwalton Fen NNR: the second most important patch of fenland, with its own special rare plants and a reintroduced stock of large copper butterflies *Lycaena dispar*.

The South-Eastern Chalk Ridge

The south-eastern 'shore' of the Fenland is an extension of the Chilterns, the chalk being covered in many places by a thick layer of boulder clay. It is traversed by England's ancient main highway, the Icknield Way (which also runs at the foot of the Chilterns), across which, some time in the Dark Ages, were constructed the **Devil's Dyke** and **Fleam Dyke**, now both important habitats for chalk-loving plants. Many of the woods in this area contain the true oxlip *Primula elatior*.

Gog Magog Hills: chalk hills just south-east of Cambridge, with still some stretches of open grassland, sometimes with good displays of perennial flax *Linum anglicum*.

Hayley Wood: a good oxlip wood, now one of the best understood woods in Britain, thanks to the detailed research of Dr Oliver Rackham and the hard work of members of the Cambridgeshire and Isle of Ely Naturalists' Trust.

ESSEX

A largely arable county, whose main wildlife interest lies on the coast, with little original turf remaining on the outcrop of chalk in the north west.

The Thames Estuary

Ducks and waders occur in fair, sometimes large numbers from East Tilbury downwards.

Aveley-Wennington Marshes: an immense rubbish disposal area, the happy hunting ground of botanists interested in aliens.

Rainham Marsh: good for waders; ruffs often winter there.

Grays has a large chalkpit with several uncommon plants.

South Ockendon: ivy-leaved toadflax *Cymbalaria muralis* still grows on the walls where it was originally introduced to Britain by William Coys in the early 17th century. It has now spread to walls almost everywhere.

Leigh Marsh: the nearest brent goose flock to London.

Great Wakering: the driest place in Britain, with only 17 in. of rain a year, an amount scarcely exceeded in many semi-desert areas of the world.

Foulness has some fine saltmarshes and brent geese, but is still closed to the public by the Ministry of Defence.

The Coast

Much indented by the estuaries of the Roach, Crouch, Blackwater, Colne, Hamford Water and Stour, most of them with good saltmarshes, waders and wildfowl, including brent geese.

Bridgemarsh Island, Crouch estuary: a saltmarsh reserve.

Blackwater estuary and Dengie Flats: especially good for brent geese.

Northey Island is a good saltmarsh reserve of the Essex Trust.

Bradwell on Sea: site of a small bird observatory.

Abberton Reservoir: one of the top wildfowl resorts in Britain, with a duck ringing station run by the Wildfowl Trust.

Fingringhoe Wick: a reserve of the Essex Trust, with an excellent information centre.

Copperas Bay, Stour estuary: a saltmarsh reserve of the RSPB, good for waders.

Inland Essex

The Lea Valley from Waltham Abbey northwards has numerous flooded gravelpits that are much watched by London birdwatchers for winter wildfowl.

Epping Forest: one of London's

principal lungs, saved for the public by the City Corporation in the mid 19th century; famous for its ancient pollard hornbeams and old established herd of dark fallow deer, believed to have been introduced 450 years ago.

Hatfield Forest: remains of another ancient forest, now owned by the National Trust, with some areas of coppiced hornbeam.

Hales Wood NNR and Quendon Wood: two of the remaining oxlip *Primula elatior* woods of north west Essex, a southward extension of the larger oxlip area in Cambridgeshire.

Hanningfield Reservoir: another first-class reservoir for winter wildfowl, also, like most other large Essex reservoirs, with a large winter gull roost.

Danbury Common and Woodham Walter Common: two of the best of the heathy and wooded Essex commons on the low hills in eastern Essex, whose elevation of 100m or so is popularly supposed to be the highest point eastwards to the Urals. Woodham Walter has oak/hornbeam woodland and a bog.

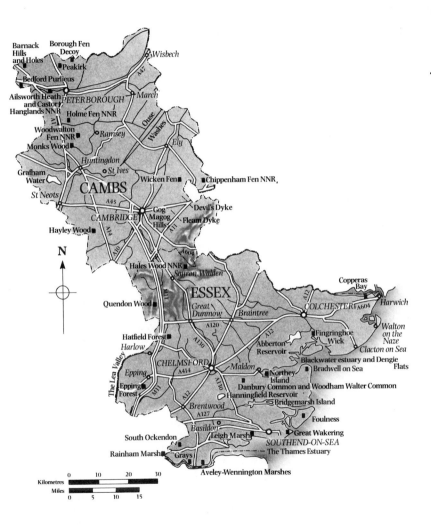

East Anglia

EAST ANGLIA (Norfolk, Suffolk)
The richest region of England for wildlife, with one unique area, the Breckland of south west Norfolk and north west Suffolk, a magnificent low-lying coast of dunes and shingle, the Norfolk Broads and in between them one of the most quintessentially agricultural countrysides in Britain.

Breckland
A remarkable stretch of sandy heathland, supporting, as a result of its continental climate, the campion *Silene otites* and several other plants found nowhere else in Britain. It has been extensively planted with conifers, so that Thetford Forest is now one of our largest coniferous forests, but some important patches of open grassy heath, both calcareous and acidic, remain, e.g. **Cavenham Heath, Horn and Weather Heaths, Thetford Heath** and **Lakenheath Warren** in Suffolk, and **East Wretham** and **Weeting Heaths** in Norfolk. **Wangford Warren,** Suffolk, is a remarkable area of inland sand dunes. These heaths and the sandy arable fields around them, together with the conifer forests and lines of old pines along the roads and field borders, are noted for three special breeding birds: stone curlew, ringed plover and crossbill. In addition there are a number of shallow meres, which often dry out in summer, including **Langmere, Ringmere and Fowlmere,** which are always good for waterfowl, such as the very local gadwall, and have good plants as well. **Scoulton Mere,** with its black-headed gullery, and **Hingham Sea Mere,** which is nowhere near the sea, lie just to the north of the Breckland proper. **Roydon Common,** Norfolk, on a northward extension of the breck

sands, is a particularly rich mosaic of habitats with many uncommon plants. **Dersingham Heath,** further north still, has a fine bog.

High Norfolk and Deep Suffolk
Only the extreme richness of the rest of East Anglia could make the agricultural uplands seem dull, for they do in fact have many choice sites, such as the ancient Norfolk woodlands of **Swanton Novers**, with may lily *Maianthemum* and Wayland Wood with its echoes of the babes-in-the-wood folk-tale, and in Suffolk **Wolves Wood, Bradfield Woods** near Bury St. Edmunds with their medieval management regime still intact, and the reverted deer park of **Staverton Forest** with the extraordinary old hollies in The Thicks. The rivers that cross the area still have several important valley fens, notably along the Yare, Waveney, Wissey and Ouse. The outstanding sites are **Lapham and Redgrave** Fens in Suffolk with their rare raft spider *Dolomedes plantarius*, the largest British spider, and **Surlingham** and **Wheatfen** on the Yare in Norfolk.
Norfolk Wildlife Park at Great Witchingham, with the Pheasant Trust's collections, and the **Otter Trust** at Earsham, Suffolk, are two notable places to visit.

The Broads
This group of flooded medieval peat diggings in the Bure valley still has an outstanding assemblage of uncommon and rare wild animals and plants, despite the ravages of pollution and eutrophication from the surrounding farmlands. The major sites are **Horsey Mere** and the Broads of **Alderfen, Barton, Hickling, Ranworth and Sutton,** but all the broads are interesting, with the possibility of

encountering bearded tit, bittern, marsh harrier and garganey, among other unusual birds, as well as otters, swallow-tail butterflies and numerous winter waterfowl.

The Coast
The Wash to Weybourne: the low-lying northern coast of Norfolk, broken only by the red chalk cliffs of Hunstanton, has many important stretches of saltmarsh, sand dune and shingle, notably **Holme Marshes, Scolt Head Island, Burnham Overy dunes, Blakeney Point** and **Cley Marshes.** Scolt and Blakeney have well known terneries and the whole coast is full of avid bird-watchers during the spring and autumn migrations. Common seals can often be seen off Blakeney Point. Immediately behind the coast are such important sites as **Holkham Park,** with its colony of Egyptian geese, **Kelling and Salthouse Heaths,** still good for nightjars, and an interesting heath and woodland area at **Holt Lowes** with good plants.
Sheringham to Yarmouth: from Sheringham to Happisburgh (pronounced 'Haisbro') the low cliffs, with nesting fulmars, are in many places crumbling into the sea, with both houses and roads at risk. From Happisburgh to Great Yarmouth there are dunes, often with sea buckthorn *Hippophaë* scrub, including the **Winterton Dunes NNR.**
The Suffolk Coast: south of Yarmouth Suffolk challenges Norfolk with a succession of outstanding sites: **Benacre Broad and Ness, Walberswick and Dunwich Marshes,** the RSPB's **Minsmere,** perhaps the finest single nature reserve in Britain, **Thorpeness, Havergate I,** the unique shingle promontory of

Orfordness with **Shingle Street** across the R. Ore, and finally the wildfowl-rich estuaries of the Deben, Orwell and Stour. A visit to the Suffolk coast rapidly gives the naturalist indigestion, for he finds most of the Norfolk birds, together with avocets nesting at both Minsmere and Havergate. Inland are the good heaths of **Westleton** at Minsmere and **North Warren** at Thorpeness. Right on the Essex border comes **Flatford Mill,** immortalised by Constable, now the first and most famous of the chain of field centres established by the Field Studies Council from the late 1940s onwards.

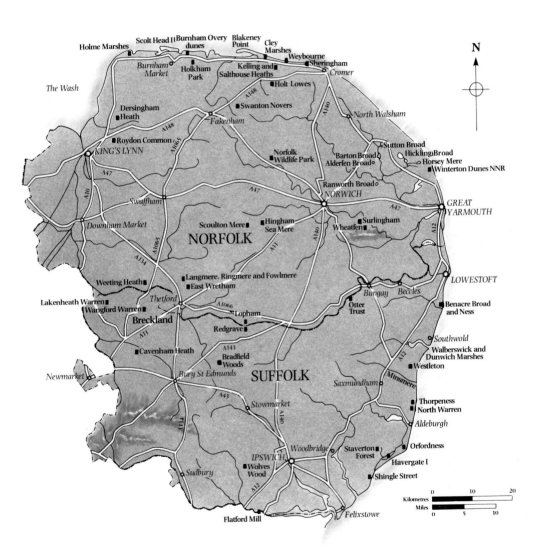

N

The Wash

Holme Marshes
Scolt Head I.
Burnham Overy dunes
Blakeney Point
Cley Marshes
Weybourne
Sheringham
Cromer

Burnham Market
Holkham Park
Kelling and Salthouse Heaths
Holt Lowes

Dersingham Heath

Swanton Novers

Fakenham

North Walsham

Roydon Common

KING'S LYNN

Norfolk Wildlife Park

Sutton Broad
Hickling Broad
Barton Broad
Alderfen Broad
Horsey Mere
Winterton Dunes NNR

Ranworth Broad

NORWICH

Swaffham

GREAT YARMOUTH

Downham Market

Scoulton Mere
Hingham Sea Mere

Surlingham
Wheatfen

NORFOLK

Weeting Heath
Langmere, Ringmere and Fowlmere
East Wretham

LOWESTOFT

Bungay
Beccles

Lakenheath Warren
Wangford Warren
Thetford

Lopham

Benacre Broad and Ness

Breckland

Redgrave

Otter Trust

Cavenham Heath

Southwold
Walberswick and Dunwich Marshes
Westleton

Bradfield Woods

Newmarket

Bury St Edmunds

SUFFOLK

Saxmundham

Minsmere

Thorpeness
North Warren

Stowmarket

Aldeburgh

Woodbridge

Staverton Forest

Orfordness

IPSWICH

Wolves Wood

Havergate I.

Sudbury

Shingle Street

Flatford Mill

Felixstowe

	0	10	20
Kilometres			
Miles			
	0	5	10

Shropshire, Staffordshire, Cheshire, Derbyshire

SHROPSHIRE

A western Midland county with many Welsh affinities and well known geological sites; its most notable features are the grassy and heathery hills of the west and the meres of the north east.

Clun Forest: one of the finest of the Shropshire hills; others are the **Clee Hills,** the **Longmynd, Stiperstones** and **Wenlock Edge,** all with at least some acid moorland and grassland remaining, but also all too many planted conifers. The easternmost have some limestone. Wild snowdrops *Galanthus nivalis* occur by streams in Clun Forest, buzzards are not uncommon and there are still red grouse on the Longmynd and Stiperstones.

The Meres: a series of shallow natural pools grouped around Ellesmere (**Cole Mere, Blake Mere, Crose Mere, White Mere**), Baschurch (**Marton Pool**) and Bayston Hill (**Bomere Pool**). They are good for winter wildfowl and aquatic plants in summer. White Mere has a cormorant roost.

Whixall Moss on the Welsh border is the best of the now few remaining north Shropshire peat bogs or mosses. **Brown Moss,** Whitchurch, is another.

Wyre Forest: a fine ancient oakwood shared with Worcestershire. Here, and elsewhere in the woods in the west of the county, pied flycatchers breed.

STAFFORDSHIRE

A midland county with the accent definitely on the north, where it verges on the Peak District.

Cannock Chase: a southern outlier of the moors of northern England, now much afforested with conifers, but still with good stretches of heather moor and some cowberry *Vaccinium vitis-idaea* as well as bilberry *V. myrtillus*.

Chartley Moss: a famous peat bog, one of the best examples of a floating peat mat, which sits on 9m of water. The nearby Chartley Park gave its name to a famous herd of old English wild white cattle.

Coombes Valley near Leek: an important oakwood bird sanctuary of the RSPB.

Dovedale: shared with Derbyshire, has splendid ashwoods, limestone grassland, dippers in the Dove and echoes of Isaak Walton.

Manifold Valley: like Dovedale, a westward extension of the White Peak of Derbyshire, with good woodland and semi-natural grassland.

Reservoirs are numerous and the best in the west Midlands for winter wildfowl. They include **Belvide, Blithfield** and **Cannock Chase Reservoirs** and **Gailey Pools,** especially noted for large flocks of the introduced North American ruddy duck. **Rudyard Lake** and **Aqualate Mere**, outliers of the Cheshire and Shropshire meres, are also good.

The Roaches: a wild stretch of moorland near Leek, with both native blackgame and alien wallabies.

The **Upper Dane Valley** has some fine oakwoods.

CHESHIRE, including Greater Manchester and Merseyside south of the Mersey

A very agricultural county, which fringes on the Pennines in the east and reaches Liverpool Bay in the west with its protruding Wirral finger.

Alderley Edge: a wooded ridge south of Manchester, much frequented at week-ends. **Cotterill Clough** and other oakwoods in the Bollin valley form additional Manchester lungs.

Canals: the **Macclesfield Canal** between Romiley and Bosley and the **Shropshire Union Canal** from Ellesmere Port to Audlem are both good for water plants.

The **Dee estuary,** shared with Flintshire, has a very extensive stretch of mudflats at low tide, with many wildfowl and waders. **Hilbre Island** off the north west tip of the Wirral is low-lying and accessible at low tide. Grey seals can usually be seen, and huge flocks of oystercatchers, curlew, dunlin and other waders gather there at high tide.

Delamere Forest: remnants still exist of the former deciduous woodlands, but most is now under conifers. There are several small bogs with sphagnum moss and cranberry *Vaccinium oxycoccos*. **Black Lake, Hatchmere** and **Oakmere** are three interesting fresh waters in the Forest.

Eastwood, Stalybridge: one of the oldest urban nature reserves in Britain, owned by the RSPB.

Macclesfield Forest: a stretch of moorland forming the best part of the Cheshire Pennines, with a herd of red deer.

Meres: in the south Baddiley, Bar, Cholmondeley and Comber Meres are outliers from the Shropshire meres; in the north the best is **Rostherne Mere NNR,** together with Great Budworth, Knutsford, Tabley and Tatton Meres and Marbury Reedbed.

Mersey estuary: shared with Lancashire, is more industrialised than the Dee, but still has good spots for wildfowl and waders, notably **Ince Marshes.**

Nantwich: salt deposits are worked in this area and some of these workings and natural springs have a saltmarsh flora, normally found on the coast, e.g. **Sandbach Flashes.**

Parks: Lyme and Tatton Parks are two of the finest of the Cheshire parklands, with old oaks and other trees. **Dunham Massey Park** has a herd of fallow deer.

The Wirral: the surviving heaths of the peninsula, such as Bidston Hill, Irby Heath and **Thurstaston Common** are lungs for Liverpool and Birkenhead. Marsh gentian *Gentiana pneumonanthe* still occurs.

Wybunbury Moss NNR is a good example of the unusual type of bog which floats on water, with a fen vegetation round its edge.

DERBYSHIRE

One of the counties that can be divided into three: the Trent valley in the south, a slice of the ordinary farming Midlands; the White Peak in the middle, composed of Carboniferous limestone; and the Dark Peak in the north, the Peak District proper, at the southern end of the great Pennine chain, whose dour moorlands lie mostly on the millstone grit.

The Dark Peak

This northern part of the Peak District National Park is itself divided in two by the A625 Manchester–Sheffield road, the **High Peak** lying to the north and the **East and West Moors** to the south. Here, rising to the curiously unimpressive summits of **Bleaklow Hill** and **Kinder Scout,** are extensive tracts of wild moorlands, still a Naboth's vineyard between the shooting men who seek the red grouse, the ramblers who seek the wild open spaces, and the water authorities who really prefer nobody to sully the purity of their reservoirs' gathering grounds. Ring ouzels, golden plover and dunlin are northern breeding birds at or near their southern limit in England.

The White Peak

So called from the contrast of its pale limestone with the soot-covered millstone grit, the southern part of the national park, shared with Staffs, is one of the scenic glories of England. Botanically its grasslands and ashwoods are exceptionally rich; Jacob's ladder *Polemonium caeruleum*, for instance, is commoner here than anywhere else in Britain, and some southern plants, such as dwarf thistle *Cirsium acaule* occur only on south-facing slopes. Lead-mine spoil-heaps have their special plants, such as alpine penny-cress *Thlaspi alpestre* and spring sandwort *Minuartia verna*. The best of the dales are **Dovedale** (see Staffordshire) and the central group: Lathkill, Monsal, Cressbrook and Miller's Dales.

Chatsworth Park: a fine old park, one of the half-dozen best in England.

The Caves: a special feature of the Dales is the series of caves with their spectacular stalagmites that point upwards and stalactites that hang downwards, both formed of calcium carbonate. Those open to the public include the **Blue John Mine** and the Peak, Speedwell and Treak Cliff Caverns, near Castleton; Bagshawe Cavern near Bradwell; Poole's Cavern, Buxton; Cumberland, Masson and Rutland Caverns at Matlock Bath; and the Fern and Roman Caves at High Tor, Matlock. Blue john is a beautiful purplish form of fluorspar (calcium fluoride), still used for making ornaments; its name is said to be corrupted from the French *bleu-jaune*.

The Trent Valley

Has a number of lakes and reservoirs worth a visit for their winter wildfowl: Allestree, Kedleston, Locko and Osmaston lakes and **Staunton Harold Reservoir.**

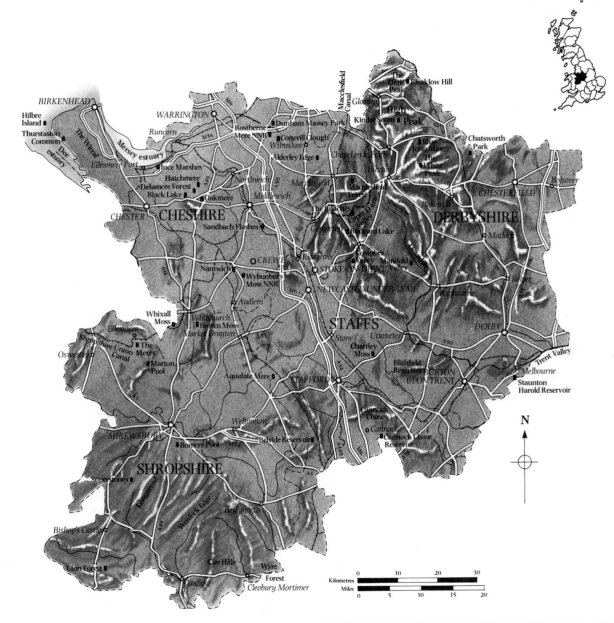

Leicestershire & Rutland, Nottinghamshire, Lincs. & S. Humberside

LEICESTERSHIRE AND RUTLAND

Like most Midland counties, a meeting place for northern and southern forms of wildlife, but also a largely farming countryside, less affected by industrial development than most of the Midlands.

Bradgate Park: an ancient park outside Leicester, with fine old oaks, rough grassy slopes and a herd of red deer; often described as a relic of the medieval landscape. Now a country park.

Charnwood Forest: the first outpost of northern England as you head north on the M1, still with a good patchwork of semi-natural habitats, oakwood, rough grassy moorland, marsh and bog. It is an island of ancient rocks, pre-Cambrian and igneous, protruding through the Triassic plain of the Midlands.

Donington Park has a fine herd of red deer.

Leicester University's **Botanic Garden** is at Oadby.

Rutland Water: the largest of numerous reservoirs in the area, most of them good for winter wildfowl; others are **Blackbrook, Cropston, Eye Brook** and **Swithland Reservoirs** and **Groby Pool.**

Vale of Belvoir: a fine stretch of farming countryside, parts recently scheduled for development as a coal-field, with a wooded escarpment overlooking it on the east and a good flora.

NOTTINGHAMSHIRE

One of the more industrialised Midland counties, most of whose surviving wildlife interest lies along the River Trent, on the Magnesian limestone ridge that traverses it from north to south, and in what remains of Sherwood Forest.

Attenborough Gravel Pits: the most notable of a series of flooded gravel pits in the Trent valley, now a county trust reserve. Common terns breed.

Creswell Crags: this famous archaeological site lies on the Magnesian limestone but is of only rather mild botanical interest. Nor are there more than a few patches of limestone flora elsewhere.

The Dukeries: a group of large parks, once largely inhabited by dukes, in the northern part of Sherwood Forest: Clumber, Rufford, Thoresby and Welbeck. Most still have deer, and Canada geese and other waterfowl breed on their lakes, which are good for winter bird-watching.

Laxton: a village which is still farmed in the medieval way, with strips rotating between different farmers each year and no hedges.

Sherwood Forest: little remains of the once dense oakwoods which sheriffs of Nottingham penetrated at their peril, but there are still some fine ancient oaks and stretches of heathy grassland embedded in extensive plantations of conifers.

Nottingham catchfly *Silene nutans* once grew on Nottingham Castle rock.

LINCOLNSHIRE & SOUTH HUMBERSIDE

Only fragments remain of the semi-natural habitats, heathland, woodland, calcareous grassland, saltmarshes and sand dunes, of this large and now almost wholly agricultural county. Apart from the coast, it consists largely of two longitudinal strips of calcareous rocks: the chalky wolds, which, after sinking beneath the clays and peats of the Fenland, link the Chilterns and East Anglia with the Yorkshire Wolds, and the Jurassic limestone 'heath', which similarly links the Cotswolds and the Northamptonshire oolite with the Howardian Hills and the North York Moors.

The Coast

Half the **Wash,** with its mudflats, grey and common seals, brent and pink-footed geese and huge flocks of waders, is in Lincolnshire. At its northern tip is **Gibraltar Point,** an important dune system, well known as a bird migration watchpoint, with an observatory, extensive sea-buckthorn *Hippophaë* scrub and important flora and breeding birds, including the increasingly scarce little tern.

Further north is another important dune system with sea-buckthorn scrub, **Saltfleetby-Theddlethorpe NNR,** where the rare natterjack toad survives.

More northerly still is **Donna Nook,** another migration watchpoint, with seal haulouts, close by the saltmarshes of **Tetney Haven.**

The **Humber estuary,** shared with Yorkshire, also important for pink-footed geese and waders, has a fine wildfowl refuge at **Read's Island** and valuable wildfowl sites also at flooded clay or gravel pits at **Killingholme** and **Barton-upon-Humber.** Bitterns breed in this area.

The Chalk and Limestone Uplands

Only the tiniest patches of semi-natural chalk and limestone grassland remain, e.g. at **Goulceby Red Hill,** where the chalk, as at Hunstanton, Norfolk, is red, and at a few road verges, chalkpits and limestone quarries, especially on the oolite around Ancaster, where pasque flower *Pulsatilla vulgaris* reaches its northern limit and the rare Continental subspecies of thrift *Armeria maritima elongata* occurs.

The woodlands, however, are more interesting, with many old oakwoods in Kesteven and ancient limewoods, especially near Bourne, Brigg (**Broughton Wood**), Gainsborough (**Bass Wood**) and Wragby. Overlying the limestone are some stretches of acid sand, as at **Linwood Warren, Scotton Common, Stapleford Moor** and **Twigmoor Warren,** and also around Woodhall Spa. Laughton and Scotton Common have black-headed gulleries.

In the north west, where the limestone sinks beneath the peats and clays of the lower Trent, are some fragments of the ancient oak and alder woodlands of the **Isle of Axholme,** which has a peat-digging tradition like Sedgemoor in the south west. **Epworth Turbary** is a county trust reserve.

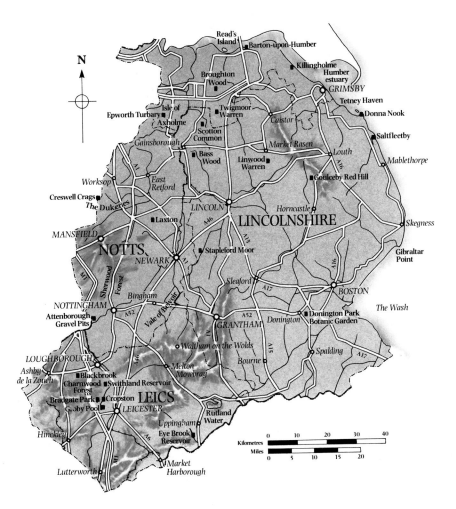

N

Read's
Island
Barton-upon-Humber
Killingholme
Humber
estuary
Broughton
Wood
GRIMSBY
Tetney Haven
Isle of
Axholme
Twigmoor
Warren
Donna Nook
Epworth Turbary
Caistor
Saltfleetby
Scotton
Common
Market Rasen
Louth
Gainsborough
Bass
Wood
Linwood
Warren
Mablethorpe
East
Retford
Goulceby Red Hill
Worksop
Creswell Crags
The Dukeries
LINCOLN
Horncastle
Skegness
MANSFIELD
Laxton
LINCOLNSHIRE
NOTTS.
Stapleford Moor
Gibraltar
Point
NEWARK
Sleaford
BOSTON
Sherwood
Forest
Bingham
The Wash
NOTTINGHAM
GRANTHAM
Donington
Donington Park
Botanic Garden
Attenborough
Gravel Pits
Waltham on the Wolds
Spalding
LOUGHBOROUGH
Bourne
Ashby
de la Zouch
Blackbrook
Charnwood
Forest
Swithland Reservoir
Melton
Mowbray
Bradgate Park
Cropston
Groby Pool
LEICS
LEICESTER
Hinckley
Uppingham
Rutland
Water
Eye Brook
Reservoir
Kilometres
Miles
Lutterworth
Market
Harborough

Lancashire, Cumbria

LANCASHIRE, including Greater Manchester and Merseyside north of the Mersey

After losing its detached northern portion to Cumbria, the county now has two main areas of wildlife interest, the western spurs of the mid-Pennines (now augmented by the Forest of Bowland from Yorkshire) and the coast with its sand dunes and estuarial mudflats.

The Coast
Ainsdale and Freshfield Dunes: a magnificent dune system with a rich flora, sand lizards, natterjack toads and a red squirrel colony in the pinewoods.
Alt estuary: a small estuary near Formby noted for the year-round presence of little gulls.
Morecambe Bay: a vast stretch of sand and mudflats, one of the five top wildfowl feeding areas in Europe, with up to 50,000 waders sometimes visible from Hest Bank.
Ribble estuary: another of the five top European wildfowl areas, with the second largest British group of pink-footed geese, on its extensive mudflats and saltmarshes, together with the fifth largest British black-headed gullery, the fourth largest concentration of common terns, and immense numbers of waders, especially at the Crossens roost, where 150,000 may be present.

Inland
Blackstone Edge, above Littleborough: one of the best Pennine moors in the county.
Forest of Bowland: a western promontory from the main Pennine chain, still with good heather and grass moorland.
Gaitbarrow, Silverdale: a fine limestone pavement, an outlier of the main area in Cumbria, now a NNR.
Hesketh Park, Southport, has a good lake for winter wildfowl.
Holden Clough, Oldham: an interesting urban nature reserve on the edge of industrial Lancashire.
Knowsley Park: a Liverpool lung, with another good lake for winter wildfowl.
Leighton Moss: an important RSPB refuge close to Morecambe Bay, especially noted for its breeding bitterns and bearded tits.
Martin Mere: now a Wildfowl Trust refuge, in the centre of the farmland frequented by the pink-footed geese of the Ribble estuary; up to a quarter of the world population may roost here.
Pennington and Astley Flashes, near Leigh: the best of many colliery subsidences that have flooded; good for winter wildfowl.
Rivington Pike and Reservoir: a Manchester lung, with moorland vegetation and winter wildfowl.

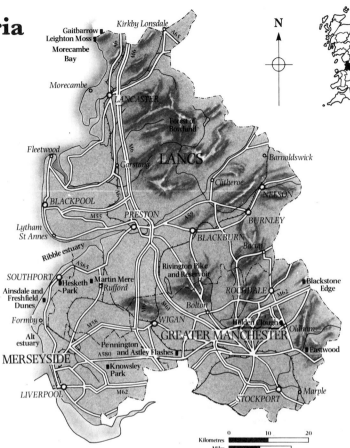

Gaitbarrow
Leighton Moss
Morecambe Bay
Kirkby Lonsdale
Morecambe
LANCASTER
Forest of Bowland
Fleetwood
LANCS
Barnoldswick
Carstang
Clitheroe
NELSON
BLACKPOOL
PRESTON
BURNLEY
Lytham St Annes
BLACKBURN
Bacup
Ribble estuary
Rivington Pike and Reservoir
SOUTHPORT
Hesketh Park
Martin Mere
Rufford
ROCHDALE
Blackstone Edge
Ainsdale and Freshfield Dunes
Bolton
Formby
WIGAN
Holden Clough
Oldham
Alt estuary
GREATER MANCHESTER
Pennington and Astley Flashes
Eastwood
MERSEYSIDE
Knowsley Park
LIVERPOOL
Marple
STOCKPORT

Kilometres 0 10 20
Miles 0 5 10

CUMBRIA (Cumberland, Cartmel, Furness, Westmorland)

A largely upland area, exceptionally rich in wildlife. Although the hills and mountains have mainly acid soils, an important band of limestone runs along its southern edge. The coast has good dune systems and saltmarshes.

The Lake District
The largest and most dramatic national park of England and Wales, containing the only true mountain range in England.
The most interesting alpine plants occur on **Fairfield Crags, High Street** crags, **Helvellyn,** mainly on the eastern side, the **Pillar** in Ennerdale, **Scafell Pike,** the highest English mountain, and **Wasdale Screes,** where the best gullies are inaccessible to non-climbers. The special Lakeland alpine is alpine catchfly *Lychnis alpina*, found only on **Hobcarton Fell** and above Glen Clova in Angus.
Although there are now a few golden eagles, the bird life is less rich than that of the Scottish Highlands. There is a herd of red deer on the **Martindale Fells.**
Woodlands: conifer plantations are widespread, especially in **Hardknott National Forest Park** and above Thirlmere, but there are still some fine old oakwoods, notably **Naddle Low Forest** near Hawes Water, **Glencoyne Wood** overlooking Ullswater, and in Borrowdale the **Keskadale Oaks,** a famous scree oakwood.
The Lakes themselves range from extreme oligotrophic waters such as **Wastwater** to the small eutrophic **Esthwaite Water** with its interesting fen, a NNR. **Windermere** is the largest lake in England and Wales.
Derwentwater, Ennerdale Water

and **Coniston Water** are all still largely unspoilt.

The North Pennines

An extensive tract of largely acid moorland with the highest summits, rounded in contrast to the Lakeland peaks, at the northern end.

On the Scottish border is the **Border Forest Park.**

Cross Fell reaches 893m with high-altitude limestone bringing a good alpine flora, though exposed to grazing due to the lack of cliffs; interesting breeding waders.

Howgill Fells: grassy hills of acid soils, but with fine scenery and some good flora, especially at Cautley Spout.

Moor House NNR at the top of Teesdale: an extensive blanket bog.

The Westmorland and Cartmel Limestone

A northward extension of the Craven Pennines, very rich in limestone crags and pavements, which are known to Continental botanists as karstlands.

Hutton Roof, Underbarrow Scar and **Whitbarrow Scar:** noted limestone crag or pavement sites, the last-named with an important juniper colony. Many unusual plants grow in the deep cracks or grykes of the pavements.

Humphrey Head, on Morecambe Bay, has several rarities, such as spiked speedwell *Veronica spicata* and goldilocks aster *Aster linosyris*.

Orton Fells: low limestone hills with a rich flora.

Roudsea Wood and Mosses on the shores of Morecambe Bay are a fascinating complex of limestone oakwood, raised and valley bogs and saltmarshes, with a good flora and some rarities.

There are famous daffodil colonies in **Brigsteer Wood** near Kendal and in **Gowbarrow Park.**

The Coast

Walney Island: a complex of mudflats, saltmarsh, sand dunes and shingle, with famous gulleries and the well known pink variety of the bloody cranesbill *Geranium sanguineum*.

Duddon estuary with Sandscale and Roanhead Dunes: another fine complex of sand flats, dunes and saltmarsh.

Drigg Point and Ravenglass: another dune system with one of the largest black-headed gulleries in Britain and a colony of natterjack toads.

St Bees Head: high sandstone cliffs with famous seabird colonies.

Siddick Pond: good for winter wildfowl.

The Solway: the English side of the estuaries of the Rivers Eden and Esk has very fine marshes, notably at **Morecambe** and **Rockcliffe,** the winter haunt of thousands of pink-footed, greylag, barnacle and other wild geese. **Grune Point,** Skinburness, is good for both birds and plants.

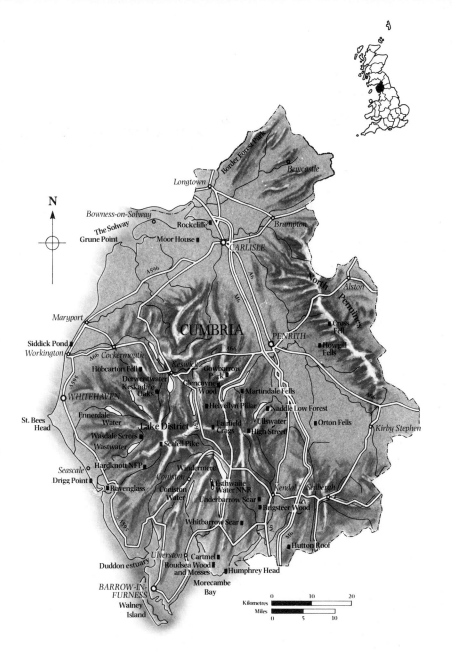

Yorkshire

YORKSHIRE, including North Humberside and South Cleveland

England's largest county has four distinct areas: the chalk of the south-eastern wolds, with its associated coastline; the Vale of York, flanked on the west by a strip of Magnesian limestone; the limestone, sandstones and shales of the Howardian Hills and North York Moors, also with a coastline; and the great western block of the Pennines, mainly of acid rocks but including the important Carboniferous limestone region of Craven.

The South-East

The Yorkshire Wolds, once with wide stretches of chalk grassland, have now mostly been ploughed for barley, but the northernmost escarpment, overlooking the Vale of Pickering, has some remnant grassland, e.g. at **Duggleby Wold,** and several steep valleys in the northern part, e.g. **Waterdale,** have not been ploughed. Several abandoned quarries, e.g. **Wharram** and **Kiplingcotes,** also have a good chalk flora. There is a good ashwood at **Great Givendale** with baneberry *Actaea spicata*.

The Coast: where the chalk meets the sea at **Bempton Cliffs** and **Flamborough Head,** it produces a wall of magnificent cliffs, Bempton with many breeding seabirds, including the only gannetry in England or on the British mainland. **Filey Brigg** is a noted bird migration watchpoint. From Hayburn Wyke to Ravenscar the shale and clay cliffs, up to 350 ft high, are covered with scrub oakwood, with wood vetch *Vicia sylvatica* abundant. **Spurn Point,** the terminus of the Yorkshire coast, is an unstable 3½-mile sand and shingle spit, curving one-third of the way across the **Humber** estuary. It is famous for its bird observatory, for both migrant birds and the great many wildfowl and waders that spread across the extensive Humber mudflats (see Lincolnshire). Bearded tits breed at **Blacktoft Sands.**

Hornsea Mere: a shallow eutrophic lake surrounded by reedbeds, where bearded tits also breed; good for winter wildfowl.

The Vale of York

Askham Bog: a small deciduous woodland and fen lying on an old bog earlier cut for peat, with many rare plants and insects.

Brockadale: a county trust reserve with some of the best surviving Magnesian limestone grassland.

Hatfield and Thorne Moors: the largest and most diverse area of lowland peat vegetation in northern England. The peat has now mostly been cut commercially, but there are still rare plants and unusual birds.

Knaresborough: the R. Nidd cuts through the Magnesian limestone here to make a famous gorge, still with some interesting plants.

Potteric Carr: an area of mining subsidence bounded by railways, near Doncaster; the mixture of open water and reedswamp gives a very rich bird fauna, especially in winter. A similar important bird reserve due to mining subsidence is **Fairburn Ings** in the lower Aire valley.

Skipwith Common: an extensive wet heath with a very rich insect fauna and good birds.

Strensall Common: another large wet lowland heath with a good flora, including marsh gentian *Gentiana pneumonanthe*.

Wheldrake Ings: the R. Derwent floods each winter and the open water here and elsewhere in the Derwent floodplain attracts Bewick's swans and hundreds of other wildfowl.

The North-East

The Howardian Hills: attractive wooded hills with some limestone grassland. **Castle Howard** has a lake with Canada geese, and other wildfowl in winter.

North York Moors National Park, extending to the Cleveland Hills overlooking the Tees estuary: a mixture of limestones, sandstones and other Jurassic rocks produce a varied scenery, with steep wooded valleys and an extensive plateau covered with heather moorland, including the well known landmark, the Hole of Horcum, southernmost outpost of dwarf cornel, *Cornus suecicus*. The limestone outcrops mainly along the southern edge of the Park, overlooking the Vale of Pickering and the **Hambleton Hills.** Many of the rivers, notably in Kirkdale, disappear into swallow-holes in dry spells.

Dalby Forest: extensive conifer forest with a rich bird fauna.

Farndale: very well known for its spring display of wild daffodils *Narcissus pseudonarcissus*, calling for one-way traffic in April.

Forge Valley Woods: fine ash and oak woods with alder in the valley bottoms.

Gormire Lake: a small lake lying beneath the impressive limestone cliffs of Sutton Bank, with an interesting flora, including the shy-flowering tufted loosestrife *Lysimachia thyrsiflora*.

Newtondale: a glacial valley along which the North York Moors railway runs. **Fen Bog** is a remote outpost for many northern plants.

Ryedale Woods: similar to Forge Valley Woods, especially around Rievaulx Abbey and Helmsley, where mountain currant *Ribes alpinum* is abundant.

The Coast is dominated by shelving, rather than sheer, cliffs, reaching nearly 700 ft at **Boulby,** the highest in England. **Robin Hood's Bay** is famous for fossils.

The Pennines

The **Yorkshire Dales National Park** consists of the higher parts of the valleys of five rivers, the Aire, Wharfe, Nidd, Ure and Swale, the last three of which join to become the Ouse at York. Its north west end, the Craven Pennines, is dominated by the stark outlines of the 'Three Peaks' of Ingleborough, Whernside and Pen-y-ghent, with their perpendicular limestone escarpments; on the first and last of these purple saxifrage *Saxifraga oppositifolia* flowers abundantly in early spring. The Carboniferous limestone of this area gives a rich flora, especially notable for the frequency of the charming birdseye primrose *Primula farinosa*, with famous limestone pavements and many caves and pot-holes, such as White Cross Caverns.

Austwick Moss: a small peat bog with some unusual plants.

Brimham Rocks: good moorland with curious natural standing rock piles.

Colt Park: a famous ashwood on limestone pavement, now a NNR; at the foot of Ingleborough, which has many other fine limestone pavements on its east and north-west slopes, notably **Scar Close.**

Fountains Abbey: its ruined walls have some botanical interest; good woodlands around the well kept grounds.

Gouthwaite Reservoir: noted for winter wildfowl, as is also **Wintersett Reservoir.**

Malham: the heart of the Craven Pennines; among the best sites are **Malham Tarn and Fen,** a large high-level lake and fen with many rare species; **Malham Cove** and **Gordale Scar,** two spectacular cliffs with waterfalls; and a fine series of limestone pavements with a very rich flora, including baneberry *Actaea spicata.*

Semerwater: larger and deeper than Malham Tarn, with a fine setting, less good flora and unique insect fauna. Not far away are **Aysgarth Falls** and the dramatic limestone hill of **Addleborough**, with a good flora on its summit ledges. All these are in **Wensleydale,** the upper valley of the Ure.

Upper Swaledale: the northernmost and most unspoilt of the dales, with limestone cliffs at Oxnap Scar and a dramatic gorge around Kisdon Hill with fine mixed woods. Old lead mines are frequent, with their specialised flora, including mountain pansy *Viola lutea.*

Upper Teesdale: the Yorkshire section of this mainly Durham dale has its own special rare plants on Cronkley and Mickle Fells, including alpine forgetmenot *Myosotis alpestris*, mountain avens *Dryas octopetala* and spring gentian *Gentiana nivalis.*

Wharfedale from Bolton Abbey upwards has many superb ash, elm and oak woods are some rare plants. The Strid is a narrow defile where one can step across the river.

South Pennines: the northern edge of the Peak District National Park, between Sheffield and Huddersfield, has a very fine stretch of moorland, though rather unexciting botanically.

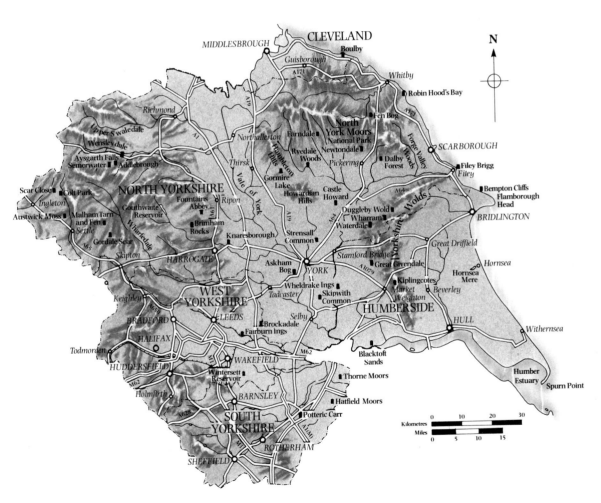

Durham

DURHAM, including the northern
part of Cleveland and the southern
part of Tyne & Wear.
A county which mixes extremely
important sites, notably Upper
Teesdale, with a predominantly
uninteresting (for the naturalist)
countryside on the Coal Measures and
a strip of Magnesian limestone.
Cassop: some good limestone grassland and ash woodland in this area.
Castle Eden Dene: the largest and
most unspoilt of a series of wooded
valleys running down to the coast and
cutting deeply into the limestone.
Hawthorn Dene, a county trust
reserve, is another.
Durham University has a botanic
garden.
Heugh Battery, Hartlepool: a good
migration watchpoint; Souter Point is
another.
Hurworth Burn Reservoir: the best
reservoir for winter wildfowl, with a
regular autumn assembly of little gulls.
Jarrow Slake on the Tyne: good for
waders.
Marsden Rock, South Shields: a
seabird colony (kittiwakes, cormorants)
clearly visible from the main coast
road. Both South Shields and
Sunderland have large urban breeding
colonies of herring gulls.
Teesmouth: one of the most
important sites in north England for
wildfowl and waders, especially
shelduck and sanderling, despite the
pollution of the Tees estuary. **Cowpen
Marsh,** a RSPB sanctuary, and **Seal
Sands** are key areas.
Thrislington Plantation: the best
remaining limestone grassland in the
north-east.
Upper Teesdale: the chief glory of
Durham for the naturalist, including
the famous botanical site of
Widdybank Fell with many arctic

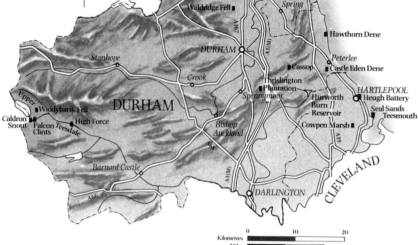

plants surviving from the aftermath of
the Ice Age on its curiously crumbly
sugar limestone (spring gentian
Gentiana verna can be seen from the
public path); **Falcon Clints,** a
whinstone cliff above the Tees; and
Caldron Snout, a waterfall just

below the new Cow Green Reservoir,
whose construction caused such a
furore in the 1960s and which like
most upland reservoirs is of little
interest ornithologically. Along the
Tees between Caldron Snout and the
much better known falls of **High**

Force are numerous bushes of the
shrubby cinquefoil *Potentilla fruticosa*.
Waldridge Fell: one of the best
moorlands outside Teesdale, with some
good alder carr.
Washington has one of the Wildfowl
Trust's fine collections of waterfowl.

Northumberland

NORTHUMBERLAND, including the northern part of Tyne & Wear. A largely upland county with three main areas: the hills and moors of the north and west, many now afforested with conifers; the coastline in the east; and the more lowland Tyne valley in the south.

The Hills

The Cheviots: the rounded, mainly grassy hills that form the Border between England and Scotland, reaching 815m on the Cheviot itself, and largely within the Northumberland National Park. **Tosson Hill** is an important site. The best botanical sites are in the ravines of **Dunsdale** and **Henhole** west of Wooler.

Catcleugh Reservoir, by the Carter Bar road (A68) was the largest area of water in the county until the giant **Kielder Reservoir** filled in 1982; like most upland reservoirs they are disappointing for winter wildfowl. **Colt Crag Reservoir** is more fruitful.

Chillingham Park: famous for its herd of 50–60 'wild white' cattle, which are certainly wild in their behaviour but are probably descendants of domesticated Roman cattle.

Irthinghead Mires: a fine group of extensive blanket bogs, partly within the national park.

Kielder, Rothbury and Wark Forests: three extensive tracts of moorland, now partly under conifers or farmland, partly in the national park and partly in the Border Forest Park.

Northumberland Loughs: five natural lakes north of Hadrian's Wall, in limestone country and so with interesting plants and better birds than the waters of the acid moorland: Broomlee, Crag, Greenlee, Grindon and Halleypike loughs.

The Coast

Coquet Island has the southernmost breeding eiders on the east coast and large terneries and gulleries.

Cliffs: best developed from Cullernose to Dunstanburgh, both with seabird colonies.

Dunes: the many fine dune systems include, from north to south, Cheswick and Goswick Sands, Holy Island, Ross Links, St Aidan's and Shoreston Links, Embleton Links and Cresswell Dunes.

Farne Islands: the most famous seabird colonies in England, with puffins, razorbills, guillemots, kittiwakes, shags and the historic eider colony known since St Cuthbert lived on the Inner Farne in the 7th century. The large (c8000) colony of grey seals is visited by many holidaymakers from Seahouses.

Hauxley: a bird sanctuary based on an open-cast mining site. **Cresswell Ponds** are also good for winter wildfowl and have little gulls in summer.

Holy Island or Lindisfarne: an island at high tide only, set in the middle of extensive mudflats, including Budle Bay with an important winter flock of brent geese and innumerable waders. There are good plants on the dunes.

The **Tweed estuary:** assembling point for salmon before they ascend the Tweed, being preyed on by both man and the grey seal.

The Tyne Valley

Allen Banks, Haydon: wooded banks and crags by the River Allen.

Gosforth Park, close to Newcastle, has a good lake for winter wildfowl.

Holywell Ponds, Seaton Delaval, and **Hallington Reservoir** are also good.

Newcastle-upon-Tyne, North Shields and Tynemouth all have large urban herring gull colonies.

Dyfed

DYFED (West Wales: Cardiganshire, Carmarthenshire, Pembrokeshire)

The Coast
A national park protects most of the coastline of the old county of Pembroke.

Cliffs, especially at **St David's Head,** are full of interest, and have breeding choughs, peregrines and grey seals; also **Pen Deri** (grey seals); Dinas Island, a peninsula; Strumble Head; and in the south from **Linney Head** to **St Govan's Head,** including **Stack Rocks** (parts of this stretch are sometimes barred off by the military).

Estuaries are numerous, and most have good wildfowl and waders, at least in winter: notably those of the Towy (with the Taf, Gwendraeth and Burry Inlet), Teifi, Dyfi, Gann (at Dale) and Angle Bay.

Dunes: especially **Laugharne and Pendine Burrows, Freshwater West** and Towyn and Pembrey Burrows.

Newgale Sands: a fine stretch of sandy beach in St Bride's Bay.

The Islands: the Pembrokeshire islands are renowned for their fine seabird colonies, notably **Skokholm** and **Skomer** with their guillemots, razorbills, puffins, kittiwakes, Manx shearwaters and storm petrels; **Grassholm** with its fine gannetry, the only one south of the Trent; **Ramsey** (grey seals), Caldey (also with a few seals) and St Margaret's Islands off Tenby and Cardigan Island with its Soay sheep.

The Hills
The soils of western Wales are mainly acid, so the botanical interest is less than in North Wales.

Black Mountain: an upland massif with limestone pavements and cliffs and a good flora; an exception to the rule.

Borth Bog (Cors Fochno): one of the finest lowland raised bogs, adjacent to the Dyfi estuary with its fine complex of mudflats, sand dunes and salt-marshes.

Devil's Bridge: the steep wooded gorge of the Rheidol River has some of the finest oakwoods in Wales.

Dowrog and Tretio Commons: a fine lowland heath on the St David's peninsula, with an important wetland in Dowrog Pool.

Dynevor Deer Park has both red and fallow deer.

Fresh Water: Bosherston Pools, Marloes Mere, Rosebush Reservoir, Llyn Brianne, Orielton Decoy. Otters occur on many rivers.

Gwenffrwd and Dinas: a wooded RSPB reserve in the heart of the kite country; red kites still breed nowhere else in Britain but the hills of mid-Wales.

Mynydd Presceli: a small mountain massif included in the national park and overlooking St Bride's Bay.

Plynlimon: an extensive massif of grassy moorland, shared with Powys.

Tregaron Bog (Cors Goch Glan Teifi): a very fine raised bog, with a wintering flock of white-fronted geese.

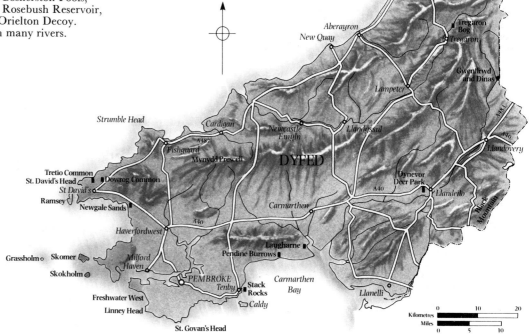

Glamorgan

GLAMORGAN
Apart from its large industrialised tracts, Glamorgan has three main ecological regions: the coastline along the Bristol Channel, the largely agricultural Vale of Glamorgan, and the moorlands of the north, still with some fragments of ancient woodland.

The Coast
Nash Point: the key sector of the limestone cliffs of south Glamorgan, with much wild cabbage *Brassica oleracea* among other interesting plants.
Kenfig Dunes: the best dune system in south Wales, rich in plant life, including the increasingly rare fen orchid *Liparis loeselii*. Other dune systems are at Margam; Newton Dunes, Porthcawl; and Jersey Marine, which also has saltmarshes.
Flatholm: an island off Lavernock Point with nesting gulls.
The Gower Peninsula, extending west from Swansea, holds many of the finest sites in the county, especially the limestone cliffs terminating in **Worms Head** with its fine seabird colonies and the extensive dune system of **Whiteford Burrows.** Other important dune systems are at Broughton, Llangenith, Oxwich and Penard, several with adjacent saltmarshes.
Penard Castle and nearby cliffs: the only British site of yellow whitlow-grass *Draba aizoides*, which flowers in March.
Broad Pool and **Oxwich Ponds:** interesting freshwater sites in the Gower. Clyne and Fairwood Commons, **Rhossili Downs** and Mead Moor are all heaths. The Bishopstone valley has good woodlands.
The Burry Inlet: an important estuary for wildfowl and waders, noted

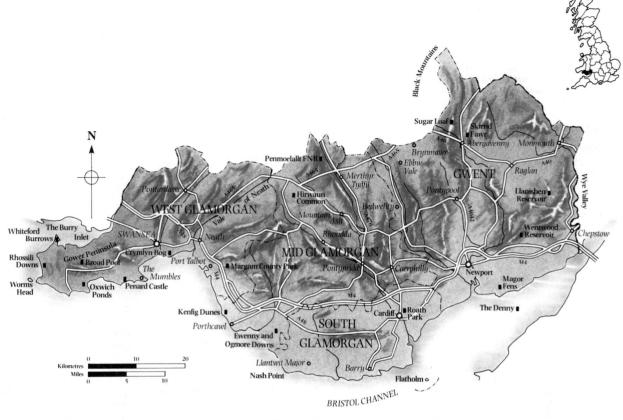

for the conflict between oystercatchers, cockles and cockle fishermen; shared with Dyfed (Carmarthenshire).

Inland
Cardiff has a large urban colony of herring gulls; so have Hirwaun and Porthcawl.
Crymlyn Bog: an important swampy site on the outskirts of Swansea.
Ewenny and Ogmore Downs: limestone grassland.
Hirwaun Common with Craig-y-llin: a good moorland stretch.
Llanishen Reservoir and **Roath Park,** Cardiff: good for winter wildfowl.

Margam County Park: a herd of 600 fallow deer.
Vale of Neath has important oak and mixed deciduous woodlands.

GWENT (formerly Monmouthshire)
The main natural interest of this south-easternmost Welsh county lies in the valleys of the Wye and Usk, together with the Severn estuary and the moorlands in the north.
Black Mountains: extensive tracts of moorland shared with Powys; the attractive valley above Llanthony Abbey has some interesting oakwoods, such as Strawberry Cottage Wood.

Magor Fens: a wet meadow reserve of the county trust.
Newport has a large roof-nesting colony of herring gulls.
Skirrid Fawr and the **Sugar Loaf,** Abergavenny: moorland areas owned by the National Trust.
The Denny: a small island in the Severn estuary off Renwick, with nesting gulls.
Wye valley: the fine limestone gorge with its rich mixed woodlands is shared with Gloucestershire, but the Forest Nature Reserves of Blackcliff and Wyndcliff are in Gwent.
Wentwood Reservoir: good for winter wildfowl.

Gwynedd

GWYNEDD (Anglesey, Caernarvonshire, Merioneth)
The north-western corner of Wales is most conveniently discussed in three sections: the mountains, most of which are in the Snowdonia National Park, the coastline and the large island of Anglesey.

The Mountains
Snowdonia: the core of the national park consists of the highland massif divided into three blocks by the Llanberis Pass, which separates Snowdon itself to the south from the Glyders, and Nant Ffrancon, which separates these from the still more northerly Carneddau. The whole massif is exceptionally rich in both common and rare alpine plants, including the Snowdon lily *Lloydia serotina* in its only locality north-west of the Alps, and six species of saxifrage. Wild goats are found in several places.
Snowdon (Y Wyddfa) at 1086m is the highest mountain in England and Wales and the only high mountain on the British mainland with its own railway. The best botanical sites are Cwm Glas, Clogwyn Du'r-arddu, Crib-y-ddysgl and Clogwyn-y-Person.
Glyder Fawr and **Glyder Fach** are the highest peaks of the middle section of Snowdonia, which includes the stupendous cliffs of **Cwm Idwal,** cleft by the narrow crack known as Twll Du or the Devil's Kitchen, and with Llyn Idwal at its foot. Cwm Idwal and Y Gribin are the two best botanical sites, and the Snowdon lily is more easily seen at the Devil's Kitchen (with the aid of binoculars if you are not a rock climber!) than anywhere else.
Carnedd Dafydd and **Carnedd Llewellyn** are the highest peaks north of Nant Ffrancon, where the massif has the most extensive summit plateau

in Snowdonia, and an impressive cliff, **Ysgolion Duon,** with many fine alpines, some of which also grow on Braich-tu-du, both on Carnedd Dafydd.
Woodlands: Snowdonia is one of the most wooded mountain areas in Britain, especially since recent plantings of conifers, with a number of exceptionally fine ancient oakwoods. They include **Coed Maentwrog,** on the southern flank, a complex of woodland mainly on acid soils and very rich in mosses and liverworts; a fine series in the Conwy valley on the north-eastern side of the massif, notably Coed Dolgarrog and Coed Gorswen; and some good oakwoods and a fine waterfall in the Aber valley.
Cadair Idris: a scenically dramatic mountain in the south of the national park, rising to nearly 900m, with a magnificent corrie, **Cwm Cau,** high cliffs a deep lake, Llyn Cau, and a fine alpine flora. There are some oakwoods on the lower slopes. **Tal-y-llyn,** a shallow lake in a glacial valley, lies at its southern foot.
Rhinog Fawr is the highest peak in the Rhinogs, the mountains that lie between Cadair Idris and Snowdonia, and are lower, less frequented and less grazed than both, although they have a herd of wild goats. On their lower slopes are two superb ancient oakwoods with rare mosses and ferns: **Coed Ganllwyd** and **Coed Crafnant,** the latter not to be confused with Cwm Glas at Crafnant in Snowdonia.
Yr Eifl: a dramatic range of hills supporting both choughs and feral goats but, having acid soils, botanically dull.
Fresh Water: among the more notable waters not already noted are **Bala Lake** (Llyn Tegid), the largest lake in Wales, with several rare fishes,

and **Llyn Trawsfynydd,** a huge area flooded for the benefit of a nuclear power station.

The Coast
Bardsey Island: noted as an observation post for bird migration, with breeding Manx shearwaters and choughs and interesting plants.
Bird Rock, Craig yr Adeyrn, on the Dysynni estuary above Towyn is named from the only inland cormorant colony in England and Wales.
Estuaries: the Dyfi, Mawddach, Glaslyn and Conwy estuaries and Foryd Bay all have good birds in winter, and the Glaslyn also has good plants.
Great and Little Orme: two limestone headlands near Llandudno with fine limestone cliffs, pavements and grassland, rich in unusual plants. **Gloddaeth Hill** is similar. There are feral goats on the Great Orme.
Lleyn Peninsula has a number of small coastal fens and marshes (Ystummllyn, Abersoch, Cors Geirch and Edeyrn) and dune systems, and ends in Braich-y-Pwll, a headland with fine views towards Bardsey.
Morfa Dyffryn and **Morfa Harlech:** two extensive dune systems with uncommon plants and good associated saltmarshes. Morfa Bychan, Portmadoc, is a smaller dune system and the West Shore at Llandudno smaller still.
St Tudwal's Islands have seabird colonies but are not easily accessible.

Anglesey (Ynys Mon)
Although scenically rather dull, except as a foreground to dramatic views of the Snowdon range (when cloud cover permits), Anglesey has some of the best wildlife areas in Wales.

Bwrdd Arthur: an ancient fort on a low limestone plateau overlooking the sea, with some rare plants including hoary rockrose *Helianthemum canum*.
Cemlyn Pool: a brackish lagoon with the largest ternery in Wales, very good for winter wildfowl.
Cors Goch has an astonishing array of habitats, from acid heath through limestone grassland to base-rich fen and open water, and a good flora, including marsh gentian *Gentiana pneumonanthe*.
Holyhead Mountain: a tract of moorland on Holy Island.
Llyn Coron and **Llyn Llywenen:** two of a number of small lakes with interesting breeding wildfowl, the latter with a black-headed gullery. Canada geese are now widespread.
Malltraeth: the estuary here has mudflats, salt and brackish marshes and good lagoons for migrant waders.
Menai Strait: mainly of interest for winter bird-watching.
Newborough Warren: an extensive dune system, now largely afforested to conifers, but still with mobile and fixed dunes, fine dune slacks and a superb flora. It terminates in **Ynys Llanddwyn,** a rocky promontory (an island at high tide) with some good plants not found on the Warren, such as bloody cranesbill *Geranium sanguineum*, and seabirds breeding on offshore rocks.
Porth Diana, Trearddur Bay: an interesting heathland and grassland reserve.
Puffin Island: off the north-east tip, has no puffins, but a large herring gullery, which extends on to the cliffs beyond Penmon Point.
South Stack, on Holy Island: steep cliffs with nesting guillemots and other seabirds and good plants, some rare, in the surrounding area, including annual rockrose *Tuberaria guttata*.

Tywyn Aberffraw: a stretch of fixed sand dunes with a fine flora, the head-quarters in Britain of the rare tiny early sand grass *Mibora minima*. Nearby Tywyn Trewan at Rhosneigr is also good.

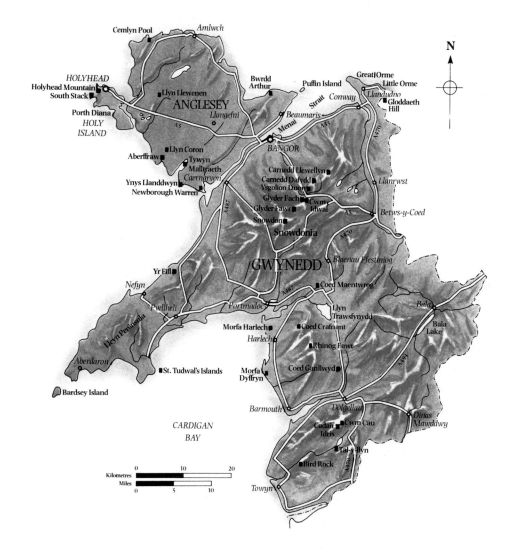

Cemlyn Pool

Amlwch

Bwrdd Arthur

Puffin Island

Great Orme
Little Orme

HOLYHEAD

Holyhead Mountain
South Stack

Llandudno
Gloddaeth Hill

Llyn Llewenen

Strait
Conway

ANGLESEY

Porth Diana
HOLY ISLAND

Llangefni

Beaumaris

Menai

Aberffraw

Llyn Coron

BANGOR

Tywyn
Malltraeth

Caernarvon

Carnedd Llewelyn

Llanrwst

Ynys Llanddwyn
Newborough Warren

Carnedd Dafydd
Ysgolion Duon

Glyder Fach
Cwm Idwal

Betws-y-Coed

Glyder Fawr

Snowdon

Snowdonia

GWYNEDD

Blaenau Ffestiniog

Yr Eifl

Nefyn

Coed Maentwrog

Pwllheli

Portmadoc

Llyn Trawsfynydd

Bala

Bala Lake

Morfa Harlech

Coed Crafnant

Harlech

Llŷn Peninsula

Rhinog Fawr

Aberdaron

St. Tudwal's Islands

Morfa Dyffryn

Coed Ganllwyd

Bardsey Island

Barmouth

Dolgellau

Dinas Mawddwy

Cadair Idris
Cwm Cau

CARDIGAN BAY

Tal-y-llyn

Bird Rock

Kilometres
Miles

0   10   20
0   5   10

Towyn

N

Powys, Clwyd

POWYS (Breconshire, Montgomeryshire, Radnorshire)
Comprises a large part of the hill country of mid Wales, including the Brecon Beacons National Park, and so borders on the kite country, together with the upper reaches of both the Wye – perhaps the least spoilt large river in Britain – and Severn.
Berwyn Mountains: this fine (and threatened) stretch of moorland extends into the north of the area from Clwyd.
Brecon Beacons: the core of the national park, which also includes the similar but somewhat less interesting **Black Mountains** (shared with Gwent). The Beacons proper contain the best hill habitats in South Wales, where some plants are at the southernmost point of their world range: fine limestone cliffs, an extensive summit plateau and upland woods with rare whitebeams, notably at **Craig Cerrig Gleisiau** NNR on the old red sandstone.
Craig Breidden, near Welshpool: a limestone quarry cliff with a remarkable group of rare plants, including spiked speedwell *Veronica spicata* and sticky catchfly *Lychnis viscaria*.
Craig y Cilau and **Cwm Clydach:** two NNRs south of the Black Mountains, with a fine limestone escarpment, large-leaved limes *Tilia platyphyllos*, rare whitebeams (one confined to this spot), an extensive cave system and, in Cwm Clydach, the only self-regenerating mature beech-wood in Wales.
Elan Valley, Radnorshire, and **Lake Vyrnwy,** Montgomeryshire, are rather uninteresting reservoirs for Birmingham and Liverpool respectively.
Llanbwchllyn Reservoir, south-east

of Builth Wells: good aquatic plants.
Llangorse Lake: good for winter wildfowl.
Penmoelallt: a small limestone wood with a very diverse tree canopy, including rare whitebeams *Sorbus*.
Plynlimon: see Dyfed.
Radnor Forest: now extensively afforested with conifers, but still with much open rolling grassy moorland.
Rhos-goch Common, Clyro: a very fine bog with a large black-headed gullery.
Stanner Rocks: a limestone escarpment just inside the Radnorshire border with an array of plant rarities to rival Craig Breidden, including both the catchfly and the speedwell.

CLWYD (Denbighshire, Flintshire)
The **North Wales limestone** is the key feature for wildlife in Clwyd. It runs in a great arc from Colwyn Bay past the interesting coastal quarry at **Penmaen Head** to near Abergele and then swings south through the Elwy valley and past Denbigh and Llanarmon to end in the magnificent terraced escarpment of **Eglwyseg Mountain** near Llangollen. It has some limestone pavements with many uncommon, and a few rare, plants on both rocks and grassland.
Berwyn Mountains: see Powys.
Clwydian Hills: a range of unspoilt heather-covered hills, rising to over 550m on Moel Famau. On their east side the valleys cut into the limestone, producing narrow gorges, such as the **Alyn valley,** which has a disappearing stream, and several good limestone woods.
Dee estuary: see Cheshire. Interesting saltings at Shotton.
Fenn's Moss: an extensive bog in the detached part of former Flintshire, now almost dried out into heathland.

Fresh Water: includes Alwen and Llyn Brenig Reservoirs, Hanmer Mere, Llyn Helig and Padeswood Pool.
Prestatyn to Point of Air: sand dunes, now much overrun with holidaymakers.
Woodlands: Cilygroeslwyd Wood, Ruttin, and Hafod Wood, Erddig Park, Wrexham, are mixed hardwood reserves of the North Wales Naturalists' Trust.

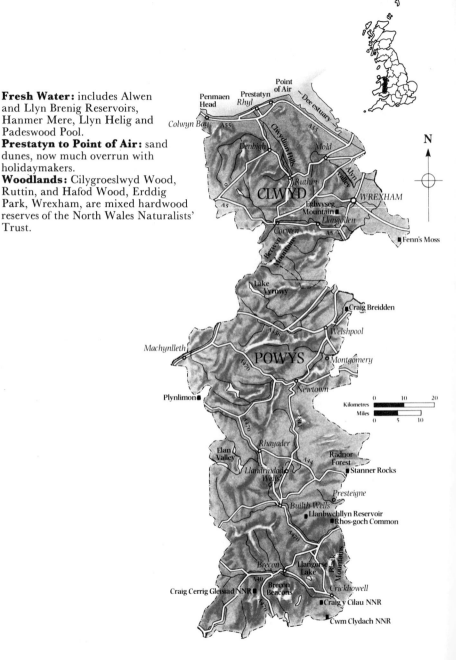

Dumfries & Galloway

DUMFRIES & GALLOWAY
(Dumfriesshire,
Kirkcudbrightshire,
Wigtownshire)

The Coast
Balcary Point: nesting seabirds.
Burrow Head: a low headland with
nesting seabirds and a good watchpoint
for bird migration.
Estuaries: the Cree and Nith
estuaries, with Auchencairn, Fleet,
Kirkcudbright, Luce and Wigtown
Bays and Loch Ryan are all good for
winter wader and wildfowl watching.
Little Ross Lighthouse: a good
migration watchpoint.
Mochrum Loch has the only inland
cormorant colony in Scotland, and
with nearby Castle Loch is good for
winter waterfowl.
Mull of Galloway: fine cliffs,
migration watchpoint, the best seabird
colonies in Galloway, and with an
interesting flora, a curious mixture of
northern and southern species, several
at their respective limits.
Portpatrick: black guillemots nest in
the harbour wall.
Preston Merse: a good saltmarsh.
Scar Rocks: seabird colony,
including a small gannetry.
Solway Firth, shared with Cumbria,
is one of the outstanding areas in
Britain for winter waders and wildfowl.
The Wildfowl Trust's Eastpark
Wildfowl Refuge at **Caerlaverock** is a
superb place to see wild geese,
including barnacles, and other
wildfowl in winter, and even better at
the start of the return goose migration
in April.
Torrs Warren: a well developed
dune system with a good range of
slacks, but inaccessible to the public.

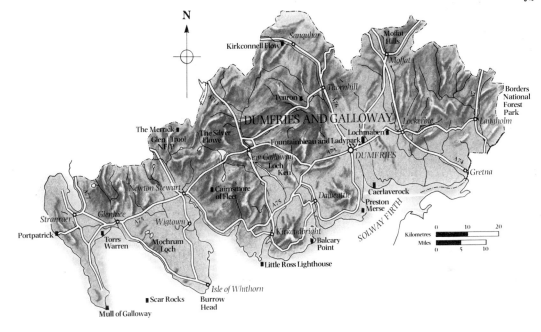

The Hills
Borders National Forest Park,
shared with Borders: the grassy hills
are now largely afforested to conifers.
Cairnsmore of Fleet: the summit of
a range of hills covered with acid
moorland, with a large herd of red
deer and breeding golden eagles.
Fountainbleau and Ladypark: a
good birchwood in Nithsdale.
Glen Trool National Forest Park:
the major, and now largely conifer-

planted, part of a range of acid-
moorland hills, which reach their
summit in **the Merrick,** the highest
hill in southern Scotland; also has a
herd of red deer and still some
oakwoods. **The Silver Flowe** is a
famous series of peat bogs.
Kirkconnell Flow: a large raised bog
mainly covered with naturally
regenerating pine.
Loch Ken: good for geese and other
winter wildfowl. Lochs Dee and Car-

lingwark are also of interest. L. Moan
has a large black-headed gullery.
Lochmaben has a group of four
interesting lochs with unusual fish
species.
Moffat Hills: an impressive massif
reaching over 800m and including a
famous waterfall, the Grey Mare's
Tail, L. Skeen just above it, and base-
rich cliffs with a good alpine flora.
Tynron: a remarkable juniper wood,
with bushes up to 6m high.

Borders, Lothian, Strathclyde South

BORDERS (Berwickshire, Peeblesshire, Roxburghshire, Selkirkshire)

Bemersyde Moss with its large black-headed gullery is one of a large series of mosses (mainly peat bogs), for which the region is noted, and including Carnwath, Dunhog, Gordon, Hule, Hare and Whitlaw Mosses. Most are reserves of the Scottish Wildlife Trust.

Borders National Forest Park, shared with Dumfries & Galloway: includes Newcastleton and Wauchope Forests and is now more plantation than moorland.

Cheviot Hills, shared with · Northumberland, are largely grass moors. The Cheviot itself (815 m) is a very flat dome on the English side.

Duns Castle policies and **The Hirsel,** Coldstream, are two large wooded estates open to the public for walking and birdwatching.

Ettrick Forest: one of the many ranges of grassy hills in the region.

Lammermuir, Moorfoot and Pentland Hills: ranges of grassy moors shared with Lothian, with breeding golden plovers.

Paradise Wood, Whiteadder Water: a good oakwood.

St Abbs Head: one of the outstanding British seabird colonies, with many thousands of guillemots and kittiwakes and fewer razorbills, fulmars, shags and puffins.

St Mary's Loch: one of the largest of the region's numerous lochs; other notable ones are Akermoor (black-headed gullery), Hoselaw, Portmore and Yetholm Lochs, West Water, Lindean and Watch Reservoirs, and Junction Water, Kelso.

Tweedsmuir Hills, just north of the Moffat Hills, lack their base-rich cliffs and so have a much less interesting flora, but hairy stonecrop *Sedum villosum* is commoner here than anywhere else in Britain.

LOTHIAN (East Lothian, Midlothian, West Lothian (part))

Firth of Forth

Aberlady Bay: a noted haunt of winter wildfowl and waders, with good sand dunes at **Gullane** and **Luffness Links** nearby.

Bass Rock: an impressive volcanic plug, site of a world-famous gannetry and with many other breeding seabirds.

Craigleith, Eyebroughty, Fidra, Inchkeith, **Inchmickery** and the Lamb: a string of islands in the Firth, one or more of which (especially Inchmickery) usually has a ternery; other seabirds also breed and the Lamb has a cormorantry.

Leith Docks have a ternery on a caisson.

Musselburgh: a good watchpoint for winter wildfowl and waders.

Seafield: a sewer outfall where nearly one-third of the British wintering scaup gather to feed on grain waste, along with large numbers of goldeneye and eiders.

Tynninghame: a good estuary for wildfowl and waders, with a heronry.

Inland

Berwick Law: a volcanic plug that dominates the East Lothian landscape.

Duddingston Loch: a bird sanctuary close to Holyrood Park, with good wildfowl at all times of year and a grassy meadow at Bawsinch.

Gladhouse Reservoir: one of the best places in the region for winter wildfowl, including thousands of pink-footed geese. Other good reservoirs are **Threipmuir** (with Bavelaw Marsh) and **Milkhall.** Cobbinshaw Reservoir has a black-headed gullery.

Linlithgow Loch is always worth a winter visit.

Holyrood Park: Edinburgh's chief lung, a stretch of grassy moorland close to the city centre, with an interesting rock flora on King Arthur's Seat and Samson's Ribs, including sticky catchfly *Lychnis viscaria* and forked spleenwort *Asplenium septentrionale.*

Lammermuir, Moorfoot and Pentland Hills: three ranges of grassy hills shared with Borders, with some woodland, good breeding birds and locally a good flora that includes birdseye primrose *Primula farinosa.* The Lammermuirs and Pentlands have more heather than the Moorfoots.

East Lammermuir Deans are base-rich glens, the finest being Sheeppath Dean.

Phantassie Dovecote: a famous old dovecote at East Linton.

Red Moss of Balerno: a good bog.

Tailend Moss, West Lothian, is another.

Roslin Glen: good oak/ash woodland.

Pepper Wood, on the edge of Edinburgh, is another woodland reserve.

Thornton Glen: a wooded gorge in East Lothian.

Tynninghame and Whittinghame: two East Lothian estates with more (planted) woodland than elsewhere in the region, and so the only part of Scotland where the hawfinch breeds.

STRATHCLYDE SOUTH (Ayrshire, Lanarkshire, Renfrewshire)

The Coast

Ailsa Craig: a rocky island in the Firth of Clyde with important seabird breeding colonies on its steep cliffs, including a gannetry almost as famous as the Bass Rock.

Ballantrae has a line of rugged cliffs and the estuary of the Stinchar with a shingle bar at its mouth.

Dipple estuary has a large population of eiders.

Horse Island and **Lady Island** both have terneries.

Irvine has a saltmarsh.

Turnberry Point: a good migration watchpoint. Nearby are some good sand dunes.

Inland

Auchalton Meadow: a calcareous grassland reserve of the SWT.

Falls of Clyde Woodlands: mixed deciduous woodlands along the wooded gorge of the Clyde, including the Bonnington birchwoods and Corehouse, with some limestone and good plants.

Feoch Meadows, Barrhill: another grassland reserve of the SWT.

Hamilton High Parks have some fine old oaks.

Lochs and Reservoirs are numerous. The more interesting include Castle Semple and Barr Lochs and Loch Macaterish, all with large black-headed gulleries; Crane Loch, Carnwath; Loch Doon, bordering on the Glen Trool National Forest Park in Galloway; Loch Libo with good water plants; Loch of the Lowes, not to be confused with its namesake in Perth-shire; Lochwinnoch, the RSPB reserve; Martnaham and Shankeston Lochs near Ayr; and Stanley Reservoir with whooper swans in winter.

Moorland: southern Ayrshire abuts on the hills of Galloway and the Glen Trool National Forest Park, and is mostly grass moorland, as is the moorland of Lanarkshire.

Possil Marsh: a well known marshland reserve near Glasgow.

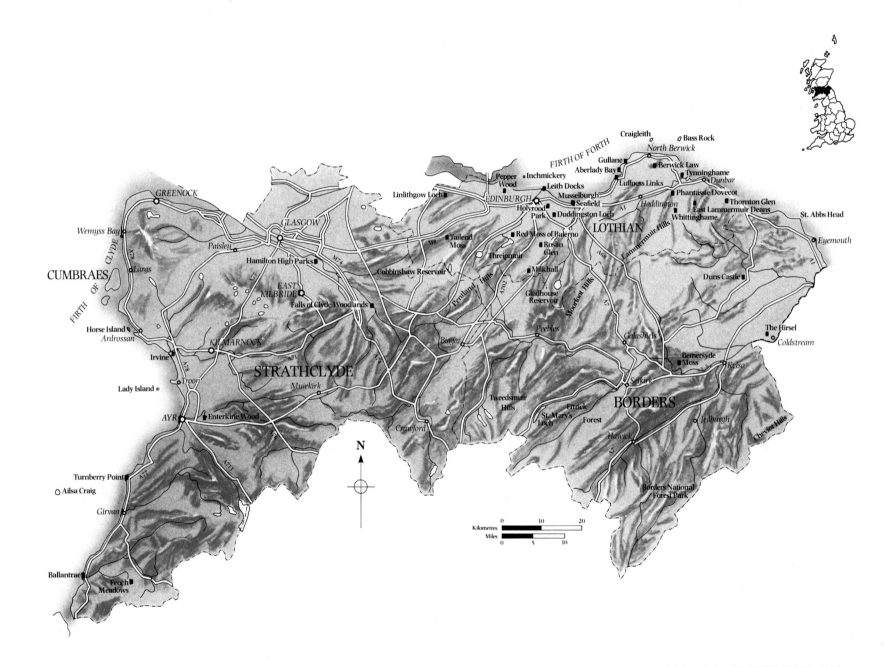

FIRTH OF FORTH

Craigleith
Bass Rock
North Berwick
Gullane Berwick Law
Aberlady Bay Tynninghame
Pepper Inchmickery Luffness Links Dunbar
Wood Leith Docks Phantassie Dovecot
Linlithgow Loch EDINBURGH Musselburgh Haddington Thornton Glen
Holyrood Seafield East Lammermuir Deans
Park Duddingston Loch LOTHIAN Whittinghame St. Abbs Head
GREENOCK Tailend Red Moss of Balerno Lammermuir Hills Eyemouth
Moss Roslin
GLASGOW Threipmuir Glen
Wemyss Bay Duns Castle
Paisley Milkhall
Hamilton High Parks Cobbinshaw Reservoir Moorfoot Hills
Largs Gladhouse The Hirsel
CUMBRAES Reservoir Peebles Galashiels
EAST Pentland Hills Coldstream
KILBRIDE Bemersyde
Falls of Clyde Woodlands Biggar Moss Kelso
Horse Island Selkirk
Ardrossan KILMARNOCK STRATHCLYDE BORDERS
Irvine Tweedsmuir
Hills Ettrick
Lady Island Troon Muirkirk St. Mary's Forest Jedburgh
Loch Cheviot Hills
AYR Enterkine Wood Hawick
Crawford
Turnberry Point N
Ailsa Craig Borders National
Forest Park
Girvan
Kilometres 0 10 20
Miles 0 5 10
Ballantrae
Feoch
Meadows

Central Region, Fife, Tayside

CENTRAL REGION (Stirlingshire with Clackmannanshire and parts of south-west Perthshire and West Lothian)

Ballagan Glen: an ashwood belonging to the National Trust for Scotland.

Ben More: the best mountain in the region for alpines.

Dollar Glen: a wooded glen belonging to the NTS.

Doune Ponds: good for winter wildfowl.

Falls of Leny: a famous waterfall on the road from Callander to Killin.

Flanders Moss with Gartrenish Moss: the extensive remnants of what was once the largest area of raised bog in Britain, covering much of the Forth valley above Stirling; a large black-headed gullery.

Forth estuary: excellent for winter wildfowl and waders; the best spot is **Skinflats,** but Kennet Pans at the mouth of the River Devon and Kinneil mudflats are also good; see also under Fife. Whooper swans feed in riverside fields between Stirling and Alloa.

Gartmorn Dam: a reservoir good for winter wildfowl.

Lake of Menteith: good for winter wildfowl.

Loch Dochart often has whooper swans in winter.

Loch Lomond: see Strathclyde North.

Queen Elizabeth Forest Park, centred on the Trossachs, a famous tourist honeypot, is a mosaic of moorland, mountain (Ben Lomond), lochs (Loch Ard), conifer plantations and the fine oakwoods that still survive along the east side of Loch Lomond.

Tailend Moss: a bog belonging to the NTS.

Tyndrum has an ancient pinewood.

FIFE

Bankhead Moss: a raised bog with heather, birch and gorse, a reserve of the Scottish Wildlife Trust.

Ferry Hills, North Queensferry: one of the few patches of calcareous grassland in east Scotland.

Forth estuary: Largo Bay is good for little gulls, and Torry Bay for waders, many of which roost on ash settling pans at Kincardine and Longannet power stations. Many scaup gather in winter at the Leven sewer outfall. See also under Central Region and, for the islands, Lothian.

Isle of May: a rocky island with a well known bird observatory, large colonies of breeding seabirds and a growing grey seal rookery.

Lochs: the best for waterfowl are Kilconquhar Loch, good for little gulls, and Lindores Loch and Morton Lochs, which are also good for aquatic plants.

St Andrews: the famous golf links have some interesting sand dune plants.

Tentsmuir: a fine stretch of rather acid sand dunes, with several rare plants, lying between the estuaries of the Tay (see also Tayside) and Eden, linking their extensive mudflats, which are all good for winter birdwatching.

TAYSIDE (Angus, Kinross-shire, Perthshire (part))

The Mountains

Atholl Forest: a block of hills north of Blair Atholl little explored botanically, though it contains one of the sites for the (now extinct in Britain) arctic bramble *Rubus arcticus.*

Balnaguard Glen: a birchwood with the finest stand of juniper wood in the region.

Ben Lawers: the hills between Strathtay and Glen Lyon, including both Lawers itself and **Meall nan Tarmachan** to the west, are the *locus classicus* for alpine botanists in Britain; its highly calcareous schists produce an unrivalled flora, including both alpine forgetmenot *Myosotis alpestris* and alpine gentian *Gentiana nivalis*. Much of it is owned by the National Trust for Scotland, which runs an information centre.

Ben-y-Vrackie: a fairly low mountain north of Pitlochry with calcareous rocks yielding some rarities missing from the Lawers range. It has an outlier on Meall an Daimh.

Black Wood of Rannoch: one of the finest surviving fragments of the old Caledonian pine forest, noted for its insect fauna. Other ancient pinewoods in the region are the Old Wood of Meggernie, Glen Lyon, and in Glen Falloch.

Caenlochan and **Glen Clova:** the only area in the Highlands to rival the Lawers range for the richness of its alpine flora, especially the willow scrub. Caenlochan is an impressive precipitous corrie with calcareous cliffs at the foot of Glas Maol (1078m). Glen Clova splits at the top into Glen Doll and Glen Fee, both worth a visit, as is the summit plateau with the only Scottish site for alpine catchfly *Lychnis alpina*.

Cairnwell: a peak on the Grampian border, whose alpine rarities can be fairly painlessly approached by a ski-lift.

Killiekrankie Pass: a steep-sided wooded gorge with a rich flora in its oakwoods, and good breeding birds.

Keltneyburn has a similar wooded gorge, with the rare whorled Solomon's seal *Polygonatum verticillatum*. The wooded banks of the **Linn of Tummel,** however, are much flatter.

Pitlochry has a fish pass, where migrating salmon can be seen. Others are at Clunie, Stronuick and the Falls of Lochay.

Rannoch Moor, shared with Strathclyde: an extensive blanket bog, studded with pools and lochans, as bleak as anywhere south of Sutherland. It has rare plants and insects, including the only remaining site of Rannoch rush *Scheuchzeria palustris*, which can be seen quite near the railway station.

Schiehallion: a strikingly shaped isolated mountain, with some limestone pavement on its north-east flank.

Sow of Atholl: noted as a site of the very rare blue heath *Phyllodoce caerulea*.

The Lowlands

Balgavies Loch: good for aquatic plants and in winter for wild geese.

Cleish Castle has a famous yew avenue.

The Den of Airlie: a red sandstone gorge with mixed deciduous woodland.

Loch of Kinnordy: a large black-headed gullery and, in winter, 15,000 greylag geese.

Loch Leven: a large, shallow, very fertile lake, with many trout and other fish species and the largest concentration of breeding waterfowl in Britain, with large numbers also roosting in winter. Nearby **Vane Farm** is a reserve and nature centre of the RSPB.

Loch of Lintrathen: good for aquatic plants and winter flocks of wild geese.

Loch of the Lowes: famous for its breeding ospreys, shown to the public by the Scottish Wildlife Trust. Nearby **Loch of Craiglush** has a good fringing marsh and woodlands.

River Earn floods south of Perth are good for wild geese in winter.

The Coast

Barry Links: an extensive sand dune system, largely under military occupation.

Firth of Tay has by far the largest winter aggregation of eiders in Britain (*c*20,000) and, especially at Monifieth, is a good place to see little gulls. There are some fine reedbeds at **Port Allen,** where the mudflats are good for waders. **Invergowrie Bay** is also good for winter birdwatching.

Montrose Basin: a curious, almost enclosed estuary, with extensive mud-flats at low tide and good numbers of wintering wildfowl.

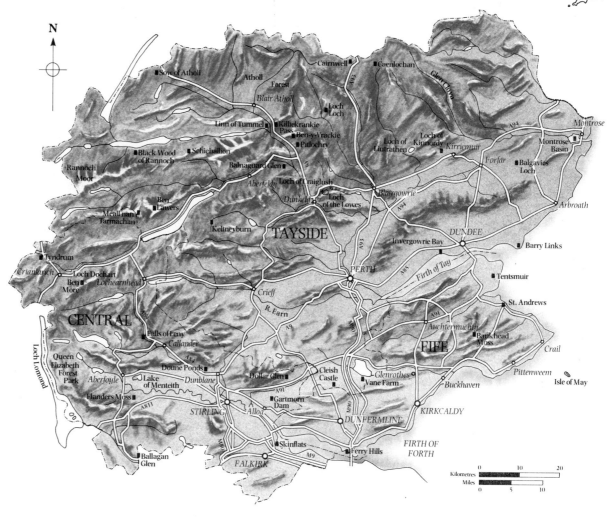

N

Strathclyde North

STRATHCLYDE NORTH (Argyll (part), Dunbartonshire, Buteshire)

The Mainland

Argyll National Forest Park, west of Loch Long and around Lochs Eck and Goil, includes moorland, conifer plantations and some surviving oakwood.

Black Mount: a deer forest in north Argyll, one of the more notable of the huge stretches of moorland in the region, accessible from the main Glasgow–Fort William road (A82); has some patches of native pinewood.

Clyde estuary, opening into the Firth of Clyde: good for winter wildfowl and waders, especially the mudflats and foreshore at **Ardmore.**

Crarae Forest Garden, Minard (Forestry Commission) and **Younger Botanic Gardens,** Benmore (Royal Botanic Gardens, Edinburgh): two fine arboreta.

Kintyre: an extensive dune system at Machrihanish and dramatic and inaccessible cliffs thence to the Mull of Kintyre, where the Irish coast is clearly visible. Limestone outcrops near Largybaan have an interesting flora; oysterplant *Mertensia maritima* is abundant near Southend.

Knapdale: the coast has rich oakwoods with good ferns and mosses; alpines grow quite low down on Sliabh Gaoil.

Loch Awe: the longest British loch, at 41 km, is also narrow.

Loch Lomond: the largest area of fresh water in Great Britain, 71 km²; some of its unspoilt wooded islands, such as Inchcailloch, are nature reserves, and the sandflats and marshes at the mouth of the River Endrick are good for waders; good reedswamps and oakwoods along its shores, many of the woods in the Queen Elizabeth Forest Park (see Central Region).

Mountains: calcareous or basic rocks (good for alpines) occur on **Ben Lui,** Ben Cruachan, Beinn an Dothaidh, **Bidean nan Bian** (the highest peak in Argyll, 1140 m above the magnificent vistas of Glencoe), Ben Sgulaird and Buchaille Etive Mor.

Oak Woodland: fragments of the original west coast forest cover survive, notably **Enterkine Wood** and **Glasdrum Wood** at the head of Loch Creran, which grade from alder and ash at the low levels through oak and birch to open moorland above. **Taynish Woods** are a fine undisturbed coastal oakwood. **Glen Nant Forest Nature Reserve** near Taynuilt is mixed old coppice. The shores of the **Kyles of Bute,** opposite the island of Bute, are well wooded with oak and birch.

Rannoch Moor: a very extensive boggy moor extending into the Tayside region, and crossed by the main west coast road and railway.

The Islands

Arran: extensive moorland and rugged mountains, rising to 874 m on Goat Fell, with Glen Rosa; a NNR for rare whitebeams *Sorbus* at Glen Diomhan in the north; a herd of red deer on the Sannox estate in the northeast; a flock of Soay sheep on Holy Island in the south-east; Brodick Wood (National Trust for Scotland) with a heronry; and a large winter flock of greylag geese at Shiskine.

Bute has lochs and mudflats for waterfowl and waders, nesting eiders and many wintering greylags.

Coll: has good machair; arctic skuas and other seabirds breed; Loch a'Mhill Aird is a good freshwater loch.

Colonsay: grey seals on Eilean nan Ron; corncrakes still numerous.

Danna: off Knapdale, has calcareous rocks and a rich flora.

Gigha has a very fine garden with subtropical plants.

Great and Little Cumbrae: two small islands at the mouth of the Firth of Clyde, the larger with a famous marine biological station at Millport, Little Cumbrae with large gulleries and breeding cormorants and shags.

Iona: very famous historically, has superb white-sand beaches and machair, barnacle and white-fronted geese in winter, and still many corncrakes in summer; the west coast is best for waders.

Islay: winter flocks of barnacle and white-fronted geese, especially around the complex of dunes and mudflats at Loch Gruinart; good machair on the Atlantic coast; more choughs than anywhere else in Scotland; and good seabird colonies on the rocky headlands of the Mull of Oa and the Rhinns.

Jura: a very barren but beautiful island, with common seals on offshore islands and a famous whirlpool in the straits.

Lismore has some limestone grassland.

Mull: largely moorland, with Ben Mhor (screes but no cliffs) as its highest point, but small outcrops of metamorphosed chalk on Inchkenneth and elsewhere. **Ardmeanach** is a wild hilly peninsula with rare plants on its cliffs, Iceland purslane *Koenigia islandica* on its barren summits, a herd of red deer and a famous fossilised tree. Good spots for waders around the coast, notably Loch Don, Fidden on the Ross of Mull, Loch Scridain, the south side of Loch na Keal (the best waterfowl loch), the very sheltered Loch Spalve and the head of Loch Cuin. Calgary has some sand dunes.

Oronsay: famous for its grey seals.

Pladda: nesting terns, eiders, redbreasted mergansers and Manx shearwaters.

Scarba: a colony of common seals, also on nearby Luing.

Staffa: the well known Fingal's Cave is formed of hexagonal basalt columns, like the Giant's Causeway in Northern Ireland.

Tiree: a very flat island, noted for its long hours of sunshine, with good machair on the Atlantic coast and still many corncrakes.

Treshnish Islands: good seabird colonies, especially on Lunga and Dutchman's Cap. Lunga has both Manx shearwaters and common seals.

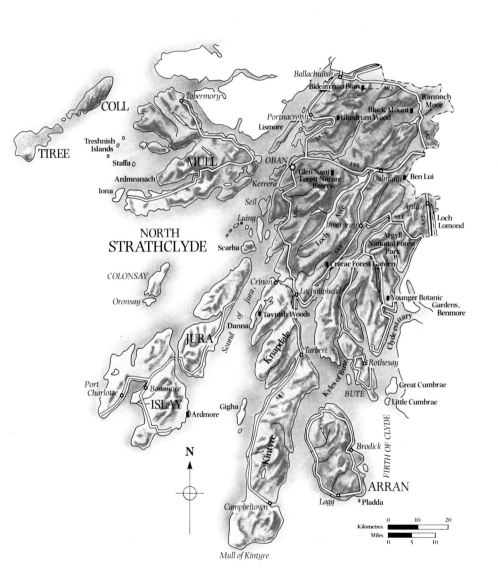

Highland (south), Grampian

HIGHLAND, SOUTH OF THE GREAT GLEN (Inverness-shire (part), Morayshire (part), Nairnshire)

A natural region that consists essentially of Strathspey with its associated mountain ranges of the Cairngorms (shared with Grampian) and the Monadhliaths.

Abernethy and Rothiemurchus Forests: the core of the wildlife attractions of Strathspey, the largest continuous surviving fragment of the ancient Caledonian forest, with a rich shrub layer, including much juniper, and many rare and uncommon plants and insects. Red and roe deer are common, with crossbill, crested tit, capercaillie and greenshank among the unusual birds for which the region is famous. The other ancient pinewoods of Strathspey are Dulnan and Glen Feshie, parts of which are included in the **Glenmore National Forest Park.**

Ben Nevis: the highest point in Britain, 1347 m, lying just south of the Spey watershed, made of largely acid rocks and so much less rich in alpines than the Cairngorms; nor is its sub-arctic plateau so extensive. Glen Nevis has an ancient pinewood.

Cairngorms: the largest area of land above 1200 m in the British Isles, dominated by the four, rather flat and rounded, 'peaks' of **Braeriach, Cairn Gorm, Cairn Toul** and **Ben Macdui**, which at 1313 m is the second highest British mountain. The massif is cleft by several deep, steep-sided valleys, Glen Avon (pronounced A'an), Glen Einich and the celebrated pass of the **Lairig Ghru,** the ancient track from Aviemore to Braemar that connects Rothiemurchus with the almost equally important Mar and Glentanar

Forests on the Grampian (Aberdeen-shire) side. The high plateau of the Cairngorms, including Carn Ban Mor to the south, is the nearest approach to what most of Britain must have looked like during the Ice Age, or to what the Arctic tundra looks like today; it has a rich Arctic flora and such montane birds as golden eagle, ptarmigan, dotterel and often snow bunting. A semi-domesticated herd of reindeer joins the native red deer on the high tops in summer. This is the one part of Britain that can successfully challenge Norfolk with its wildlife.

Craigehlachie NNR: a species-rich birchwood with good birds and insects.

Drumochter: the hills around the pass south into Perthshire (Tayside) have a good summit heath vegetation and breeding bird population.

Gaick Forest: a tract of wild and mountainous moorland, famous for its red deer herds, at the head of Glen Feshie.

Insh Marshes: an extensive reed-swamp and marsh by Loch Insh with characteristic northern fen plants and a rich bird fauna, including wintering whooper swans. The adjacent **Lynachlaggan Birchwood** is also a RSPB reserve.

Loch Garten: famous as the RSPB osprey reserve; it was here that the RSPB managed to beat the egg-thieves in the early 1960s to allow the osprey to re-establish itself as a Scottish breeding bird – a northern counterpart to its triumph with the avocet in East Anglia. Ospreys now breed widely through the Highlands and may also be seen feeding at nearby Mallachie, Morlich and Pityoulich lochs, and even sometimes at their ancient haunt of Loch an Eilein in Rothiemurchus, the most romantic loch in the eastern Highlands with its ruined castle on an

island, where egg collectors exterminated the local ospreys at the turn of the century. In winter up to 1000 greylags roost on Loch Garten. Further north is another group of lochs, Alvie, Cran, Flemington and Loy, where waterfowl are a greater attraction than ospreys.

Monadhliath Hills: a very large area of comparatively low rounded hills between the Spey and Loch Ness, largely unexplored, especially by botanists.

Nairn Bar on the Moray Firth has up to 1000 roosting greylags in winter and is good for seabirds and waders at all times of year.

River Spey: a famous salmon river, unique in having long stretches of slow-flowing stream, with extensive shingle banks, at a high altitude above Grantown. Lupins *Lupinus nootkatensis* grow wild on some of these banks. There is a fish pass at **Tromie,** where leaping salmon can be seen; others are at Invergarry and Dundreggan on the River Ness.

GRAMPIAN (Aberdeenshire, Banffshire, Kincardineshire, Morayshire (part))

Inland

Ballochbuie: a surviving fragment of the ancient Caledonian pine forest; others are Crathes, Glentanar, Glen Avon and Man.

Cairngorms: see Highland, south of the Great Glen.

Corby, Lily and Bishop's Lochs: three good freshwater lochs just north of Aberdeen.

Deeside: otters are common along the River Dee.

Dinnet Oakwood NNR: a rare example of a Highland oakwood.

Hatton Castle, Turriff: the centre of

the largest complex of rookeries in the British Isles. Arnage Castle had at one time a single rookery of over 2000 nests.

Hill of Towan: interesting low-lying serpentine hill with a curious flora and insect fauna.

Lochnagar: an impressive, rather isolated mountain, with unusual alpine plants and rather dangerous cliffs and screes.

Morrone Birkwoods NNR: an upland birchwood, ungrazed and so with a rich flora, passing uphill into species-rich grassland; the finest subalpine wood on basic soils in Britain.

Pitfour Loch: the second most important winter wildfowl roost in Buchan, after the Loch of Strathbeg.

St. Fergus Moss has a large mixed gullery.

The Coast

Bullers of Buchan: the cliffs have important seabird colonies, especially the Longhaven Cliffs and Whinnyfold.

Culbin Sands: the largest dune system in Britain, the result of a series of storms which overwhelmed a village more than 300 years ago; now largely planted with conifers, but still with many rare and unusual plants, of both dunes and pinewoods.

Findhorn Bay: the mouth of the River Findhorn, adjacent to the Culbin Sands; the sands and mudflats here and at the mouths of the Lossie and Spey are excellent for winter birdwatching. Huge numbers of long-tailed duck and common scoter winter offshore, especially in Spey Bay and Burghead Bay.

Fowlsheugh: spectacular seabird colonies, with thousands of kittiwakes and guillemots and hundreds of razorbills and fulmars; a RSPB reserve.

Loch of Strathbeg lies behind a very varied dune system with both fresh and salt marshes; most important for winter wildfowl, especially wild geese and swans; only rescued with difficulty from being a gas-pipe terminal, now a RSPB reserve.
Rattray Head: a good migration watchpoint.

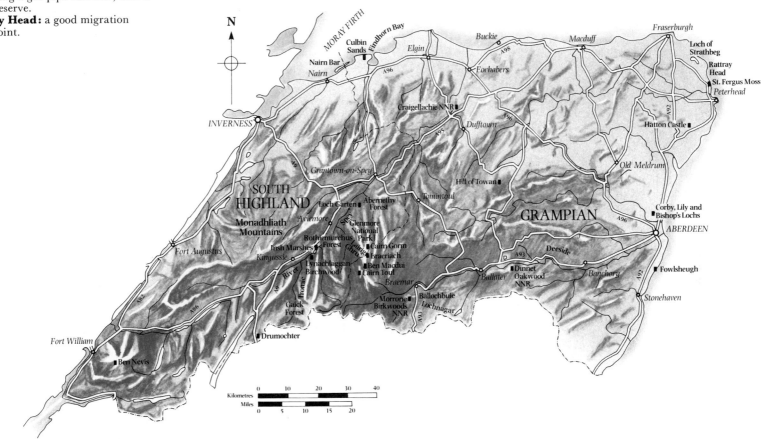

N

MORAY FIRTH

Findhorn Bay

Fraserburgh

Culbin Sands
Buckie
Macduff
Loch of Strathbeg

Nairn Bar
Elgin
A98
Rattray Head

Nairn
A96
Fochabers
St. Fergus Moss

Peterhead

Craigellachie NNR
Dufftown
A96
Hatton Castle

INVERNESS
A95

Old Meldrum

Grantown-on-Spey
Hill of Towan

SOUTH HIGHLAND
Tomintoul
GRAMPIAN
Corby, Lily and Bishop's Lochs

Loch Garten
Abernethy Forest
A96

Monadhliath Mountains
Aviemore
Glenmore National Park
ABERDEEN

Fort Augustus
Rothiemurchus Forest
Cairn Gorm
Deeside

Insh Marshes
Braeriach
A93

Kingussie
Lynachlaggan-Birchwood
Ben Macdui
Dinnet Oakwood NNR
Banchory
Fowlsheugh

River Tromie
Cairn Toul
Ballater
Braemar

Gaick Forest
Morrone Birkwoods NNR
Ballochbuie
A93
Stonehaven

Lochnagar

A82
A86
Drumochter

Fort William

Ben Nevis

	0	10	20	30	40
Kilometres					
Miles	0	5	10	15	20

Highland (north)

HIGHLAND, NORTH OF THE GREAT GLEN (Argyll (part), Inverness-shire (part), Ross & Cromarty, Sutherland)

North Argyll and West Inverness-shire

Ancient Pinewoods: fragments of the old Caledonian forest occur in three groups: Ardgour in north Argyll; Barisdale, Glengarry, Glen Loy, Glen Loyne, Glen Moriston and Loch Arkaig with Glen Mallie, in south Inverness-shire; and Glens Affric, Cannich and Strathfarrar with Guisachen and Congie in Strathglass.

Ardnamurchan: the westernmost part of the British mainland has interesting volcanic rocks at the tip of the peninsula. Ben Hiant is the highest hill.

Arriundle Oakwood: NNR: the gem of the extensive oakwoods along the south side of Loch Sunart, which have an immensely rich moss, liverwort and lichen flora.

Beauly Firth: the moult migration ground of Canada geese; very good for wildfowl and waders in winter, e.g. over 2000 red-breasted mergansers and over 1000 goosanders in December.

Claish Moss: a long and rather specialised type of raised bog on the south side of Loch Shiel, a deep oligotrophic lake with Nessie-type traditions.

Glen Affric: a relatively unspoilt valley with extensive pine and birch-woods, golden eagles, wild cats and crossbills.

Loch Arkaig: the last breeding place of the osprey in Britain, in 1902 (with a single bird surviving till 1910), before it returned to Speyside in the 1950s.

Loch Morar: the deepest lake in Britain, at 310m, separated from the sea only by a low neck of land; some of its islands have good ungrazed pine woodland. Another loch with frequent reports of Nessie-like 'monsters'.

Loch Ness: the most famous loch in Scotland, not so much for its great bulk – its 7895m^3 is the greatest volume of fresh water in Britain – and depth to possibly 280 m, as for an animal whose existence has never been scientifically proved, although Nessie has been given the scientific name of *Nessiteras rhomboideus*. Otherwise, though spectacular scenically, it is a rather dull loch for the naturalist.

Rahoy Hills: a magnificent mosaic of Highland habitats in Morvern, now a nature reserve; two of the peaks, Beinns Iadain and nah-Uamha, are good for alpine plants.

Sandaig: the Camusfearna of Gavin Maxwell's 'Ring of Bright Water'.

The Inner Hebrides

The following Inner Hebridean islands were dealt with under Strathclyde North: Coll, Colonsay, Iona, Islay, Jura, Mull, Oronsay, Pladda, Scarba, Tiree and the Treshnish Islands.

Canna: good seabird colonies, including Manx shearwaters.

Eigg: a rich mixture of habitats, mountains, some of them lime-rich uplands with alpines, moorland, mixed woodland, scrub, lochans. A large Manx shearwater colony on the Cleasdale cliffs. Golden eagles breed.

Raasay: remarkable for its fertile soils and mild climate; good cliffs on the south-east coast.

Rhum: a large island now devoted to scientific research, especially on its red deer herd, the sheep having all been removed. Two fine mountains, Fionchra and Ruinsival, with interesting plants and a huge (over 100,000) montane colony of Manx shearwaters. Golden eagles breed and the experiment of reintroducing the white-tailed sea eagle seems to be succeeding. Good seabird colonies.

Skye: the largest and finest island of the Hebrides, with two notable mountain ranges, the **Cuillin,** craggy climbers' hills with alpine rock-cress *Arabis alpina* in its only British locality and other rarities; and **the Storr** in the Trotternish peninsula, lower but with other interesting plants. There are some fine limestone pavements, the best in Scotland, and several excellent woods in Sleat, notably **Tokavaig,** and a beechwood at Dalavil. Golden eagles may be seen.

Ross and Cromarty: Easter Ross

Ancient Pinewoods: Amat, Glen Einig, Rhidorroch and Strath Vaich.

Beauly and Moray Firths: good for winter wildfowl and waders; see also under Highland, South, and West Inverness-shire.

Ben Wyvis: a massive flat-topped hill with mainly acid rocks so that the flora is poor, but the different types of mountain vegetation are very well represented.

Black Isle: mainly low-lying and agricultural, but has some interesting grassy cliffs, Drummondreach Oakwood (a reserve of the Scottish Wildlife Trust) and Monadh Mor, pinewood and bog.

Castle Leod has the first wellingtonias *Sequoiadendron giganteum* ever planted in Britain, in 1853. Nearby Ardross Castle has the next oldest, in 1855.

Conon River: fish-passes at Torr Achilty, Meig and Luichart, where migrating salmon can be seen.

Dornoch Firth: Skibo and Whiteness are the best areas for waders and wildfowl.

Loch Eye: a sanctuary for greylag geese and whooper swans.

Ross & Cromarty: Wester Ross

Ancient Pinewoods: Achnashellach, Coulin, Loch Maree and Shieldaig.

An Teallach ('The Anvil'): a famous mountain with magnificent scenery and some good arctic-alpine plants.

Beinn Dearg: one of the most important hills in Scotland for the botanist, with its high, wide summit areas, rich calcareous cliffs and impressive list of arctic-alpine plants, together with most of the rarer upland birds and mammals.

Beinn Eighe NNR and Liathach: a magnificent steep mountain rising from Loch Torridon, with a good display of mountain plants, a herd of red deer, pine martens and golden eagles.

Benmore Coigeach: a mountain exceptionally rich in wildlife, including red and roe deer, wild cat, pine marten and golden eagle, with some fine birchwoods.

Corrieshalloch, Braemore: a steep gorge with a fine waterfall and extensive woods.

Five Sisters of Kintail: a fine stretch of mountain (Beinn Fhada) and moorland, owned by the National Trust for Scotland, which also has the nearby Falls of Glomach.

Gairloch: the coastline here is well wooded and rich in mosses and liverworts.

Inverewe: famous subtropical gardens.

Inverpolly: a fascinating area with odd-shaped mountains and many rare plants. The best cliffs are by the road at Knockan; Cul Mor and some of the other hills have unusual alpines. Loch Scionascaig has black-throated divers.

Loch Maree: a beautiful loch with

ancient pinewoods at Coille na Glas
Leitre, much juniper on its southern
shores and its many islands, and
undisturbed oakwoods on its north
shore.

Loch Torridon: a most impressive
sea loch, one of the wildest and least
spoilt stretches of the west Highland
coastline, as there are no roads along
the shore near its mouth.

Rassal Ashwood, Kishorn: an
unusually northerly ashwood on a
limestone outcrop. Limestone also
outcrops at Alltnan Carnan, Apple-
cross, Lochan Fada and Loch Coulin.

Summer Isles: a remote group of
islands with caves, cliffs, lochans,
breeding seabirds and greylag geese
and otters.

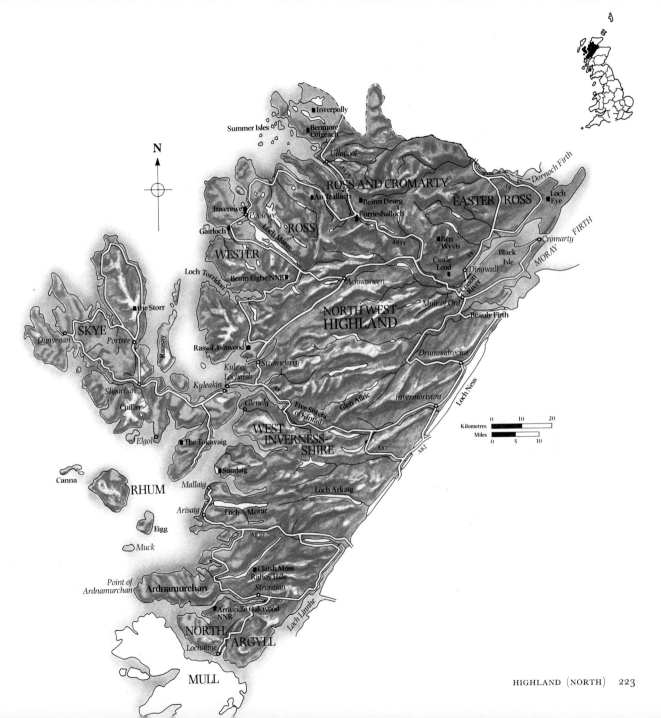

N

Inverpolly

Summer Isles

Benmore
Coigeach

Ullapool

ROSS AND CROMARTY

An Teallach

Beinn Dearg

Corrieshalloch

EASTER ROSS

Loch
Eye

Inverewe
Poolewe

Gairloch

Loch Maree

ROSS

WESTER

Ben
Wyvis

Cromarty

Black
Isle

MORAY
FIRTH

Castle
Leod

Dingwall

Loch Torridon

Beinn Eighe NNR

Achnasheen

Conon
River

NORTH WEST
HIGHLAND

Muir of Ord

Beauly Firth

the Storr

SKYE

Dunvegan

Portree

Raasay

Rassal Ashwood

Stromeferry

Drumnadrochit

Kyle of
Lochalsh

Kyleakin

Sligachan

Glenelg

Five Sisters
of Kintail

Glen Affric

Invermoriston

Loch Ness

Cuillin

Elgol

The Tokavaig

WEST
INVERNESS-
SHIRE

Sandaig

Canna

RHUM

Mallaig

Loch Arkaig

Arisaig

Loch Morar

Eigg

Muck

Claish Moss
Rahoy Hills

Strontian

Point of
Ardnamurchan

Ardnamurchan

Arriundle Oakwood
NNR

Loch Linnhe

NORTH

ARGYLL

Lochaline

MULL

Kilometres
0   10   20

Miles
0   5   10

Highland (north-east), Outer Hebrides

Sutherland
Badcall has a salmon farm.
Ben Hope: a high isolated hill with good alpine flora. **Ben Loyal** is similar but less interesting.
Brora: good watchpoint for wildfowl at sea.
Bettyhill: a fine dune system with with many good plants.
Cape Wrath: the northwesternmost point of the British mainland, the culmination of **Clo Mor**, a magnificent stretch of north-facing cliffs, with huge colonies of nesting seabirds, birds of prey and interesting plants, including Scots primrose *Primula scotica*, which is found nowhere else in the world but Sutherland, Caithness and Orkney. The western part of the Cape Wrath peninsula, known as **the Parphe**, is accessible only on foot and is very beautiful, with good dune systems at **Sandwood Bay** and **Oldshore.**
Faraid Head has a puffin colony.
Foinaven, Arkle and Meall Horn: a characteristically lumpy group of mountains, with a rich flora and fauna.
Handa: a small island well known for its breeding seabirds and as a RSPB reserve.
Inchnadamph: a relatively low-lying area including Loch Assynt and an extensive tract of limestone with many rare plants.
Invernaver: a good dune system with some rarities.
Kylestrome: a virtual sanctuary for common and grey seals.
Loch Eriboll: a sea loch where great northern divers assemble for their spring passage to Iceland. Some fine birchwoods adorn its head.
Loch Fleet: a magnificent coastal reserve of the Scottish Wildlife Trust, with very good wildfowl and waders, especially eiders; flanked by pinewoods, **Balblair, Ferry and Ferry Links Woods** with such uncommon plants as creeping lady's tresses orchid *Goodyera repens* and twinflower *Linnaea borealis*.
The Mound Alderwoods NNR: extensive alderwoods formed on the tidal saltmarshes of Loch Fleet after an embankment shut it off from the sea.
Rabbit Island, Kyle of Tongue, has a dune system and numerous breeding sea and other birds.
River Shin: fish-passes and Diversion Dam and Lairg.
Strathy Bog: a group of interesting peat bogs on the flank of the Strathy valley.

Caithness
A county which is as flat and unspectacular inland as Sutherland is dramatically mountainous.
Ackergill and Keiss Links: good dune systems; also at Dunnet, Freswick and Reay.
Berriedale Cliffs: a magnificent range of cliffs with enormous seabird colonies, including the largest guillemot colony (126,000) in mainland Britain.
Dirlot Gorge: an area of woodland and scrub near Thurso.
Duncansby Head: headland with a superb spring floral display and a fine seabird colony; other major colonies are at Skirza Head, Holbourn Head, Noss Head, Stack o'Brough, Iresgoe, Ulbster, Bruan, Halberry Head, An Dun, Inver Hill and Badbea.
Dunnet Head: this, not John o'Groats, is the most northerly point on the British mainland; a fine seabird colony.
Loch Watten: a small well vegetated eutrophic lake, with extensive marshes between it and Wick.

Loch of Winless has a marginal fen.
Stroma: an island in the Pentland Firth with breeding terns and other seabirds.

OUTER HEBRIDES
Barra: the southernmost island of any size, has the rare Irish lady's tresses orchis *Spiranthes romanzoffiana*.
Benbecula: the flattest island, between the Uists, has splendid machair (grassland on fixed dunes with a very rich flora) on its Atlantic side, more Irish lady's tresses and still many corncrakes. Loch na Liana is a good botanical loch.
Berneray: the southernmost island of all, has nesting seabirds.
Deasker: a large cormorant colony.
Flannan Islands: very remote, one of the five British colonies of Leach's petrel.
Gasker: grey seals, barnacle geese.
Harris: the southern part of the Long Island, with Clisham, the highest hill in the outer isles, has, in its own southern part, one of the barrenest landscapes in Britain. There are grey seals on **Coppay,** nesting seabirds on Husinish Point, and two good estuaries: Traigh Seilebost and Luskentyre.
Haskeir: grey seals, puffins, terns and other seabirds.
Lewis: the northern part of the Long Island, with important sites at the **Butt of Lewis** (seabirds, migration watchpoint), **Melbost Sands** (nesting terns, wintering wildfowl), **Tiumpan Head** (nesting seabirds) and **Stornoway Castle grounds** with the only (artificial) woodland on the Long Island, apart from a few trees in Glen Valtos. Good machair in **Uig** and elsewhere in the west.
Mingulay: seabird colonies.
Monach Islands: grey seals, seabirds.

North Rona NNR: extremely remote, with a huge grey seal colony.
North Uist: some of the finest machair on its Atlantic coast; **Narstay** has common seals and greylag geese; **Vaccasay** has a ternery; **Loch an Tomein** has one of only three inland cormorantries in Britain; **Loch Obisary** is good botanically; and corncrakes are still common.
Pabbay: large ternery, introduced red deer.
Shiant Islands: noted for seabirds, including storm petrels.
St Kilda: remotest of all, with the highest cliff in the British Isles and immense seabird colonies, especially gannets (three colonies, 60,000 pairs), fulmars (40,000 pairs) and puffins (250,000 pairs). Soay sheep, a primitive Norse breed, still breed on Soay, and feral Scottish blackfaces on Boreray.
Shillay: grey seals.
South Uist: perhaps the most important island in the main chain, with splendid machair on its west coast; **Loch Druidibeg** NNR, the headquarters of breeding greylag geese in Britain; **Balranald** RSPB reserve, with important water-bird breeding lochs and marshes, and grey seals on nearby Causamul; **Loch Bee** also for waterfowl; **Loch Roag** as an important botanical site; good moorland on **Beinn Mhor** and **Hecla;** and a small aspen wood in Allt Volagir. Corncrakes are still common and some red-necked phalaropes still nest.
Sula Sgeir NNR: gannetry, Leach's petrels.

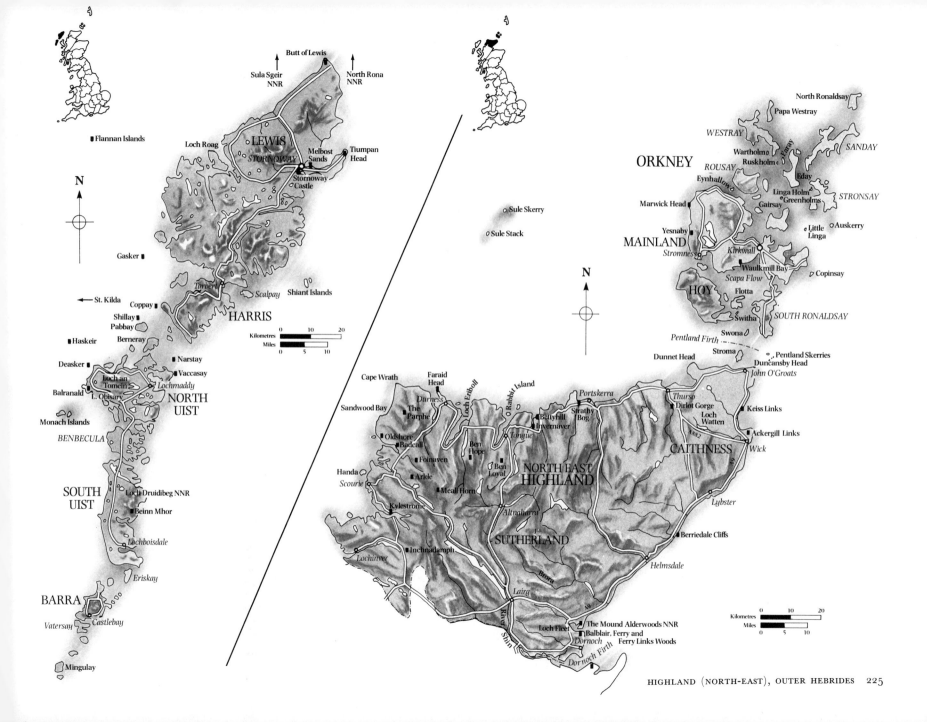

Butt of Lewis

Sula Sgeir
NNR

North Rona
NNR

■ Flannan Islands

LEWIS

Loch Roag

Melbost
Sands

■ Tiumpan
Head

STORNOWAY

Stornoway
Castle

Gasker ■

Tarbert

Scalpay

Shiant Islands

← St. Kilda

Coppay ■

HARRIS

Shillay ■
Pabbay ■

Berneray

■ Haskeir

Narstay ■

Vaccasay ■

Deasker ■

Loch an
Tomein

Lochmaddy

Balranald ■

L. Obisary

NORTH
UIST

Monach Islands

BENBECULA

SOUTH
UIST

Loch Druidibeg NNR

■ Beinn Mhor

Lochboisdale

Eriskay

BARRA

Vatersay

Castlebay

Mingulay

Sule Skerry

Sule Stack

North Ronaldsay

Papa Westray

WESTRAY

SANDAY

ORKNEY

Wartholm ■
Ruskholm ■

Eday

ROUSAY

Eynhallow

Linga Holm
Greenholms

STRONSAY

Marwick Head

Gairsay

Yesnaby

Little
Linga

Auskerry

MAINLAND

Kirkwall

Stromness

Waulkmill Bay

Copinsay

Scapa Flow

HOY

Flotta

Switha

SOUTH RONALDSAY

Swona

Pentland Firth

Pentland Skerries

Dunnet Head

Stroma

Duncansby Head

John O'Groats

Cape Wrath

Faraid
Head

Loch Eriboll

Rabbit Island

Portskerra

Thurso

Dirlot Gorge

Keiss Links

Sandwood Bay

Durness

The
Parphe

Strathy
Bog

Loch
Watten

Bettyhill
Invernaver

Ackergill Links

Oldshore
Badcall

Tongue

CAITHNESS

Handa

Foinaven ■

Ben
Hope

Ben
Loyal

NORTH EAST
HIGHLAND

Wick

Scourie

Arkle ■

Lybster

Meall Horn ■

Kylestrome

Altnaharra

SUTHERLAND

Inchnadamph

Berriedale Cliffs

Lochinver

Brora

Helmsdale

Lairg

River Shin

The Mound Alderwoods NNR

Loch Fleet

Balblair, Ferry and
Ferry Links Woods

Dornoch

Dornoch Firth

The Northern Isles

THE NORTHERN ISLES (Orkney, Shetland)

Orkney (map p. 225)
Flatter and less hilly than either Shetland or the Outer Isles, with a much more fertile soil than either, so that it has much more farmland and less moorland.
Auskerry: terneries.
Copinsay: RSPB reserve as a memorial to James Fisher, with fine seabird colonies.
Eday: seabird colonies on the Calf of Eday.
Eynhallow: a notably rabbit-free island with nesting terns and other seabirds.
Faras: grey seals on North Fara and Faraholm.
Flotta: terneries; common seals are numerous in Scapa Flow.
Gairsay: nesting fulmars and other seabirds; grey seals, including on Sweynholm and Grassholm.
Greenholms: the main grey seal colony.
Hoy: the second largest island, with the third highest cliffs in Britain; breeding terns and other seabirds; golden eagles; some heather moorland.
Linga Holm: a flock of seaweed-eating North Ronaldsay sheep.
Little Linga: grey seals.
Mainland: the largest island, with some heather moor, e.g. in RSPB reserves at Birsay Moor, Dee of Durkadale and Skelday. Other habitats include cliffs with seabird colonies, e.g. Costa Head, **Marwick Head;** saltmarsh, e.g. **Waulkmill Bay;** sand dunes, e.g. Dingyshowe Bay and Aiker Ness; and freshwater lochs, e.g. Loch of Isbister and Loch of Skaill. **Yesnaby** is a well known site for Scots primrose *Primula scotica*.
North Ronaldsay: noted for its

seaweed-eating breed of sheep.
Papa Westray: fine seabird colonies, including terns and skuas; two of the last British great auks killed here in 1813.
Pentland Skerries: terneries.
Rousay: seabirds on Skaeburgh Head, terneries, some heather moor.
Ruskholm and **Wartholm:** grey seals.
Sanday: storm petrels breed.
South Ronaldsay: seabird colonies, grey seals.
Spurness: grey seals.
Stronsay: seabirds breed.
Sule Skerry and **Sule Stack:** twin islands, remote and very rich in seabirds, including a gannetry on the stack.
Switha and **Swona:** two small islands off Hoy with breeding seabirds.
Westray: seabirds breed on Noup Head.

Shetland

The northernmost part of the British Isles, much of it north of the 60th parallel, and nearer to Norway than to Aberdeen. Largely consists of moorland, but has spectacular coastal scenery, e.g. at Foula, Noss, St Ninian's Isle, Sumburgh Head and Whiteness.
Bressay: seabirds, skuas, terneries.
Fair Isle: the most famous migration watchpoint in Europe with a great many rarities seen annually; also many nesting seabirds, storm petrels and a small gannetry.
Fetlar: with **Hascosay** the most important area for wintering waterfowl; grey seals, Manx shearwaters, terneries, still a few non-breeding snowy owls.
Foula: the Kame is the second highest cliff in the British Isles; immense seabird colonies, including the largest

British colony of bonxies (great skuas), also storm petrels, terneries and a small gannetry; grey seals.
Gruney or Haaf Gruney NNR off south coast of Unst; seabirds, grey seals.
Mainland: numerous seabird colonies, including **Sumburgh Head, Fitful Head** and **Ronas Hill** NNR, the highest point in Shetland; many lochs, including **Loch of Spiggie** (whooper swans, black-headed gullery) and **Pool of Virkie;** Esha Ness has superb maritime cliff-top grassland; good sand dunes at Quendale; grey and common seals.
Mousa: off south-east coast of Mainland: seabirds, common seals.
Muckle Holm in Yell Sound: common seals.

Noss: huge seabird colonies, including a gannetry.
Out Skerries: grey seals.
Papa Stour off west coast of Mainland: seabirds, terneries, grey seals.
Ramna Stacks off north end of Mainland: Leach's petrel colony.
Samphrey in Yell Sound: common seals, storm petrels, terneries.
Unst: northernmost island with large seabird colonies at Hermaness, including a gannetry, great and arctic skuas and grey seals; a black-browed albatross regularly visits the gannetry.
Baltasound has a famous outcrop of serpentine rock with unusual plants.
Uyeasound is a wintering place for whooper swans.
Whalsay: common seals.
Yell: seabirds; **Loch of Lumbister,** RSPB reserve, for waterfowl.

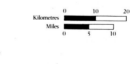

Ireland

IRELAND

The outstanding wildlife attractions of Ireland are found along its coastline, especially the teeming seabird colonies of its cliffs and offshore islands and the huge flocks of wintering wildfowl and waders, notably barnacle and Greenland white-fronted geese. Much of the remaining wild part of the interior still consists largely of bog or peat-covered moorland. Both choughs and corncrakes are much commoner in Ireland than in Britain.

The Coast

Cliffs with seabird colonies are found all round the coast: the outstanding ones are Rathlin I, Antrim; the Cliffs of Moher and Loop Head, Clare; the Old Head of Kinsale, Cork; Horn Head, Donegal, perhaps the finest headland with the largest seabird colonies in Ireland; Lambay Island and Howth Head, Dublin; Puffin Island, Kerry; Bills of Achill, Clare Island, Downpatrick Head and the Stags of Broadhaven, Mayo; and the Saltee Islands, Wexford. There are large gannetries on the Bull Rock, Cork, and Little Skellig, Kerry. Grey seals breed all along the rocky coasts and common seals on both kinds of coast. The hexagonal basalt columns of the **Giant's Causeway** are a spectacular and world famous feature of the Antrim coast.

Low-lying coasts with dunes, mudflats, saltmarshes and shingle: Shannon estuary, especially Poulnasherry and Clonderlaw Bays and Fergus estuary, Clare; Cork and Youghal Harbours; Lough Swilly, Donegal; Lough Foyle, Donegal and Londonderry; Carlingford and Strangford (common seals, brent geese) Loughs, with Downpatrick Marshes, Down; Malahide (Swords) and Rogerstown estuaries and the North Bull sanctuary, Dublin; Tralee Bay, Kerry, especially Castlemaine Harbour; Dundalk Bay, Louth; Inishkea, Mayo, with more than half the Irish wintering barnacle geese; Sligo Bay, also good for barnacle geese; Dungarvan and Tramore Bays, Waterford; and Wexford Harbour and Slobs (marshes), famous for geese, with Lady's Island and Tacumshin Lakes, Wexford. The shingle bar at Lady's Island Lake has the only surviving colony of cottonweed *Otanthus maritimus* in Ireland or Britain.

Bird Observatories: Cape Clear Island, Cork; Copeland Islands, Down.

Inland

Fresh Water: Ireland is studded with loughs, most of which have good winter wildfowl watching: the best are Lough Neagh in the north-east, the largest in Ireland; Shane's Castle Lake (a RSPB reserve), Antrim; Ballyallia Lake, Clare; Lough Erne, Fermanagh; the River Shannon from Lanesborough, Roscommon, to Portumna, Galway, including Loughs Derg and Ree and the goose sanctuary at Little Brosna River flats, Offaly/Tipperary; Rahasane turlough, Galway (a turlough is a deep hollow in limestone, which may dry out in summer; this one does not); Loughs Carra, Conn, Corrib and Mask, Mayo; Lough Gara, Roscommon, with a large flock of Greenland white-fronts; and Poulaphouca Reservoir, Wicklow.

Woodland: Randalstown Forest Park (red deer) and Shane's Castle, Antrim; Tollymore Forest Park, Newcastle, Down; Castlecaldwell, Fermanagh, a RSPB reserve; and the extensive oak and other woodlands around Killarney, Kerry, including Bourn Vincent National Park, The Killarney area has native strawberry trees *Arbutus unedo*, the only Irish yew wood in Reenadinna Wood, the only native red deer in Ireland, and the now more numerous sika deer, introduced from the Far East.

Mountains and Moorland: the most important area in Ireland is the Burren, a tract of limestone hills and pavements in Clare, with a magnificent floral display in spring and many rare plants, in a unique mixture of Arctic, Atlantic and Mediterranean species. Other good mountain districts for wild flowers are the Kerry-Cork highlands and Ben Bulben, Sligo. Slieve League, Donegal; the Mourne Mountains, Down; the Galtees, Tipperary; and the Wicklow Mountains, the largest area of continuous high ground in Ireland, are all less fruitful botanically, but have interesting birds. Western Mayo has a fine stretch of mountain, moorland and bog, including Achill Island, Croagh Patrick, the pilgrims' mountain, and the great Bog of Erris. Connemara in western Galway has many rare and unusual plants.

Botanic Garden: Glasnevin, Dublin.

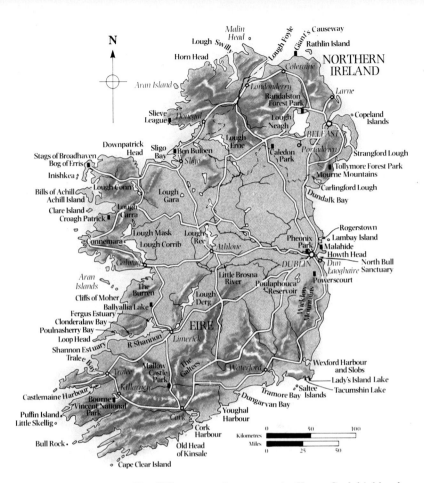

Isle of Wight, Isles of Scilly

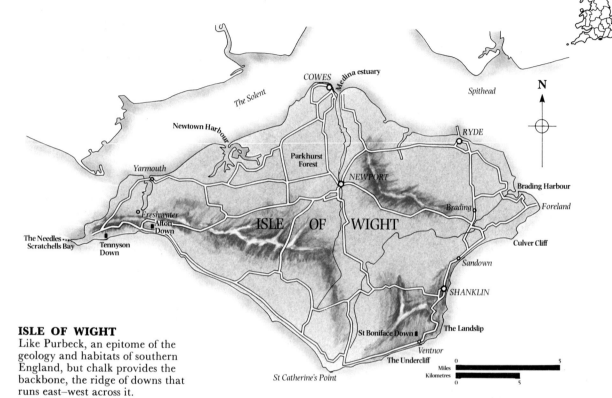

COWES
Medina estuary
The Solent
Spithead
N
Newtown Harbour
Yarmouth
Parkhurst Forest
RYDE
NEWPORT
Brading Harbour
Freshwater
Afton Down
Brading
Foreland
ISLE OF WIGHT
The Needles
Scratchells Bay
Tennyson Down
Culver Cliff
Sandown
SHANKLIN
St Boniface Down
The Landslip
Ventnor
The Undercliff
St Catherine's Point

Miles 0 ... 5
Kilometres 0 ... 5

ISLE OF WIGHT

Like Purbeck, an epitome of the geology and habitats of southern England, but chalk provides the backbone, the ridge of downs that runs east–west across it.

The South Coast

The Needles: a series of chalk stacks at the west end of the island are a famous landmark.

Scratchells Bay: the most important seabird colony, which continues east along the steep chalk cliffs of High Down to Freshwater Bay. Here are the easternmost nesting ravens, peregrines, puffins, guillemots and razorbills along the south coast of England.

Tennyson Down: the westernmost of the downs that stretch eastwards to near Carisbrooke, many of them still

with much good chalk turf, with spring gentian *Gentianella anglica* and other colourful chalk plants and butterflies. Hoary stock *Matthiola incana* grows on the cliffs of **Afton Down**.

The Undercliff and the Landslip, Blackgang to Luccombe: similar to the Axbridge–Lyme Regis undercliff, where scrub and trees cover many falls of rock and clay; the headquarters of the rare Glanville fritillary butterfly *Melitaea cinxia*, especially near Niton.

St Boniface Down, above Ventnor, now has a large colony of naturalised holm oak *Quercus ilex*.

Culver Cliff: the eastern outcrop of the chalk cliffs sometimes has nesting ravens and peregrines.

The North Coast

The Solent shore has many good saltmarshes, notably those around **Newtown Harbour**, along the **Medina estuary** and in **Brading Harbour**, all of which have good winter wildfowl and waders.

Parkhurst Forest: an old established oak woodland, especially notable for the frequency of narrow-leaved lungwort *Pulmonaria longifolia*.

ISLES OF SCILLY

A very interesting archipelago with plants and animals not found elsewhere in Great Britain.

Annet: the best known seabird island in Scilly, with breeding puffins, storm petrels and Manx shearwaters. Other, less accessible seabird colonies include Gorregan, Mincarlo and Rosevear.

St. Agnes has a bird observatory.

Tresco: well known for the remarkable gardens and planted grounds of Tresco Abbey, with many subtropical plants.

Western Rocks have the largest colony of grey seals in south west England.

Round Island
St Helen's
White Island
Tean
ST MARTIN'S
BRYHER
TRESCO
Samson
Eastern Isles
Hugh Town
ST MARY'S
St Mary's Sound
Annet
ISLES OF SCILLY
Gugh
ST AGNES

Miles 0 ... 2
Kilometres 0 ... 2

Isle of Man, Channel Isles

ISLE OF MAN

The wilder habitat of the island is either largely acid moorland, and so of comparatively little botanical interest, or around the coast.

Ballaugh Curraghs: interesting marshlands.

Calf of Man: an island off the south end of Man where choughs and Manx shearwaters and other seabirds breed; a good bird migration watchpoint.

Fresh water: Eairy Dam, Kionslieu Dam, Mooragh Park, the Ayres.

Langness: another bird migration watchpoint.

Maughold Head has seabird colonies; also at Black Head, Chasms and Spanish Head.

Point of Ayre: good dunes and shingle.

Ramsey Mooragh: another dune system.

Snaefell: at 622 m, the highest point in Man.

THE CHANNEL ISLES

Jersey, Guernsey, Alderney and the smaller islands really belong to the Continent from the wildlife viewpoint, but as many people visit them from Britain and several plants grow there that are rare or absent in Britain, such as the loose-flowered orchid *Orchis laxiflora*, we give a few very brief notes.

Burhou: a small island off Alderney with storm petrels and other breeding seabirds.

L'Ancresse Common: an area of dune grassland on Guernsey with many rare and unusual plants, e.g. the tiny Guernsey centaury *Exaculum pusillum*.

Les Etacs: rocks off Alderney with 2000 pairs of breeding gannets.

Ortac: another gannetry island off Alderney, with 1000 pairs.

St Ouen's Bay: the chief sand dune area of Jersey, with St Ouen's Pond nearby, the largest piece of natural fresh water in the islands and the site of a bird observatory.

Sark, Herm and Jethou: three of the smaller islands well worth a visit for their heaths, dunes and cliffs.

Vazon Bay: another dune area in Guernsey.

Three unusual small breeding birds to look out for are short-toed treecreeper, which does not breed in Britain, Dartford warbler and cirl bunting. Stonechats are common on the gorsy cliffs.

Point of Ayre

Jurby

Ballaugh Curraghs

Ramsey Mooragh
RAMSEY

Sulby

ISLE OF
MAN

Maughold
Head

Snaefell

Peel

Laxey

St John's

N

DOUGLAS

Port Erin

Castletown

Port
St Mary

Langness

Calf of Man

Miles

Kilometres

0   5

0   5

Index

Page numbers in *italics* refer to illustrations and those in **bold type** indicate an entry in the countryside calendar.